D1308180

Divine Towels: The Spiritual Way to Solve Problems

"And greater works than these will he do because I go to the Father." – John 14:12

By

Beau Jason McGlynn

Table of Contents

This is dedicated to my dear Mother. It is my prayer that "Divine Towels" will make her vision of a healing ministry a reality.

ACKNOWLEDGMENTS

Writing a book like this is not something that I could have done on my own. I want to thank all the people who were behind me and helped me every step along the way. I especially want to thank my dear Mother who inspired me to write this.

There were also countless other people who offered moral and spiritual support and encouraged me to keep on plugging away. Among them were my friends at work who read countless revisions: Steve Beamer, Eric Lowy, Michelle O'Leary, Cindy Justis-Reichelt, and Georgia Herring. I also want to thank Carol Conely-Klahorst, Jim Datz, Jon Christopher, and Tom Sykes for the many hours they spent working on the cover of this book. Finally, I owe much gratitude to Dr. Richard George and Dr. Peter Norberg of Saint Joseph's University and to my editor, Terri Breslin. I am so grateful for all those who were instrumental in helping me get this work of love published.

SCRIBE'S NOTE

A scribe's job is to transcribe what he is instructed to write down. Just as God directed and inspired the authors of the Bible, so was His instruction and inspiration given to me for the writing of *Divine Towels*.

Some may consider the concepts written about in *Divine Towels* to be extreme or underdeveloped. However, my goal is the planting of seeds in the souls of those who read it. Each person reading Divine Towels will need to contemplate how they can apply its concepts to their own lives and creatively address their own spiritual concerns. Too often I have found that Christian books tell a story, but do not necessarily challenge readers to dig deep into the soil of their own spiritual gardens to cultivate what needs to be growing there. As a writer, I feel bound not just to tell a story, but to offer people something substantial that will help them discover the fruits of the spirit in their own unique search for God.

We live in a time when we are inundated with responsibilities and find ourselves pressed for time and multi-tasking just to make it through the challenges that each day brings. While the majority of us have good intentions, we never quite seem to get around to doing the work that we know deep in our hearts that Christ has called us to do. At times, we feel we are on automatic pilot and would do anything to break free from the chains of our busy routines. My sincere prayer is that those who read this book will "be still" in the hope of discovering the presence of the Divine within them in the spiritual garden of the soul. Christ did so when he drew away from the crowds. Ultimately, taking time to quiet the mind and "seek first the kingdom and its righteousness" provides the Holy Spirit with the opportunity to empower and renew us so that we can cultivate the fruits and gifts of the spirit that have been given to us to use for the highest good of those placed in our path by God.

PREFACE

Reading the Gospels and the Acts of the Apostles can be an electrifying experience -- for they fill the soul with wonder and create a sense of awe in relationship to carrying out the Great Commissions of the Bible: preaching, teaching, and healing. Learning about the disciples who stood up to the injustices that plagued society provides a sense of encouragement as well as an example of what people are capable of accomplishing when empowered by the Holy Spirit. Such stories inspire us to venture from our safe surroundings and to be Christ's hands, feet and heart to a broken world by living the gospel and spreading unconditional love.

To realize the ultimate gift of eternal life, Christ calls us to follow his teachings and commandments in our thoughts, words and deeds, both consciously and unconsciously. However, sometimes when we look at the acts that the early Christians performed and compare them to what we are doing, we feel a sense of failure and inadequacy. These early followers seemed to be filled with a sense of mission that somehow seems to elude us in this fast-paced and hi-tech world that expects instant gratification and results. Lately, the world seems to have an "all -about –me-as-the -center -of the –universe credo.

The Gospels call us to be watchful and to live bold lives that are full of passion to follow Christ but also to have compassion and empathy for those less fortunate than ourselves. I have observed that people, even those who consider themselves to be Christians, seem to be living in a state of unconsciousness – holding the form of religion but denying its power. It is sad to see people who appear to be feeling not only powerless to change their circumstances, but permeated with a sense of hopelessness as well. These feelings have insidiously crept into our current-day society as the result of a vast array of variables, including difficult economic times, broken family structures, a decline in morals and accountability for our actions, etc. The more society seems to unravel at its seams, the more difficult it seems to recapture a sense of spiritual fulfillment and grasp the meaning of what it means to truly follow Jesus of Nazareth and his teachings.

Study the faces and body language of those around you when you are at work, walking down the street, shopping etc. The majority of people seem preoccupied with multi-tasking, manipulating hi-tech equipment or just staring blanking into space as a result of fatigue, depression and overload. In fact, people are so weighed down with just trying to keep themselves afloat, they don't realize that they have drifted away from the source of the soul's true source of peace, security, and guidance – total submission and reliance on the Lord.

If we are to live lives full of passion and serve as beacons of light in a dark world, and if we are supposed to be all about doing our "Father's business," something within us needs to be spiritually rekindled and redirected. It seems that a dark and negative force is exerting itself in the hope of drawing us into an ever downward spiraling maelstrom. This force would love to separate us from the love of Christ by keeping us in a constant state of anxiety and plagued with problems that keep us in a constant state of turmoil and confusion. Some would call this negative force Satan. Other would refer to it as evil. Whatever the label, the result is one of creating a world of people plagued with problems that prevent them realizing the Christ consciousness within them.

There was a time when being a Christian was more than a label. It meant you had a strong moral backbone and you were seen as a reckoning force. Perhaps, the real question we need to ask ourselves --and a question that *Divine Towels* seeks to answer -- is how can people reclaim their spiritual connection to Christ and refocus their lives to become children of the Light for Him and the world.

There is a small voice within us that knows when things are not right both within us and in the world around us. What we need to do is turn off the noise around us and tune into that "still small voice" to change not only ourselves but to be instruments of good for a troubled world. At first this "tuning in" might prove difficult, but I believe that it is never too late to change a negative and spiritually unproductive lifestyle into a positive and Christ-centered one. The message of *Divine Towels* has evolved slowly for me over twelve prayerful years. One day, twelve years ago, I felt drawn to sit down at my computer and write. In preparation, I put my head down and prayed for guidance. The Lord Jesus Christ gave me some thoughts and words to put down. I thought to myself, "Oh, this is such a beautiful and wonderful experience! Thank you, Lord for filling me with these wonderful words to write for you." The next time I sat down to write, I, again, went into prayer and asked for guidance, and more words and thoughts were given to me. This process has continued over twelve years and the message of Divine Towels has been the result! It has been an experience of bonding with Christ that I never believed could happen to me! I hope that in reading what He gave to me will also create a bond and a new sense of call within your life. *Divine Towels* tells a tale of how we can become empowered Christians and claim our moral authority, the peace that passes understanding and the ability to truly become not only "hearers of the word but doers of it".

To My Beloved Soul Mate:

The journey Christ has taken us on has been both extraordinary and bittersweet. To say the least, it has been filled with inexplicable joy and sorrow. Throughout the years, many people have watched what we have accomplished despite the countless obstacles and barriers that we have had thrown in our paths. In fact, people have marveled that we have achieved what we have. Indeed, Christ has given us the strength to overcome tremendous earthly and spiritual difficulties. He has consistently provided us with a spiritual parting of the Red Sea. I am very thankful that God has allowed us to walk through this life together.

While Christ has certainly blessed us and has always made a way, one thing continues to weigh heavily on my heart: Many years ago, you shared a spiritual experience that you had with me. You explained to me that one day you were sitting in church after communion and Christ appeared to you and said, "You were baptized with the name of 'Lucille' which means 'bearer of Light.' Now, I lay my hands upon you, Lucille, so that you might lay yours upon those in need of my Light and healing." For years and years you struggled to start a healing ministry. Each time you did, something came along to prevent it from happening. At Christ's guidance you still continued to offer the gift you were given to others -- and wondrous healings continued to occur. However, something would come along again and again to try to stop you. You continued this struggle to be obedient to this calling, but the harder you tried, the more obstacles came to stop you. I have watched you go through this struggle for over thirty years and I know that nothing will ever stop you from offering your gift to others -- at Christ's direction. BUT, it has pained me to see you have so great a gift to offer and so great a struggle to share it. I have often thought that some evil force has chosen to block you from sharing Christ's Light with others. BUT , I have also watched your perseverance and know that nothing will ever stop you from using your gifts of the spirit to help others. I know how much you wanted to become an Episcopal priest. I know how it broke your heart to have to turn down your acceptance to the Princeton Theological Seminary so that you could ensure my college education and care for my needs. I know that you could have had any ministry you wanted if you had not made the choice to lay down your life for me and to care for your mother and sister when they were sick. I know you made these choices willingly. And I know that for these forty years of caretaking you have never complained. BUT, I also understand the great toll that making these choices have also had on you.

I know you thought it went unnoticed because I never said anything. If I ever tried to bring it up, you would always assure me that being a clinical social worker was just as much a call to vocation as being a minister of the gospel. However, I still saw the look of sadness in your eyes and knew exactly how you felt. Many times, I longed with all my heart to comfort you and to put my arms around you and somehow make it all better, but I could not. I watched the whole thing unfold, but there was nothing I could do to prevent it from happening. As you always put it, "It is what it is." I hated it! I was inconsolable, and could not bear to see it continue! When I ponder our past, I sometimes feel sick that life can be so unfair.

While we have overcome tremendous obstacles, I remain deeply troubled that you never realized your dream of having a healing ministry. In an effort to stoke the spiritual fire, I decided to use my imagination and make up the following story. It is my hope that what the Holy Spirit provided me in writing Divine Towels will prove to be the catalyst for you to finally realize the vision planted in your heart so many years ago by Christ. I truly believe that God wants you to have a healing ministry and that He has destined it to come to fruition in a way that you never imagined or expected!

What you are about to read may sound somewhat far-fetched. However, I believe God is full of surprises and has allowed it to unfold this way for a reason. As you know, it took me twelve prayerful years to write this story, typing with only two fingers. It is my prayer that after reading this story, you will see that God is faithful and that the Light of Christ is truly at the end of the tunnel. God does keep His promises even when the road looks like it comes to a dead end. May God be with you always.

Love,
Your Son and Soul Mate…Beau Jason

PART ONE: STOKING THE FIRE

THE MISSION

As a boy, whenever anything went wrong or when Ethan was feeling blue, his grandmother always uttered the platitude, "You never know what's around the corner." At the time, Ethan found this to be meaningless and cold-hearted. However, in retrospect, she was right. Given enough time, things have a way of working themselves out. The problem is that people want things when they want them. They forget that God is the one in control and has the power to change man's future whenever He chooses.

Ethan grew up and did everything that society dictated would make him a happy man. He went to college, earned his MBA, and landed a job right out of graduate school. By worldly accounts, he was living the American dream: working in corporate America, making a decent salary and increasing the company's bottom line. Indeed, by the world's standards he had a perfect life as well as a job.

The truth was Ethan felt as if he was living someone else's dream and his nightmare. He always had this feeling hanging over him that there was something that he was supposed to do with his life and somehow he would just know it when he found it. In the eyes of the world, he may have appeared to be successful, but in reality, he felt unfulfilled. Thinking back over his life, Ethan realized that things began going downhill the moment he accepted his first job. Intuitively, he knew it was a mistake to take this position because it was going to compromise his true values-- living with one foot in heaven and one foot on earth. In other words he knew it would force him to serve "two masters." He tried his best to work in this "each-man-for-himself" environment, but he was miserable and went home every night with knots in his stomach.

Somehow, Ethan always knew that God had a special plan for his life and it was certainly not working for corporate America. While he didn't know what "the plan" was, he also knew that it was important to earn his MBA. Instinctively, he realized the importance of having a working knowledge of how things were accomplished in the business world. BUT -- he also knew that his Jesuit education also made it very clear that giving back to the world was equally important. Unlike many of his colleagues in graduate school, he never wanted to work in corporate America. In fact, he wasn't interested in big businesses and bottom lines. Ethan wanted to learn fundamental business skills so he would be in a better position to make a positive difference in the lives of others and facilitate social change for those less fortunate than himself.

In spite of not wanting a job in corporate America, Ethan still ended up taking one: he had living expenses and many college loans to pay back. He told himself that while it was not his dream job, he would just have to make due until the real deal came along! Despite trying his utmost to keep focused on the tasks at hand, he continued to feel frustrated and at loose ends. Despite all his lofty hopes and pure motives, things were just not turning out the way he had dreamed they would. He desperately wanted the chance to turn his true hopes and dreams into realities.

While Ethan was certainly less than joyful about his current state of affairs, he also believed that God allowed everything to happen for a reason. BUT, he also felt as if he was becoming a spiritual yo-yo. On one hand, he would wake up every morning and say "all things work together for good for those who love God and are called according to His purpose." He would walk out the door and give God charge of his life. On the other hand, after a couple hours in his unsavory office environment, he would find himself swinging wildly into a hopeless and helpless state of thinking. It seemed that he was living a life that was an exercise in spiritual futility. In fact, Ethan was starting to feel as if he was riding the corporate merry-go-round to nowhere and could not get off, no matter how hard he tried. What was even worse was that he felt as if he was locked in a room of windows where he could see people all around him in desperate need of help, but was he was unable to get out of where he was to help and comfort them. Ethan sensed that God had put him in his present predicament for a reason. He asked himself, "Is this empty and meaningless job supposed to force me to explore new employment options and opportunities where I can be of value to a troubled world?"

Ethan continued to pray, read his Bible, and ask the Holy Spirit for guidance, but no answers seemed to miraculously manifest. His despondent mindset dragged on and he often wondered, "How much longer will I be trapped in this miserable job situation before God answers my prayers?" Suddenly, Ethan remembered something that he had seemed to forget in his frustration and impatience for an immediate answer to his prayer. He reminded himself that throughout his life he had lived through many such unhappy circumstances and God had always come through and answered his prayers when the time was right and least expected! He mulled this over in his mind and thought, "this is how things always happened in the Bible." When Sarah had given up having a baby, she became conceived a child in her senior citizen stage of life, much to her husband's utter joy and amusement. When everyone gave Jesus up for dead and gone, he resurrected and ascended into heaven. Yes, Ethan reasoned, God was filled with surprises that came out of left field when least expected. These Biblical examples reminded Ethan of the need for divine patience and to wait upon the Lord. He resolved to do something that had recently slipped from his mind: "to let go and let God." Accordingly, he surrendered his situation to God, he experienced a sense of peace that he had not known for quite a long time

On a cold and dreary Tuesday afternoon in mid-March, Ethan was sitting his office at the computer. He had just gotten into a work rhythm when the song "Hammer and a Nail" started to play on the radio. This song made his mind wander back to college. Suddenly he was experiencing all the warm and heartfelt memories that this song conjured up. The lyrics had always evoked a sense of challenge and bittersweet feelings within his heart. Suddenly, he was brought to a standstill. He found himself in a state of déjà vu in which he was reliving the valuable experiences of his Jesuit education: giving back to the community and serving others, service projects he completed in college, and the inspiring people who helped him believe that one person really could have an impact on the lives of others. The song also served as a "cattle prong" to him, for it reminded him of everything he wanted to do to help others.

In sheer frustration and desperation, he cried out for help. "Lord, I don't understand why I am here. You tell us that we are to spend our lives living the Gospel, saving souls, and doing the works you did when you were on earth. I look at my life and do not like where it is going. You put me on earth to do a mission for you and to make life better for others, not to work long hours and go home dead tired. I long to use the talents you have given me to serve you as I did when I was in college. Please send your Holy Spirit and show me how to get to the place that You have destined for me. I ask this in Jesus' name. Amen."

Suddenly, Ethan heard a voice within him say, "My son, I have heard your prayer. Because you have been faithful to me for many years, I am about to bless you in a special way. There are people who feel they spend their lives trying to climb out of a pit of quicksand. Every time they make some progress, they slip deeper into the hole. I want you to help these souls reach solid spiritual ground. Your mission is to be my "Towel boy."

Ethan knew God spoke to people and placed unusual revelations within their hearts. However, he had never experienced anything like this before. And, he wasn't quite sure if his mind was playing tricks on him or if he really heard the voice of God call him to be a "towel boy." Ethan reasoned with himself, "I know that I can have a really vivid imagination at times, but could I actually come up with the idea of being a "towel boy" for Jesus by myself! I think not." The impact of what just happened suddenly seized Ethan's heart and emotions and he can to be realization that God had actually spoken to him and given him an answer to his long-awaited prayer. But what on earth did it mean? How does one go about becoming a "towel boy" for Jesus? Ethan found himself somewhat mystified and then laughing until he was crying. He finally got a grip on himself and said, "Well, God, if you could send an angel to Mary and tell her that she would conceive a son who would be the savior of the world, I guess you could ask me to be your towel boy. I give you my trust and my obedience and will wait for your guidance on how to do this for you."

Ethan then mused over the concept of "mustard seed" faith and came to the realization that he trusted Jesus completely. He felt incredible humility at the thought of having the opportunity to do great works in His name by fulfilling the mission of being His "towel boy."At this point, Ethan started to play over the things that God asked people in the Bible to do for Him and the incredible courage and trust that was required of them. Now that God had given him this directive, could he be as brave as the Biblical characters who were also given such cryptic callings? He hoped he could with all his heart. But…what in heaven's name did a "towel boy" do for the Master of the Universe! This was truly perplexing.

Despite his apprehension, Ethan decided to be like a trusting child and follow where the Master led him. While the idea of being a "towel boy" seemed somewhat bizarre to him, he decided to think upon it as a mystical puzzle. Initially, Ethan wondered if God was being literal and wanted him to spend his life working in a spa or bath store arranging towels. Because this did not make sense, he soon thought about it in a different way. Suddenly, he recalled the story of Jesus washing the feet of His disciples. With great excitement, he realized that the Holy Spirit had just given him the first clue in the piecing together of his intriguing mission! He mulled over Jesus' foot washing ceremony that is re-enacted on Maudy Thursday during Holy Week. As he recalled how Jesus washed His disciple's feet, he was moved to think how this act captured the essence of humility and guided us as to how we are to minister to one another. Ethan had always been filled with a sense of awe and wonder at the tenderness and humility that Jesus demonstrated when he washed His disciples feet. For some reason, Ethan had always been drawn to how and why Jesus chose to do this. But how was this applicable to him? Just as Ethan was getting ready to get up and walk away to clear his mind, he closed his eyes. Suddenly, he had a clear vision as to what God meant by the word "towel boy" as well as what supposed to do to fulfill it!

"My son," Jesus said, "I realize this is scary, but I want you to quit your job and open a towel shop in town. In the store, I want you to wash the feet of people who are in need of all types of healing. If people have childlike faith and abide in me completely, I will allow my disciples to be a branch off my vine. While people have their feet washed, I will heal them in different ways according to My will. Some may be healed of their physical ailments or could be healed in other ways: being blessed with spiritual gifts and being empowered through the Holy Spirit to do mighty works or walking away feeling an overwhelming peace. Others will think differently and will have the ability to come up with unique solutions to complex problems.

"I do not want you to charge people for the healing. However, you may accept donations for all services rendered. Do not worry about how you will run the store or pay the bills. Leave the details to me. I will be with you and will show you what you need to do. At first it will be difficult, but if you trust me and do as I say, I will bless you and you will see that the business will thrive. Remember

I never sent my disciples out into the world alone but rather, two by two. Your mother has already agreed to help you in any way she can. Since you complement each other so well, I have chosen her to be your partner in this ministry."

When Ethan heard this news, he experienced a glimmer of the sheer joy Mary must have felt when Gabriel announced she would be Jesus' mother. As he considered the message Christ had given him, he was overwhelmed. Something in his spirit changed radically as if God had spiritually revived him. No longer did he feel his life was drifting with the tide but rather that Christ had a distinct purpose for his life.

The thought of serving Christ in such a special capacity with his beloved mother excited him beyond belief, for they had spent their lives preparing for this moment with great expectation. Ethan knew he would see his mother when she picked him up from work, and he could hardly wait to tell her the wondrous news.

It was wonderful to think about opening the store from a spiritual standpoint. Yet, when Ethan considered all the work that had to be done from a practical standpoint, the reality of what was happening sank in and he had doubts. The mere thought of taking a leap of faith of this magnitude without having a contingency plan was terrorizing. He realized that if he had one bad month, not only would he have to close the business but he would also be financially ruined and without a job. Furthermore, he imagined trying to rent a store and having the realtor laugh in his face when he mentioned the whole idea.

Ethan was not sure what to do. He knew in his heart he could do all things through Christ who strengthened him and if he just obeyed Christ, everything would work out. He also realized it was one thing to have faith, but another to have the courage to put his faith into action.

For years, Ethan had longed to be Christ's hands and feet on the earth. However, now that God had answered his prayer, Ethan had to decide if he trusted Christ enough to follow his heart. Was he all talk and no action? Ethan imagined being in this situation at many times in his life and thought it would be easy to make the right decision. Now that he was actually in this situation, Ethan had to decide if he was willing to act on his convictions.

Ethan wanted to do the right thing; yet, everything seemed to hit him at once and he couldn't think straight. Additionally, he was having such a wrestling match of the wills that he was weary and confused. Ethan tried to be patient and wait until the end of the day came. However, it reached a point where he could not stand it anymore.

"Hi, mom," Ethan said. "I know you're probably busy; but something very important just happened, and I must talk to you immediately! I cannot do it over the phone. I was just sitting here at work, and God gave a message that will change our lives forever. Please just come now! I feel overwhelmed, and I can't seem to get it together right about now."

Since it was nearly four o'clock, Claire was tempted to ask Ethan to wait an hour until she picked him up from work and they would discuss the matter over dinner. However, hearing the anxiety in his voice, she knew that he was deeply troubled and that he needed her help immediately. Without a moment's hesitation, she simply said, "Ethan, I'm not sure what you have to tell me, but I'll help you with whatever it is. Don't worry, it will be all right. We will get through it together, as we always do. Just hang tight. I'll be right there."

When she arrived and Ethan relayed had happened, Claire became choked up and could not believe what she was hearing. All the emotions she had buried so long ago came rushing back. For a time they just sat there speechless, thinking about this wondrous gift and the journey God had taken them on to bring them to this moment.

Ethan's journey began with the most unusual event. It occurred while he was still in heaven before entering his mother's womb. Although Ethan remembered the encounter distinctly, he was not sure if it actually happened or something he imagined.

God had invited him into an inner tent for a private conversation. "Son," He said, "I have a mission I want you to do for me on earth. I am upset with the way things are going, and I need someone special to help me. I know I can count on you to do it for me. However, before I send you, I must make sure you are up for it. I am sending you to earth one final time to accomplish a special mission and for further soul development. The assignment I have for you is a tough one; however, I feel you are up to the task."

Ethan was a bit apprehensive; nevertheless, soon he found himself in an empty movie theater with red satin walls and God was sitting next to him. Within a short time, God said, "Before I give you your assignment, I want to show you scenes from two possible lives. After viewing them, I will give you a choice if you want to live one of the two lives or remain in heaven with me.

"I will show you each movie in two parts. The first part will reveal the lifestyle that you will lead as well as the usual questions a person likes to have answered: if you are happy, healthy or sick; your character traits given different situations, and, of course, where you draw your strength. You will see how you spend your free time, what types of relationships you form, your passions, and if you are successful in a worldly sense.

"The second part will uncover a much deeper level of reality that some cannot perceive. It will show the development of your soul and the purpose of your life during your time on earth. There are many reasons why some choose to come to earth. Some come to have fun, to be famous, and to lavish in the luxuries of the world. Others come to help, to teach, and to serve others. You will also see the impact your life has on those around you, why you are attracted to certain people, and the role I want you to play in helping them in their quest.

"Your fate in the afterlife will be determined by the life you choose. Some may argue that these two parts are mutually exclusive, but they are very much interconnected, as you will soon discover. Depending on which part you choose to emphasize will determine which movie you pick."

Once Ethan understood the rules, the show began. The first movie showed a shrewd businessman named Mitch, a cardiologist in New York City. Mitch worked hard but enjoyed a very good life. He had a wife and three children who adored him. He had a house in the best part of town and summered at the Jersey shore. Mitch appeared happy and successful; yet, there was a great emptiness in his life that he never seemed able to fill. He had friends and family and he helped patients, but he always searched for some sort of nourishment to feed his starving soul. To fill this emptiness, he tried various things, but nothing satisfied him. He had money, power and love, but somehow these were never enough.

Like most people, Mitch had a dark side that he had never confronted. He seemed to be a dedicated family man, but as Mitch became successful, he ignored the family that had raised him. They were not well off and spent their lives working hard to make ends meet. Mitch could have easily made their lives easier but felt it was not his responsibility. Because of this, Mitch would be returning to see if he could get it right in the next life. He also did not practice any religion and thought religion was all just a myth people believed in because they were weak inside. What Mitch failed to realize was that it is the source of all happiness.

After a brief pause, the second movie began. At first glance, it seemed absolutely horrendous. It showed a boy born with cerebral palsy to a woman who would soon become a single parent and their lives would be filled with much suffering. Except for his mother, the boy would be considered an outcast even by his own family. Sure, the boy would have many superficial relationships, but few would truly care. Upon seeing this, Ethan made up his mind that this was definitely not the life he intended to lead. However, before Ethan made a hasty decision, God urged him to take a look at the second part.

At the time, Ethan wondered why a good and loving God would allow one of His children to be born with such affliction and have to endure such torture. Though He never answered Ethan in words, when Ethan saw a small glimpse of the second part, he understood that whatever he would have to endure in this life would be worthwhile.

After little thought, Ethan chose the second life. God smiled and told Ethan that this was the mission He had intended for him all along, but wanted to see if he was up to the challenge. Once Ethan made the choice, God explained that the life that Ethan had chosen to lead would be extremely difficult but filled with great joy. Ethan would have a mother who would be his best friend and soul mate. Their lives would be filled with much heartache and tribulation on many fronts but dedicated to helping others and bringing them to know Christ.

God explained that though Ethan would be disabled, he would have a wonderful opportunity to bear witness to others and help them look beyond the obvious and look at their own lives in a different light. By living a life of faith, Ethan and his mother would touch many lives in ways they could not even imagine. Their actions would serve their testimony and their words would nourish souls. After hearing these words, Ethan cried with joy and could not wait to start his mission. God blessed and hugged Ethan and then prepared him for the journey. He told Ethan that if he ever needed Him, all he had to do was cry out and He would be there. God sent Ethan through the birth canal to begin his mission. Being sent away from his Father and best friend was without a doubt the hardest thing he ever had to endure in his life.

THE EARLY YEARS

When the dream ended, Ethan woke up, but he felt disoriented. Indeed he was alive, but he had the oddest feeling—it was as if he was operating in two dimensions simultaneously. He may have been one of the main characters in the movie; yet many times, he felt as if he was watching himself from afar.

Like many, Ethan didn't know what happened the first three years of his life except what his mother, Claire, told him. God had given Ethan much to contend with, and his struggle began instantly. Under normal circumstances, giving birth is a joyous time for a woman. It is a beautiful event full of cherished, fond memories: hearing your baby cry, cutting the cord, and holding your baby in your arms for the first time. Claire's experience of giving birth to her 9-pound son Ethan was memorable; but unfortunately, not in the usual way.

It was a nightmare, and she was actually living it! Three days before she gave birth, she had a gut-wrenching feeling that something just wasn't right. However, by then, it was too late. The die had been cast, and there wasn't anything she could do about it. She experienced labor pains and knew the doctor should have checked on her or done something to induce labor, but that just wasn't how things were done deep in the coal fields of West Virginia.

Had there been anyone there to help, she would have screamed, but she lay in the hospital utterly alone. Initially, Claire called her husband at home, but he was sinning with a neighbor and getting tipsy the way he always did. Because she was lonely and afraid, after much hesitation, she resorted to calling her mother, Helen, who lived in Atlantic City, and pleaded with her to help. Claire had never had a close relationship with her mother and hoped that if she came to see her new grandchild, it would serve as an opportunity to make amends and start their relationship afresh.

Unfortunately, calling Helen proved to be a mistake. Even in Claire's darkest hour when she needed her mother, Helen made lame excuses why she was unable to leave Atlantic City. "Claire," Helen remarked, "why do we have to go through this yet again? I already told you I can't possibly come there. It's your brother's birthday and if I came down, who would bake him a cake? Besides, it's a long ride and you know I can't share a bathroom with anyone. You'll be fine, just stop being so melodramatic. I hate it when you get this way; it ruins my day and it's not fair! Just buck up, go outside, look at the blue sky, and smile."

If Claire thought she was depressed before, by the time she finished talking to her mother, she was so upset that she wanted to die. Based on past experience, she should have known it was not a good idea to call, for it was just like pouring salt on an open wound. Although she was deeply hurt, she had braced herself for the worst and wasn't disappointed. In the midst of her emotional anguish, two things helped numb Claire's pain: asking the nurse for some medicine and imagining that Jesus was at her side, lovingly stroking her head.

Claire had hoped those three days were just a stroke of bad luck, but unfortunately, they were a precursor of what was to come. As she lay in the delivery room, she drifted in and out of consciousness. It didn't take Claire long to discover that her premonitions three days earlier were correct. Upon undergoing natural childbirth and seeing that her newborn son was completely blue, Claire knew her troubles had just started.

The 20 minutes of sheer terror that followed would change her life forever. "Breathe, you bad baby," Dr. Kimmel kept yelling frantically, as he rushed her baby to an area across the room where he performed mouth-to-mouth. As Claire lay on the delivery table and heard what was happening, she wanted to scream. At that moment, she would have done anything in her power to stop the tragedy, but she was powerless and at the doctor's mercy. After 10 minutes Dr. Kimmel was able to revive Ethan. However, by then, the damage to Ethan's brain had been done. (Later, it was found that if Dr. Kimmel had performed a c-section, Ethan would have never had brain damage and would have been fine.)

During difficult times, our tendency is to wonder where God is and why a God of love would allow His children to suffer. It has been said that the best things in life never come easily. The fact is God often assigns the people He loves the most daunting missions to accomplish for Him during their time on earth. We may think our task on earth is to do our daily routines, but rather it is to learn and then perform the mission God has given us. Some people know from the start what God wants them to do. For others, figuring it out is a lifelong process.

As humans, we are eager to accomplish our mission and to run out of the starting gate with much vigor. Yet God in His wisdom knows that to have the stamina to run the race, He has to put us through basic training so we can acquire the skills needed to perform our mission. There are times when basic training is a grueling and painful process. Along with the times of joy, there are also many lessons we must learn in the form of trials and tribulations that every one of us must endure along the way. God knows if we knew all that we would have to endure beforehand. We would refuse to take the journey. To make the burden more bearable, He shields our eyes and promises to hold our hand as we take each step along the way.

It was a true blessing that Claire didn't know what kind of life God had in store for her, for if she had, she would have never had the strength to endure it. Initially, Claire didn't know what a tragic mistake Dr. Kimmel had made or what impact his negligence would have on every facet of her life. All of that changed within hours, when the doctors wouldn't allow her to see or hold her newborn son. Claire clearly knew something was seriously wrong. The most frustrating part was that the doctors refused to answer any of her questions, saying they wouldn't know anything until they had run a series of tests.

The doctors at the local hospital read the test results and realized that they were not equipped to handle the complexity of Ethan's medical problems. Consequently, they sent Ethan immediately to West Virginia's main hospital in Charleston, a six-hour drive away. The most astounding part of the entire ordeal was that the doctors made no attempt to explain to Claire what was happening.

At that time, as Claire's maternal instinct kicked in, she had a most uncomfortable feeling in the pit of her stomach and knew the doctors didn't know what they were talking about. If she had had any support system to help her, she would have left West Virginia and taken Ethan back to the Atlantic City area where there were good hospitals. Unfortunately, she found facing an impossible situation without a soul to turn to for comfort, support, or help.

If things were not hard enough, Claire's life was even more complicated because she had tried to stand by Jim, her husband, and do the right thing. Unfortunately, she found herself in a mess. The saying, "No good deed goes unpunished," is certainly true; unfortunately, she was living proof of that.

Jim had grown up in a strict Jehovah's Witness family, and like many young men, he rebelled because he did not like the rules. When Jim became a young man, he left home because he did not want to be indoctrinated any longer and wanted to experience the real world. For a while, Jim liked being in the real world; unfortunately, because he had been so sheltered and brainwashed, he felt as if he had stepped into a foreign land and didn't have a clue how to behave.

Jim was unable to enjoy life because he felt two conflicting emotions simultaneously. While it was a relief to be out of the environment and not be chastised for every little thing, he was nonetheless plagued with feelings of guilt and shame. He felt he had lost his identity and didn't know how much more he could stand. The worst part was that he did not have a place to go to escape the mental anguish that he felt. At times Jim considered going back to his family. However, this was not an option since his family had disowned him.

His estrangement caused him constant pain. He had no escape, so he turned to liquor and slowly evolved to more potent addictions, such as pills, pot, and cocaine as a way of self-medicating. This did help him forget, numbed his pain, and for a time, everything seemed to be okay. However, whenever the high wore off, the sorrow returned, and he became more depressed than ever.

When Claire met Jim, he was in the throes of despair. Since Claire felt abandoned by the world, she thought maybe they could provide much needed comfort and support to one another. As time progressed, Jim grew tired of feeling empty. Finally, he had reached a point where he couldn't stand it anymore After much deliberation, he decided the only way he would have any peace was to make amends with his family in West Virginia. Much to his dismay, doing this would require him to become a Jehovah's Witness again.

Moving to West Virginia was definitely a culture shock that Claire was not prepared for. In the first place, Claire knew nothing about the Jehovah's Witnesses and was in for a rude awakening.

The pace of life and mores of society were different, and she knew she was completely out of her element.

Claire was despondent and felt that her world had been shattered as she stood above the crib looking down at her son. She wasn't prepared for this and did not know what to do. The doctor had relayed the news, and it wasn't good. He said her son had cerebral palsy, was profoundly retarded and would be a vegetable. It was best to institutionalize and forget about him.

All she wanted was a fresh start and a baby to love her. As she stared at her baby, she asked herself many questions "Is this really possible? Did the doctor make a mistake? How could the doctor say this about my baby? Does he know what he is talking about? What should I do? Should I listen to him? He doesn't see the sparkle in my baby's eyes. Why is this happening to me? It isn't fair! What did I ever do to deserve this? Why doesn't God love me?"

Claire had to decide what to do. Of course, she wanted to do right by her son, but what was that? If Claire had had someone to turn to, perhaps he would have encouraged her to listen to the doctor's advice. After all, taking care of a sick child was an overwhelming responsibility, and the prognosis of his amounting to much was nil. However, it was a blessing in disguise that she was utterly alone and didn't have anyone to tell her that what she was about to do couldn't be done.

Against her better judgment, Claire stayed in West Virginia for two years and tried to make a life with Jim. However, in the end, it was futile. The reality was Jim was mentally ill and locked in a vicious cycle of torment that would never end. His plan of reuniting with his family and becoming a Jehovah's Witness again didn't help. In fact, it made his depression even worse. Sitting in those meetings for hours on end reminded Jim why he had left.

At this time, Jim just didn't know what to do and felt he was losing his mind. Nothing he did helped. He suffered such severe anguish and wished he could push a magic button and have it all go away. Jim wanted help but just didn't know how to make the nightmare come to an end. Claire was tired of being an enabler and being abused by him. Claire knew how horrifically difficult her life would be if she left him. But she had no choice. Ethan was sick and needed help, and the hospitals in West Virginia were simply inadequate. She could either give her son a fighting chance and move back to the Atlantic City area where there were good hospitals or stay in an abusive relationship with someone who didn't have any intention of changing.

It had taken Claire over two years to reach this point, but finally she had had enough and refused to take it anymore. She knew Jim, her husband, was sick and needed help. She could deal with his sickness, but everything else was unbearable. She knew she had done her best, but she realized her efforts are in vain. She had tried to help Jim, but there was no use. He was a hopeless case.

Life changed dramatically for Claire the day a woman approached her in church and recommended that she take Ethan, who was seven-years-old at the time, to a faith healer. Initially, Claire found the whole idea amusing and laughed to herself exclaiming, "Yeah, it'll be a cold day before I do that!" Her experience with faith healers had been the typical one—the phony televangelists who perform healings on television and ask people to send them money. The mere thought of taking Ethan to one of those charlatans turned her stomach.

Days passed and Claire forgot about the encounter. However, she was reminded of it when she reached into her coat pocket and found the faith healer's phone number. Claire was tempted to throw out the number, but as she looked at it, she wondered what would happen if this was real. What kind of mother would I be to turn this down if there were a possibility that God would actually heal my son? Claire called the number and ended up taking Ethan to see Joann.

Claire had gone to church all her life, went through the motions, but never had a close relationship with God. As Claire drove to see Joann, Claire took a hard look at herself and didn't like where her life was going. Claire felt weird asking God to heal her son, especially when she did not even really know who He was. She did not know what the outcome of the day would be. Nevertheless, she vowed that no matter what, she was going to change her life and do her best to be a better person.

When Ethan and Claire arrived at Joann's house, they were not sure what to expect. Joann did her best to put them at ease by explaining that she herself was useless and did not possess any power. Rather, she was merely an instrument and that Christ worked through her in whatever way He chose. Upon making this abundantly clear, Joann led Ethan and Claire to the basement and asked Ethan to lie on the couch and to make himself as comfortable as possible. At the time, Ethan walked with crutches and wore short leg braces. As the three of them prayed and Joann asked Jesus to use her as a channel in whatever way He chose, she laid her hands upon Ethan. He felt intense heat and charge go into him. While Joann had her hands on him, Claire opened her eyes and saw a massive lightning bolt go into her son's body.

After the prayer, Joann helped Ethan to his feet, and he began walking without his braces or crutches. He was amazed. Never before had Ethan experienced the feeling of being able to put one foot in front of the other without the help of an assistive device. He thanked Joann profusely for what she had done. However, before he could even get it out of his mouth, she reminded him that it was not her but Christ who worked through her. The three of them thanked God for what He had done. Surely, God was in the room with them and heard and answered. The king of the entire universe had answered Ethan's prayer.

At that time, Ethan tried to sit down and write his name on a piece of paper but could not do it. He realized then that Jesus had healed him partially to help him get around better but had not cured him completely so he would still need to be reliant on Him.

After 10 minutes of praise, Ethan asked Joann to lay her hands on his mother and ask Jesus to heal her eyes. Claire's eyesight had been bad since she was a child. Although Joann did this, her physical eyes did not improve, but Jesus blessed her with a far more glorious gift. Claire would not discover this gift until a week later after she had had a chance to think about everything that had happened that day.

When Ethan returned from Joann's, he showed his unbelieving grandmother the wondrous miracle that had taken place. She was quick to tell him that it was not Jesus who made him walk, but rather that it had been a result of his determination to walk. This angered him greatly because he had not been able to walk independently the day before and she would not accept the fact that a miracle had taken place. While perseverance is important, it alone is not enough to make something of such magnitude happen overnight.

SERIOUS COMMITMENT

Claire had always taken Ethan to church and knew the stories in the Bible. They prayed before meals, but that was really the extent of the relationship they had with God. From reading the Bible, they knew God was always with them and loved them on some level, but God seemed to be a distant being who managed the universe from afar. They also knew intellectually that God could heal people, but it wasn't until God had given Ethan the ability to walk that their eyes were opened. In that moment, they had a spiritual awakening and their lives were never the same. Their entire concept of who God is changed radically. No longer did they see God as a distant, ethereal being but rather as a loving Father who cared deeply about them.

Ethan and Claire's knowledge about God had been strictly factual up until this point. However, now that they had a personal encounter with Him, they wanted more than anything else, to get to know God better and have an intimate relationship with Him. While this was their desire, they were not sure how to go about it. Getting to know people is hard enough when you can look them in the eye and talk to them. However, it is even more challenging when you know they are there and yet you do not know how to have a dialog with them.

Getting to know God better would take work. If they were serious about wanting to have a personal relationship with Jesus, they would need to read the Bible to learn what God wants from His people and learn to have a child's faith and trust implicitly, without asking any questions. They would also need to seek to do His will above all else and to know that while they could not see Jesus in the flesh, He was there.

Despite Ethan and Claire's reservations, they prayed to their Father in a new way. No longer did they rattle off meaningless, ritualistic words. Rather, they spoke sincerely from their hearts to God, as if He was a friend who cared deeply about them. They admitted they were unable to do anything on their own without constant help. Although they were not sure if there would be any result, they were tired of living day after day and wanted more meaning in their lives.

The process of becoming one with Christ should be one of the most natural things, yet at times it can be frustrating. It is easy to pour out our hearts and ask for help, but often it is difficult to tune out the world, quiet the mind, and wait for God to respond. We know Jesus said, "Come unto me all you who are heavy laden and I will give you rest." Part of the reason why it is difficult for us to become still is that we live in a fast-paced world and are accustomed to instant gratification. When God doesn't answer us immediately, we have a tendency to become exasperated and to presume that God isn't listening. Instead of becoming frustrated, we must step back, assess the situation, and know that God will answer us in His time and in the manner He deems fit.

When Ethan and Claire began to meditate, Ethan found it very difficult to quiet his mind. Claire told him to picture Jesus; yet, he found his mind either drifted to other subjects or that he would hear a voice but could not determine if he was hearing his own voice or the still, small voice of God. This was hard enough; however, he became even more frustrated upon comparing notes with his mother and discovering that she had a completely different experience. Initially, Ethan did not understand why this was happening and wondered if he was doing something wrong. Over time, he came to understand that God speaks to people in different ways depending on where they are in life. There are certainly times God has special instructions to tell groups of people He has chosen to accomplish tasks for Him during their time on earth. However, because He has created every person for a distinct purpose, He has special things He has to tell each of His children.

At times, Ethan wished God would speak to him in meditation. He enjoyed hearing his mother tell of the wondrous inner world Christ allowed her to experience whenever she meditated. Whenever Claire would surrender herself and ask Christ to fill her with Himself, Christ came to her in a form she had never experienced before . . . in the form of pure light. Some may think this light refers to joy, but it actually is light. It is not the kind that comes from a light bulb, but spiritual light that you can see with your eyes closed when you become one with the very heart of Christ. It is a gift the Spirit bestows upon His children who truly seek to do His will above all else and to be His hands and feet on the earth.

Because Claire had never experienced anything like this before, she did not know what was happening. Initially, she was apprehensive about telling anyone what was happening for fear that they would think she was nuts. However, when it occurred every time she prayed and not at any other time, she knew she had to figure out what was happening so she could have peace of mind. Claire called Joann and prayed that she would be able to provide some insight on what was happening.

Since Claire was new at this and was not sure how to broach the subject, the first few minutes of the call proved awkward. Fortunately, Joann was perceptive and could tell that Claire was tiptoeing around the topic. After some idle chitchat, Joann put Claire at ease by saying, "I've been expecting to hear from you and have been wondering why you didn't call me sooner. Look, I'm not sure yet what has happened to you spiritually, but whatever it is, don't be afraid to tell me. I'll understand."

Claire relayed the events that had transpired over the last few weeks. During this time, Joann listened quietly and gave Claire the time to explain fully the predicament she was in.

Once Claire finished, Joann calmly said, "I realize the tremendous courage it took for you to tell me that, and I feel honored that you thought enough about me to share this with me. Be assured that in no way do I think you're crazy. Let me begin by reminding you that a few weeks ago when you were at my house Ethan asked me to lay my hands on you and ask Jesus to heal your eyes. Well, I'm pleased to tell you that Jesus heard our prayer and answered it. Oh, He did not answer it the way you thought He would. However, believe it or not, He did answer it!

"God may not have healed your physical eyes, but has He blessed you with a far greater gift. He opened your spiritual eyes and allowed you to enter into a spiritual realm where you could experience His abundant light. I know you have been wondering what has been happening, but be assured that you are highly favored by God, and He has blessed you with a tremendous gift that He only gives to His select few." Claire had suspected that this was the case all along; however, once Joann reaffirmed what she believed, the apprehension left and Claire was left with a feeling of well-being.

Claire felt that the next few months was her honeymoon with God. She would get up, give the day to the Lord and ask Him to use her as an instrument in whatever way He chose. Going about her day, Claire tried to visualize that Jesus was using her body to accomplish His will. She imagined what He would do in any given situation and act accordingly. Whenever she encountered the slightest bit of difficulty or trouble, she asked the Master for help. Unfortunately, this state of blissfulness did not last long. Because Christ had special plans for Claire, after a time of brief rest, it was time for Claire to begin her mission.

Within days, Christ came to her during her meditation dressed in a long, white robe and gave her a special mission that changed the direction of Claire's life forever. "Blessed child," Jesus said, "just as

I laid my hands on Ethan and you and healed you both, I now lay my hands on you and call you to lay your hands on others."

When Claire heard these words, she was overcome with emotion. Claire was obviously humbled, excited, and filled with great joy that Jesus had asked her to do this for Him. However, at the same time, many questions flickered through her head. Why had God selected her, of such lowly stature, to accomplish this important task? Was she really up to the task? If she told people that God had visited her and had given her this assignment, how would people react? Would people believe her or think she had turned into a freak?

Once the initial wonder of it all subsided, Claire calmed down and began to think clearly. Throughout her life whenever she faced situations that seemed impossible, Claire often thought of Peter. Jesus had asked him to get out of the boat and walk to Him on the water. From experience, Claire knew she had to learn basic lessons if she wanted God to use her and there was no way to get around learning them. Prior to committing her life to Christ, she often tried to escape from unpleasant situations by doing things her own way, hoping if she whined and stomped her feet, God would have mercy and spare her from the unpleasant lesson. Much to her dismay, this did not help, for it merely prolonged the inevitable. After she had thrown her little tantrum, she found herself right back in the spot she had been prior to becoming upset.

Claire was tired of following an unproductive routine that did not get her anywhere and surmised there had to be an easier way. Hence, she decided to try a new approach: just to do it and get it over with. Consequently, she shut her eyes and prayed, "Lord, I have been in this situation before I'm not sure exactly what you want me to do for you. However, I know if I trust you and depend on you to guide me step by step that everything will work out according to plan."

When Claire finished praying, a great sense of peace came upon her, and she knew everything would be all right. Although she had no idea where Christ would lead her, she took comfort in knowing that Jesus would never leave her side and would help her with whatever situation she encountered.

From afar it may seem noble to be Christ's hands and feet on earth, to engage in spiritual warfare, and to fight to set the captive free. Yet, Claire knew from reading the Bible that those who committed their lives wholeheartedly to carrying out Christ's will suffered greatly. Claire had always heard people say that until they decide to follow Christ, nothing that tragic happens to them. Sure, some things happen once in a while because that's just the way life works out sometimes. However, once they make a serious commitment to follow Christ, life changes drastically. For as soon as Satan sees that people are diligently trying to do God's will, Satan goes on the attack and does everything possible to make their lives unbearable. Satan hopes that by inflicting enough misery in their lives, people will become so worn down and will quit before reaching the finish line.

———————————

It has been said that God created every person for a distinct purpose and no two people are exactly alike. People know they have a distinct purpose on earth; yet, discovering what that is can often be very challenging. Some people go through their entire lives yearning with all of their hearts to discover why they were put on the earth. Christians know Christ calls us to live passionately and to perform acts of love; yet, when you ask most Christians what is going on, they act as if they are half asleep, and rattle off answers like "not much." Despite being commissioned by Christ to do this, some die feeling as if their lives were a waste because they had not discovered the purpose of their lives.

The journey with God is a delicate balancing act and if you are not careful, you will surely lose ground. On one hand, it is vital to be tenacious, persistent, and outspoken, for if you are not, you will never get ahead. At the same time, if you approach things the wrong way, you can end up alienating people. That may in turn prevent you from achieving your ultimate objective.

When Claire began her journey, she was a rookie unaware of the balancing act. She knew God had given her a special assignment, and she was determined not to let anything get in the way of accomplishing her mission! For the next several years, Claire woke up every morning with a zealous attitude of wanting to take on the world for Christ.

When Claire received the message to start a healing ministry, her life changed radically. She continued doing her daily routine; but more and more the idea of serving the Lord in this special and unique capacity became the driving force behind all she did and quickly became all she thought about. As the days dragged on, she longed to be freed from her responsibilities so she could serve her Lord and King full time.

One day, Claire just had had enough of her incessant, never-ending routine and sat down and cried out to her Father in Heaven. After telling Him how tired and weary she was of her routine, she became still and listened in a way she never had before. Although she did not feel God's actual touch, she soon felt His presence surrounding her. "My precious, beloved daughter," a voice said, "peace be with you. I understand how much you long to serve me. I promise you there will be a day when you will do this and you will do it well. I know you wish it would happen now, but daughter, it's not time yet. I plan to use you, but before I do, I must teach you some lessons. Just as a soldier attends basic training to prepare for battle, I also need to strengthen your character and make you totally dependent on me. Until you depend on me for everything and realize that apart from me you can do nothing, I cannot use you. Basic training is often grueling and is meant to push you beyond your endurance; however, it is a task I reserve for my dearest disciples. Despite what they may think, I do not do this to make them suffer, but because I love them and need them to be well trained for battle."

It is one thing to say you want to be a disciple. However, when God puts challenging obstacles in a disciple's path that are painful, do they remain faithful when things get rough or run away when the going gets tough? Over the next several years, God certainly tested

Claire's character by leading her down a hard road to prepare her for her mission.

It can be quite difficult at times to discern whether God is actually directing a person or if a person's desire is the force driving them to pursue a specific goal. We may believe in our hearts that God is the one driving us to pursue a goal. However, in actuality, we are following our own ambition. Learning to discern this difference is not easy, is frustrating, and requires a great deal of practice.

When God told Claire that He would lay His hands on her so she could lay her hands on others, Claire was excited and was raring to go. After praying and asking Jesus to direct her feet, there were times Claire sensed that God was putting her in situations to begin to lay the groundwork for a healing ministry. When this happened, her hopes soared and she put everything she had into pursuing the lead, believing this might be the opportunity she had been waiting for.

For years Claire did everything she could think of to get herself in position where she could start a healing ministry and serve her Lord and Master. Despite many fervent attempts and much to her dismay, nothing she tried ever worked out. Every time she failed, she got back up and tried again. Claire even tried to enter the seminary and become a minister.

Every fiber of Claire's being longed to bathe her mind in the Word of God, and even received a full scholarship to seminary. While she was eager to serve her Master and go to seminary, because of her commitment to doing the right thing by Ethan, she reluctantly turned down the opportunity. If Claire had had any type of support system to help her take care of Ethan, things would have been different. In the end, her role as mom won out over her own personal ambitions and desires. Making the ultimate sacrifice to forgo the seminary cut her soul to the core.

After suffering this devastating blow to her soul, Claire was so angry at God that she became like a turtle that went into its shell and shriveled up. Consequently, she accepted her lot in life and never tried to pursue starting any type of healing ministry again.

Claire's time in this wilderness was not only trying, but it lasted over 30 years. During the experience, Claire often felt like the Samaritan on the side of the road: few people aided or comforted her. Yes, they saw what her life was like and empathized with the cross she had to bear. Some tried to help; however, after a very short time, many became weary, uttered platitudes, and walked away.

On occasion, people would ask how she survived the monotony of it all without losing her mind. In truth, she spent many nights imploring God to give her the endurance to get through another long, lonesome day. While there were times when she wondered if could get through another day, she surmised there was a reason why Christ wanted her to experience this. Consequently, when she grew tired or discouraged, she remembered two Bible verses "I can do all things through Christ who strengthens me" and "Those who endure shall be saved."

Hearing Ethan's wonderful news, Claire was ecstatic. Although she had tried to make the best of a difficult situation, this was the first time she felt she could finally relax. The impediment that held her captive for so long had been lifted.

Because Claire had such a special relationship with Ethan, she understood the gamut of feelings he must be experiencing. On the one hand, he was no doubt awestruck and excited about the opportunity God was giving them to serve Christ in such a capacity. It was all they ever wanted from life, and now their dreams were about to come true. At the same time she understood how scary this was and that many variables were weighing on his mind.

She understood that it is easy for people to dream about following Jesus and being faithful to Him no matter what. Now that Jesus had actually put him to the test, Ethan faced a decisive moment. Was he a man who paid lip service or was he a man who acted on his convictions? She realized the tremendous courage it would take Ethan to lunge for the swinging trapeze bar, especially since he did not know whether there would be a net to catch him if he were to fall. While she empathized with Ethan's predicament and wanted to be as supportive as possible, Claire knew that if Ethan stood there too long, he might never have the nerve to jump. This was exactly what she wanted to avoid and thus knew her role was to help Ethan and provide him with the encouragement he needed.

Claire prayed silently for several minutes and then prayed aloud. "Father, you are an awesome God, and we are so thankful for what you are doing. The news that Ethan just told me is remarkable and does come as a surprise. We believe you had planned this for us and have wanted us to serve you in this manner since the beginning of time. We also know throughout time you have asked your servants to do many things that may have seemed impossible. However, despite their fears and doubts, they obeyed you and you used them to do mighty things for your glory. You know the situation we are in. We know if we trust you that you won't allow us to fail. We rededicate our lives to you this day. We love you and seek to be your hands and feet on earth in whatever you want. Please direct our footsteps and we will follow wherever you lead us. We ask these things in the name of Jesus."

When Claire finished praying, the Holy Spirit's presence filled the room, and a peace came over them. Although no words were uttered, Ethan was confident that the Holy Spirit was present and would direct them every step of the way.

Ethan and Claire praised God for granting them their ultimate wish of serving Him together, but they soon realized that they had to get down to work. Immediately, they sketched out a game plan, made a list of tasks that needed to be done, allocated the tasks according to who was the most knowledgeable in that area, and went to work.

Since Claire was good at writing and public relations, it seemed only natural that she would be responsible for publicizing

Divine Towels. She would not only post flyers at various community agencies and churches but also would talk to support groups at hospitals and demonstrate how God worked through the towels. Ethan, on the other hand, would run day-to-day operations and keep track of donations and expenses. While each of them was an expert in his or her respective area, they also recognized that there would be some overlapping, and they would need to rely on each other for help. Thus, they agreed to meet frequently to discuss and monitor the progress that was being made.

Once a basic framework had been mapped out, Ethan had no reservations about writing his letter of resignation and telling his supervisor that he was pursuing a "higher calling." Initially, when he read Ethan's letter, his supervisor looked at Ethan as if he had lost his mind but smiled and wished him the best of luck on his endeavors anyway.

FIRST STEPS

Now that Ethan had resigned from his job, he got to work right away and did several tasks immediately. First, he needed to find a store with a fairly cheap rent. However, finding a place like that in the Coppertown area was not an easy task. Ethan looked in the paper, but all the stores in the area wanted at least $1,500 a month rent plus a security deposit. This was simply more than Ethan could afford. Ethan then tried posting several ads on the Internet but did not get even one reply. Ethan was running out of ideas on where to look and ended up falling on his knees, as he should have done in the first place and asking for help.

After praying for a while, Ethan felt led to call his Mom and ask for her advice. Claire was a very wise woman who always seemed to make miracles happen when nothing else would work, and this time was no exception. "Why didn't you come to me sooner, you goof? I just heard in prayer meeting that the hardware store on the corner of Main Street is going out of business, and Mr. Smith the proprietor, who just so happens to be a member of the church, is looking for a tenant immediately. I know him personally and have a feeling that if you talk to him and explain the situation that he might even be willing to lower the rent. If you like, I would be happy to talk to him for you."

"I appreciate the offer," Ethan said, "but I think it would be better if I talk to him myself, especially if it comes down to money. You are good at many things, but making decisions about money was never your strong point."

"Yeah, yeah," Claire chuckled because her son certainly did know her well.

"Do you have his number?"

Before calling, Claire told Ethan that Mr. Smith had partial paralysis on his left side because of a work-related accident. Consequently, Ethan phoned Mr. Smith and agreed to swing by his house later on that day. He also decided it would also be a good idea to take a towel along and demonstrate how it worked. After all, if Mr. Smith was going to let Ethan be his tenant, he had every right to see that Ethan's business was legitimate and not a hoax.

"Hi, Mr. Smith, I'm glad to meet you. Thank you for taking the time to meet with me."

"Don't mention it. I just hope I can help. By the way, call me Jim."

"Well, I hope you can too because I'm in a difficult position, and I'm coming to you as a last resort," Ethan laughed nervously.

"Okay, lay it on me, and I'll try to do whatever I can to help."

Ethan took a deep breath and prayed that Christ would guide him on what to say. "It happened a few days ago as I was sitting at my desk at work and was bored with my routine. I had always longed to be a warrior for Christ and had been asking Him for a long time to give me an opportunity to serve Him. He finally took me up on it and told me to quit my job and become a towel boy. He then went on to say I was to open a nonprofit store, offer my services to the public, and accept only donations. At first, I thought I was going nuts, but after praying about this, I am confident that this is what Christ wants me to do. The reason I'm telling you this is I know that you own the hardware store on Main Street that is going out of business. My mother thought that if I told you my plans, you might consider renting it to me for a reduced rate."

As Ethan spoke, Jim Smith smiled to himself. Like Ethan, Jim had also longed for the same type of opportunity; however, he was never fortunate enough to have his dream become a reality. Jim had done much during his life to help others, but he always felt that he was supposed to do more but could never quite identify what it was until now. Jim was thankful that he had been so richly blessed, and he knew now was his time to give something back to his God and his community.

Jim was about to speak but never got a chance. Bang! It happened, as it did whenever he was in one position for too long. "Oh, good God, not now! Quick, Ethan, go to the medicine cabinet and get me a pill. I get these cramps every once in a while, and they are enough to make me want to die." Jim wailed with agony as he grasped his left leg. "I have been like this for five years. I was helping one of my men in that storeroom and the ceiling came crashing down on me. I have been paralyzed on my left side ever since I would give anything just to be able to move normally again. I keep asking Jesus to heal me so I can return to helping others, the way I used to before my accident. However, it hasn't worked thus far."

Seeing that Jim was in severe pain, Ethan got the medicine as fast as possible. Once Jim took his medicine, he got a gleeful look in his eye and began laughing uncontrollably, as if he understood what God was doing. Once Jim had managed to contain himself, he said, "Oh, please forgive me for the outburst. Sometimes it's just funny how God works. You know I believe God knew what He was doing when He sent you here. You said Jesus gave you the gift to heal people by washing their feet. I firmly believe if you wash my feet, I will be healed."

Ethan smiled and got to work. He filled a basin with water, prayed silently and humbly that he would become the vehicle through which Christ would work, and he immediately began washing Jim's feet. Jim was not sure what to expect. After all, there appeared to be nothing extraordinary about washing feet, merely pouring water over feet and then drying them off with a towel. However, Jim was amazed by what he experienced. From the second Ethan began, streams of intense pulsating energy, as Jim had never felt before, flowed from Ethan's hands into Jim's feet and then through his entire body. The experience was electrifying. Yet Jim was more moved by the tender and caring way Ethan washed his feet, for it reminded him of Jesus' desire to cleanse and heal his wounded and beloved lambs.

As Ethan dried his feet, Jim could not believe the sensations that he felt in his body. Not only did the cramps cease, but Jim also knew how the tin man in *The Wizard of Oz* must have felt when he was being oiled. The paralyzed side that had been rigid and tight for so long slowly began to limber. For the first time in five years, Jim was able to move with ease, and the freedom he felt was awesome. Jim could not contain the sheer joy; he began to dance and sing to the Lord. Being able to move his limbs again was incredible enough. However, when he stood up and began walking across the room without the need for his walker, Jim was simply amazed. Ethan, on the other hand, watched and marveled at the miraculous things Christ was doing through him and in Jim, but he also wondered if Jim planned to help him on the store or not.

After some time, when the shock of what happened began to wear off, Jim told Ethan to take a seat and wait for him for a few minutes. He would be right back. While Ethan waited, he noticed how black the water in the basin had become and was curious why this happened, especially when Jim's feet had appeared to be clean. As he sat there thinking, nothing came to mind, so he thought he would clean up while he was waiting.

As Ethan was about to pick up the basin to rinse it out, he heard a word of caution. "My son, because you have never done this before, I must teach you a very important process once each basin is used. The reason the water turns black is that you are doing much more than just washing their feet. In this act of washing, the feet represent the whole person, body, soul, and spirit. Therefore, when you wash a person's feet I am, in fact, cleansing the very essence of their being. All negativity, pain, and heartache

35

associated with a person's brokenness are transferred to the water. There is only one way to prevent this spiritual sludge from polluting the sewage system and being passed on to others. You must pray for the blood of Jesus to cleanse the water as you pour it down the drain. The blood will overcome the evil before it can infect anyone else."

At that moment, Jim waltzed out of other room whistling and left an envelope with Ethan's name on it on the table next to where Ethan was standing. "Here, I want you to have this as a small token of my appreciation," Jim said. A few seconds later, Ethan turned his attention to the envelope on the table.

"What is it?" Ethan asked. However, by that time, Jim had left the room. Once Ethan finished disposing of the water as he had been directed, he dried his hands and proceeded to open the envelope. Inside Ethan found four things: a key, a check for $20,000 made out to him, the deed for the store, and a letter. Ethan could not begin to understand why Jim was doing this but hoped that reading the letter might shed some light on it. It read:

Dearest friend in Christ:

I'm not exactly sure what happened today, but whatever you did worked. I realize I do not know you, but like you, I also want to devote my life to serving Christ. I have done some worthwhile things during my life, but I feel compelled to help you in your endeavor to be a towel boy. You have helped me so much and helping you in this way is the very least I can do. Christ has given you a miraculous gift; never forget that. For this reason, I would be most grateful if you would accept the deed to the store, the key, and this small check to get you started.

I know you're probably wondering why I'm giving you the store. Frankly, I'm just tired of dealing with all the hassles associated with it. I have already made a lot of money during my lifetime, and I don't know what I would do with the store even if I kept it. I want you to have it, so you can bless the lives of others with it.

In exchange for this, I ask only for two things in return. First, please don't tell anyone besides your mother that I did this. I prefer that this remain between us and God. Second, if you need anything or encounter any obstacles along the way, please call me immediately because I want to support you in any way I can.

Your brother in Christ,
Jim Smith

Ethan could hardly believe Jim's generosity and the way God had answered his prayers. Several days ago things looked bleak and hopeless, but God had turned the situation around and made it blossom into a beautiful flower. After a few moments, Ethan rose, went into the other room, thanked Jim and went on his way.

On his way home that day, Ethan could not help but smile to himself. He could hardly believe all the blessings God had lavished on his mother and him. Although he had always made himself available to be used, it was not until he stopped trying and relinquished control to God that his adventure began. Twenty-four hours before, he was a mere underling trying to climb the corporate ladder. Now Ethan and his mother were about to serve Christ in a capacity they had dreamed about for years.

Now that Ethan had a store, it was time to concentrate on the store itself. It was obvious once people learned of the healing they could receive at the store, if they truly believed, that people would soon flock to the store in droves regardless of the store's ambiance. Because Ethan and Claire were perfectionists and believed that whatever service they performed was for the Lord to help people quiet their minds and focus on what was really going on, they felt it was vital to create a warm, inviting atmosphere that was free of distractions. Fortunately, Claire had a knack for knowing how to create this type of environment.

After spending hours trying out various styles and textures, Ethan and Claire decided the store should have a naturally stained wooden floor, indirect lighting, gold-colored walls, wheat-colored area rugs, and soft, soothing music. Although they liked the look, they determined they needed a crucial element to tie everything altogether. It was not until they asked the Holy Spirit for guidance that they were directed to hang vine branches around the perimeter of the ceiling. This would constantly remind the workers in the store that God is the one with the power and without His help, we are useless. Initially, it sounded expensive; however, after pricing it out and deciding that they could do much of the work themselves with the help of a few friends, it definitely was in the realm of possibility. God was surely at work, and this was yet another sign that He had everything planned and was guiding every movement.

Once Claire had sketched out a blueprint of the store's interior, Ethan and Claire asked friends to lend a hand. Originally, when they asked for help, all were eager to participate. However, when the time came to get busy, for one reason or another, they bailed out, leaving Ethan stranded. There was so much work to be done that Ethan and Claire could not imagine how they could possibly do all the work themselves. Not knowing where to turn, Ethan recalled that Jim Smith said to call him if he ever needed anything, and Ethan decided to take Jim up on his offer.

"Hello, Mr. Smith. This is Ethan, I . . . ."

"Hi, Ethan, what's up? I've been meaning to call you. So much has changed since you washed my feet; it's simply unbelievable. People whom I associate with everyday are so shocked to see me up and about that most have to do a double take to make sure that their eyes aren't playing tricks on them. When I explained about the towels and how the power flowed from Christ through you and into me, I got mixed reactions. While some think I have completely lost my mind, most are so shocked that they don't even know what to think. I'm telling you this because many people have seen what you have done for me and are very anxious for the store to open so that they can come and see what Christ can do for them."

"Ah, I see," Ethan said, somewhat anticipating that this would be his reaction.

"So tell me, my friend, how is the store coming?" Mr. Smith inquired.

"Well, to tell you the truth, I'm calling because I'm in bind and I need some help."

"What sort of help?"

"All my friends who promised to help me get things set up and organized bailed out on me at the last minute. Now I have no one who can help me with construction, and I was hoping you might know some people who are good with their hands."

Jim laughed hysterically.

"What is so funny?" Ethan inquired.

"I'm laughing because I was just about to ask you if you needed help, and because it's kind of funny how God brings people together to do His work," Jim exclaimed while chuckling a bit. "When I had my own construction company, I formed an unusual bond with many men who worked for me. It began casually one day over lunch. Mark, one of my foremen, had been talking about how he drove through the ghettos everyday to get to work. He explained that he hated seeing people living in extreme poverty with looks of despair on the people's faces and knowing there was little hope of ever getting out of it. He wanted to help, but he felt helpless and did not know what to do except to pray that God would help them. Then, one Sunday while listening to a sermon about the Good Samaritan, his pastor made a comment that Mark never forgot. The pastor said, 'Whenever you are in a frustrating position and don't know what to do, just shut your eyes and ask yourself what type of help would you offer Jesus.'

"Just then, Mark imagined he was driving through the ghettos and that Jesus was standing outside. Again, Mark felt helpless, but he did not just want to drive by as if the person did not exist. As he looked at Jesus, Mark was reminded of the scripture, 'I was hungry, and you gave me food to eat; I was thirsty, and you gave me drink; I was a stranger, and you took me in; naked, and you clothed me; I was sick, and you visited me; I was in prison, and you came to me . . . inasmuch as you didn't do it to one of the least of these, you didn't do it to me,' and knew it applied to him. Mark realized God did not just bless him with the gift of being a master craftsman so he could merely use it at his job, but wanted him to use it in the community where it was really needed. In that moment, Mark was convinced to start a ministry in the ghetto and make repairs to broken-down houses free of charge.

"Mark recounted his story, the gang was amazed. Mark had voiced a concern that had been bothering the guys for a long time. Upon hearing Mark's revelation, the men felt the message was also for them. All of the men were eager to become involved and to help the community. Once they agreed this was something they wanted to pursue, they needed to find a way to make it reality. Initially, some men suggested calling their local chapter of Habitat for Humanity. Although they did their best to make a positive change, in the end it turned out to be a bureaucratic mess and things never progressed past the planning stage. Sure, the setback disheartened them; nevertheless, they were determined to keep on fighting. Hence, after praying about the matter, they told the pastor they felt the Lord wanted them to start this ministry and asked people to support them.

"When we got things started, we helped an average of one or two people a month. We were just getting into a rhythm when I had my accident. Although I have not been able to do the work for some time, my crew calls me weekly and keeps me abreast of what they are working on. I can tell you that since the guys started doing this, people are amazed by what the men have done to transform the ghettos. It's amazing what a little landscaping, carpentry, and painting can do to lift the mood in a neighborhood. Because the guys have done such a remarkable job, there is now a waiting list of people who want their help.

"Since the day you washed my feet, I have been meaning to go show the men what Jesus has done for me. However, I have been putting it off because I wasn't quite sure how to go about it. In talking to you, I know I must go tell them about the store and how I was healed when you washed my feet. Usually there is a waiting list of people who want our help. Yet, when I tell them how the Holy Spirit is working, not only will they make the store their top priority, but they will be eager to have their feet washed as well. Just tell us what needs to be done, and we'll do whatever we can to help."

When Jim got off the phone with Ethan, he was excited that he could help Ethan and once again work side-by-side with old friends. It was one thing to talk to the guys and find out what they were up to. It was another to spend time with them doing the work everyone loved doing together, for it was what gave them joy and made life worth living. As Jim considered what would be involved, he thought about his friend Bill who would be a tremendous asset. It had been quite a while since he had called Bill; somehow, they had drifted apart. Jim felt bad about this but working together on the store might be a way for them to reconnect and renew their old friendship.

While God longs to have a personal relationship with all His children, He does not impose Himself on us. We have free will. Yet, in an attempt to get our attention, He sometimes plants a baited hook in our path, hoping we will respond. Though many see the bait dangling in front of them, because legalism has become so pervasive in society today, it has often stifled the human spirit and has prevented many from ever swallowing the bait they so desperately need to live an abundant life. Consequently, many spend their lives nibbling at the end of the bait hoping it will satisfy their starving souls in some way.

When it came to God, Bill was very faithful and tried his utmost to please his king, so he thought. He attended church regularly, helped in the community whenever he could, and prayed every night. For a while Bill found this lifestyle quite gratifying and fulfilling. Then one day he woke up and nothing seemed to make sense to him, but he was not sure why. He still enjoyed helping people and going to church, yet he yearned to do something more with his life.

There had been a time years before when hearing the Gospel invigorated him. It made him feel that, though he was only one man, if Christ was behind him, he could go out and change lives. Bill had done much to serve others well for many years and was content, but now his soul ached and hungered for more. Bill had always read the Gospel and longed to live out Christ's Great Commission to heal the sick and give peace to those in strife. However, because of the structure of the current society, he felt there were limited opportunities to do the type of work he really wanted to do.

During the next several weeks, Bill tried to continue with his normal routine, hoping he could come up with some way to resolve his problem. No matter how hard he tried to occupy his mind with other things, the problem nagged at his heart. Bill spent several sleepless nights churning everything over without resolve. He prayed, hoping God would quiet his anguished heart. Despite his persistent attempts, nothing helped. At this time Bill became disturbed, and since he did not know what else to do, he sought the counsel of some close friends. Unfortunately, they were struggling with these same issues and could offer little insight. All they could advise Bill to do was to put it in God's hands and allow Him to handle it in His time and in His way.

In Bill's heart he truly wanted to take his friends' advice and knew he would feel better if he could only be freed from the emptiness and anxiety that plagued his soul. Yet, despite his countless prayers of supplication, because he was willful and wanted an immediate answer to his problem, he was unable to make contact with his Maker or obtain peace of mind. The most exasperating part was that Bill knew intellectually what the problem was, but he could not quiet his discontented heart. At this time, Bill felt as if he was alone in the Garden of Gethsemane and could not understand how a God who claimed to love him would not rescue him when his whole world seemed to be in shambles.

Bill remained trapped in a perpetual holding pattern for weeks. Then, one day, he looked in the mirror and realized if he intended to obtain peace of mind, he needed to take control of the situation and change his attitude. As he paced trying to figure out what he should do next, he saw his Bible lying on the coffee table. Ordinarily, Bill would not have even taken notice of it. However, as he looked at it, the words of his mother came back to him.

"Son, I have taught you a great many things over the years, and I am very proud of the man you have become. Yet, if I am to fulfill my obligation as a parent, I must teach you one more thing. Although you may not believe me right now, what I am about to say is of utmost importance and might even save your life at some point, so listen very carefully.

"Throughout the course of life, I guarantee there will be times when you will find yourself in great distress and will have no idea where to turn for help. When I have faced situations like these and wondered if I could stand to live another day, the one thing that has helped my soul has been to open the Bible and read the comforting words of Christ. Go ahead and laugh all you want. But if you become still and ask the Holy Spirit to give you wisdom and open the Bible, you will turn to the right page and will be given the food you desperately need."

Reflecting on his mother's words, Bill sensed that his prayer was about to be answered. Just when everything in his life appeared to be hopeless, God in his mercy had provided him with a much-needed lifeline. Bill had heard many fellow Christians say that reading the Bible was a great comfort to them in times of distress; however, he had never spent much time reading the Word, and he was a bit leery. As he looked at the Bible, he wondered how something that had been written over 2000 years ago for another time and people could possibly help him out of his turmoil. After a few minutes, he was tempted to dismiss the whole idea from his mind and walk away. However, the thought of living another day in this state was more than he could stand. Thus, he decided to take the plunge and listen to his mother's sound advice.

Bill took a few deep breaths, sat down, bowed his head, and prayed for guidance. As he opened his Bible and flipped the pages, he was amazed by the gripping power the words of God had and how they soothed the rumblings of his discontented heart. Though he was familiar with the passages and had been known to quote them on occasion, as he reread the stories, the Holy Spirit touched his heart and he came to see Christ in a new way.

Bill came to the realization that, though he knew the Bible well and lived a virtuous life, he had missed the essence of the Gospel and was, by all rights, a modern-day Pharisee. He also discovered, contrary to what he had been taught, that the kingdom of God could not be gained merely by following a prescribed formula. Rather, it was achieved by loving unconditionally and seeking to do the will of God above all else.

Bill still had many doubts about the future, but he decided to put his new convictions to the test. Therefore, Bill knelt and spoke to Jesus, no longer as a majestic ruler, but as a friend who was deeply concerned about him. "Father, I come tonight in a state of utter confusion and hopelessness. You know the situation and how I feel, as well as the void that's in my heart right now. Lord, everything in my life has become so confusing, and I don't know what to do or where to turn. I have sincerely tried to lead a good life and to do the right thing but nothing makes any sense right now. I have reached the point where I can't handle it anymore. It says in your Word that if a man cries out to you and asks for help, you will sup with him and give him rest. Please, Jesus, come be with me. I need you and your guidance as I have never needed it before. Send me your Holy Spirit and help me to understand why this is happening. I surrender everything in my life to you for I am powerless and know I am incapable of helping myself right now. Please just show me what to do, and I will do it."

The oppressive veil that had held Bill in a state of silent torture for so long suddenly vanished, allowing an immeasurable peace to flood his soul. Now that this weight had been lifted, Bill felt liberated and went about his business confidently trusting that the Lord would intervene when He saw fit.

Within hours, Bill's life changed dramatically when he received an unexpected phone call from Jim. "Hi, Bill," Jim replied enthusiastically. "It's Jim Smith, your former boss. How are things going?"

"Just fine, Jim, how 'bout you? Gee, it's been a long time. I've been meaning to call you to see how you've been doing, but I guess I've just been busy! Anyway, what's been happening?"

"A whole lot, actually, and that's why I'm calling you. You see, I have taken on a very exciting project that is dear to my heart, and I desperately need your help and expertise."

"Gee, Jim, thank you for asking me. I feel honored, really I do. However, I'm afraid I must decline at this time."

"Oh, why?"

Bill was about to give a general answer but then decided to come out and be honest. "I'm not sure what has gotten into me lately, but I seem to be in a funk and don't know how to get out of it. One minute everything seemed to be going along smoothly. Then, as I was sitting in church the other day listening to the sermon, I realized my life lacked passion and wasn't going anywhere. I may be a respected member of the community and do much to help those in need, but somehow it just isn't enough.

"Sometimes when I look at the throngs of people who cry out for help, there is so much more I want to do with my life. I realize

I'm only one person and can't help everyone, but I'm tired of my monotonous daily routine and yearn for a challenge. I would give anything for a chance to address the underlying concerns that prevent so many in the world today from making progress. Throughout time, many people have had this same desire and have made significant contributions to society that have had far-reaching effects. I too have a burning passion inside me and long to be a warrior in the battle of injustice and just wish the Lord would provide me with an avenue so I can fulfill my mission. Please know I'm not interested in doing this for self-glorification, but rather so a greater good can be achieved. Am I making any sense at all or am I rambling like a fool?"

"No, you are making perfect sense, and personally, I admire your goal and think you expressed your predicament rather eloquently. Believe me, I totally relate to what you're going through because I have felt that way many times throughout my life, especially this past year. I don't have a magic wand and can't resolve your dilemma, but I'm confident after listening to your story that if you came and worked on this project, you would obtain a clear understanding as to the direction God wants your life to take."

"What makes you so sure of that?" Bill asked smugly.

After clearing his throat and smiling to himself for a moment, Jim continued "Well, Bill, I'm not sure if you're aware of this or not, but as a result of the accident, I suffered some paralysis on my left side. Because of it, I was not able to volunteer my time to fix up old houses the way we used to when we worked together at the site. I know it's been a long time since we saw each other, but I often think about the good times we had together. Yes, I missed those days and spent too much time in the house feeling resentful and frustrated that I was no longer able to able to minister to people the way I used to.

"I'm sorry to hear that, Jim; I had no idea."

"Anyway, that's all in the past. I'm calling you because something tremendous happened last week, and I desperately need your help! Ever since the accident, I've been quite active in my prayer group at church and we have been actively asking God to heal me so I could once again help people the way I used to. I always thought God would heal me, but never expected it to happen the way it did. Last week, I received quite an unusual call from the son of a woman in my prayer group. I'm not sure what made him call. In any event, when I met with him and inquired as to the business he had in mind, he explained how he had been called by Christ to heal others. Christ told him to open a towel shop where people who believed could come and be healed.

"Ordinarily, I'm quite cynical when it comes to the topic of healing because of all the frauds on television. However, when I saw the purity in Ethan's eyes and heard the sincerity in his voice, something told me this is not a hoax. I was anxious to have my feet washed and experience the miracle for myself. When he washed my feet and my paralyzed side moved as though nothing was ever wrong with it, I was speechless and filled with much awe. Witnessing this miracle, my spirit told me that God had heard His people cry and once again in His endless mercy was about to stretch out His hand, perform miraculous works, and rekindle a sense of hope to this community. I also felt that it was far from coincidental that I met Ethan. From the very second I laid eyes on him, I knew that God had blessed him tremendously and that I was supposed to help my brother in any way possible so that this fantastic mission could come to fruition.

"Every time I walk down the street and someone stops me and asks, 'Aren't you the guy who . . .' I'm filled with so much joy because of what has happened to me and the miraculous works that are about to unfold. It's just as exciting and invigorating for me now as I imagine it was for the disciples in the Bible. I feel a great sense of urgency to build this store so God can begin His work and change people's lives. This, my friend, is why I so desperately need your help."

"Gee, Jim," Bill said, a bit flabbergasted, "your enthusiasm is quite contagious. I have to hand it to you; you would make a fine marketer! This offer does sound electrifying and it is exactly the type of opportunity I've been seeking to jump-start and rejuvenate my spirit. While I really would like to do this worthwhile project, I have a few reservations about becoming involved for fear it could somehow backfire and throw me into an even deeper depression than I'm already in. I hope you can understand where I'm coming from."

While it distressed Jim greatly to find his friend immersed in such a pit of despair, he was nevertheless grateful to Christ for providing him with the opportunity to minister to his wounded brother who was in desperate need of help. Seeking Christ's guidance on what to say and taking a deep breath, Jim began, "I certainly do, and I know what tremendous gumption it takes to get back up after a bad fall. However, don't be dismayed. I firmly believe that our lives are not subject to the winds of chance as many think, but are controlled rather by a loving God who is full of surprises and has very intricate plans in mind for His people. It is obvious to me that you are a beloved child of God, and you have been sent to earth to accomplish a special mission for the king. Whether or not you know it, God has been hard at work behind the scenes preparing for this momentous occasion, and now that all the components are in place, God is about to set His glorious plan into motion.

"You have taken a wonderful first step by surrendering all to Him, and I applaud your efforts. However, Bill, you need to realize that Christ doesn't always answer our prayers the way we want. Rather, He places people and events in our path who are intended to lead us to the next step in our journey. It seems obvious to me that Christ has answered your prayer and has sent me into your life so I could present this opportunity to you. You're making this much more complicated than it needs to be. Just open your eyes, realize what is happening, and be like a trusting child who allows his parent to lead the way. Besides, Bill, it's not as if the Lord is sending you to a foreign land where you don't know anybody. You will be working with most of the men you have worked with before on an unprecedented project that will change the lives of many forever."

When Bill heard these words, a transformation occurred in his mind. For the first time he realized that he was no longer wandering aimlessly, but he actually felt as if God had a special purpose for him. After a few moments of being absolutely enthralled, Bill began, "Wow, Jim! Where on earth did that come from? It was prophetic! How could I have been such a blind fool? Of course, it all makes perfect sense! I'd be a fool to pass up this opportunity, especially since this project holds such abounding promise for the future."

"Good, it's settled then. I'll see you bright and early tomorrow morning just like the old days."

Within a few hours, much to Ethan's amazement, Jim called back and announced that the men were so enthusiastic about the project and the tremendous ways that it would benefit the community that they could hardly wait to get started. Ethan was delighted to have all this help; yet everything was happening so quickly that he felt overwhelmed and did not know what to do first. Sensing Ethan's exasperation, Jim, who had much experience coordinating this type of work, offered to oversee the project.

Ethan breathed a sigh of relief and was grateful to God for sending him such a qualified individual to do the job. Ethan was talented in many respects, but renovating certainly was not his forte. Jim was willing to oversee the construction and organize the work so it could be done in the most efficient manner possible. He would need to meet with both Claire and Ethan immediately to discuss the blueprint and other design issues. They agreed to hold this meeting later that day.

Ethan was pleased with the progress he was making and felt his hard work would soon pay off. Consequently, he became further motivated to achieve this end, for the seed planted in Ethan's soul at the inception of this whole idea had taken root and was now well on its way to producing a prosperous harvest. He called his mother immediately, told her the good news, and asked her to meet him at his apartment later that day. He then jumped on the Internet and began hunting for wholesale prices on towels.

Ethan became so engrossed in his search that he lost track of time and was quite surprised at four o'clock when Claire and Jim rang the doorbell. However, by then he was bleary eyed from staring at the screen for so long and welcomed the interruption.

After chatting for a brief time, they prayed and then Jim began assessing what needed to be done. Claire was precise in drawing the blueprint, and it was quite easy for Jim to imagine what the store would look like when it was completed. Much hard work lay ahead to make the blueprint come to life; however, Jim was, nonetheless, dazzled by the store's simplicity, continuity, charm, and rich inviting elegance. Jim studied the design, made some notes, and mapped out a strategy for how they might proceed. He realized that it would be relatively easy to remodel the store.

Once Jim understood the current design and the atmosphere they were trying to create, he removed his glasses, took a deep cleansing breath, rubbed his eyes, and was ready to get to work. "First off, let me say that you did a remarkable job, and I feel extremely blessed to be able to work on this project with you. However, before we discuss the details, let's order some Chinese food? It's going to be a long night and if we are to do a good job for the Lord, we must be nourished."

While Jim was pleased with the basic design, after toying around with different options, he came up with ways to utilize the floor space that would maximize efficiency, create a more open feeling, and help with people traffic. After discussing the different options and reaching a consensus, Jim drew the final blueprints. The next step was to discuss the logistics of the project, such as what they needed to do to prepare the store for renovation, the supplies that were needed, where to get the best prices, and the tasks the workmen would need to do. They allocated chores and agreed to meet again the next night to see how well they had progressed. Throughout the entire process, they noticed that a very tranquil feeling was in the air and knew the Holy Spirit was present and was guiding their every thought.

By the time they wrapped things up, it was almost 10 o'clock. The strangest part was that, although they had worked for hours, they were not the least bit tired. They joked about this for a few minutes and surmised that the Holy Spirit had no doubt supplied them with the energy they needed to get the work done.

As Ethan lay in bed that night, he could not stop thinking about the miracles God was performing in his life. Consequently, he did not sleep at all but was raring to go at it again when his alarm clock went off. His day was booked solid; he did not have a minute to waste. He spent the morning at city hall applying for the necessary permits and the afternoon with Jim gathering supplies at hardware stores in the area. Claire, on the other hand, spent the day shopping for a sound system, gadgets, and other gismos that were needed to create a peaceful atmosphere. She also shopped for an awning to hang outside the store.

By the time Ethan, Claire, and Jim had finished their work and coordinated delivery, they were so tired they could not even think. They shared the success of the day and decided since all the big pieces were already in place they could wait until morning to resolve any critical issues.

When Jim heard that Ethan and Claire planned to be at the store as soon as he and the work crew arrived to pray with them and wish them well, he tried to convince them that it wasn't necessary. Jim knew how hard they had been working and told them that he could handle it from there. However, his persuasion didn't work. Ethan and Claire felt that if the men were going to give of their time and talent, the least they could do in return was to be there to greet them. Who knows, maybe if they felt ambitious enough, they might even pound some nails.

PREPARING THE PLACE

Thanksgiving and joy radiated from Claire's soul as she drove to the store the next morning and reflected over her life and the glorious future God had planned for her. There had been many times during her life when the roads she traveled seemed to wind up at a disappointing dead end. However, just when Claire thought God had forgotten about her, God in His wacky humor uncorked the champagne and somehow made it fizzle better than she could have ever anticipated. In retrospect, she was now very thankful to God for protecting and keeping her feet from straying. If God had allowed her to pursue every fanciful whim, Claire would never have been able to fulfill her destiny.

For years, Claire prayed and dreamed that this day would come. When she entered the store and saw the tools scattered about and heard the loud music coming from the cheap portable radio, she could not believe it was actually happening. All her hopes of opening a healing center and serving her Master were finally about to come true, and she was in ecstasy. She relished the moment by breathing in, as if it were the sweetest perfume she ever smelled.

Within minutes, Ethan walked in with his work clothes on and a box of doughnuts for the men. "Sorry I'm late. I just finished meditating and preparing for the day. Has anyone seen Jim yet?"

Just as Claire was about to answer, Jim walked up and greeted them. "Morning, guys. I don't know about you, but I certainly had trouble sleeping last night. I just could not stop thinking about the store and what a tremendous gift God has bestowed on this community. Although the men and I won't actually be doing the healings, we are humbled that God has selected us to do this work to make this store a reality. However, enough with the sentimental stuff. There is much work to be done!"

Ethan and Claire just stood there and smiled warmly at each other for Jim had so eloquently captured what they had been thinking. Within minutes Jim took charge (as he did in the old days), turned the radio off, gathered the men together for a word of prayer, and began assigning duties. At first, the men treated Ethan and his mother with deference. However, once they began working together and the men saw how genuine and eager Ethan and Claire were to roll up their sleeves and help, the men's preconceived notions vanished and soon they all found themselves working side by side as a cohesive team.

When Claire was sure everything was under control as far as construction was concerned, she stopped hammering and focused on the store itself. She felt it was important to do something to ensure that people didn't have any misconceptions or associate the towels with any form of witchcraft, alternative medicine, or new age philosophy. The difficulty, however, was how to convince people of this absolute truth in an age of moral relativism.

Claire was led by the Holy Spirit to create a pamphlet and to place it throughout the store and on the store's Website. In it, she explained how the healing process worked, the significance of the towels, and that the store's mission was to heal people of their ailments and to empower them to do the work Christ called them to do. She emphasized that the power was a gift that came from Christ and Christ alone. Ethan and she were merely the vessels through which Christ's power flowed, nothing more.

Because the hardware store had been such a prominent fixture in this small community for so long, people were saddened to see this era of service draw to a close. Yet, at the same time, they were quite eager to see what the landmark would become. Within weeks, speculation heightened when people peered through the cracks of the paper-covered window and discovered that men were working furiously. Ethan and Claire were delighted the store was generating so much interest but realized that introducing a radical, new concept of supernatural healing in the form of a business into this secular society would be controversial and cause people to ask questions. To prevent people from associating them with the charlatans who had turned this gift into a mockery for their own gain, they decided it was best to affix a copy of their mission statement to the door.

Initially their carefully crafted plan not only kept people from reaching inaccurate conclusions but also created genuine interest as well. However, within a week's time, it became evident that the public was tired of waiting and was anxious for more information. Finally, a day came when a few people who made it a point to know what was happening around town could not stand the suspense any longer. They rummaged through the store's trash one night in search of answers.

Claire was methodical and usually kept all records on her computer. However, in preparing to write the informational pamphlet, she gathered her thoughts and composed a bulleted list of core elements on a post-it note. One day, when she was midway through the process, Claire experienced writer's block. She became frenzied and began cleaning her office fanatically. Among the items she threw away was the essential post-it note that outlined the concept of the store.

Discovering the post-it note in the trash and learning what would become of the store, the people who had been so curious felt as if they were on Mars, for the ideas seemed foreign to them. True, Ethan had always been an idealist, but now he was carrying things a little too far and people were quite concerned. It was one thing to believe in God and be a helpful citizen, but Ethan was charging forward in faith and was challenging people to open their minds and put their faith into practice.

When rumors circulated about the type of store that would soon open, reaction around town was mixed. Many shook their heads, thinking it was sheer lunacy that adults were working on such a ridiculous project. They just could not understand how Ethan and Claire, who were levelheaded people, could have the audacity to believe they could evoke Christ's presence and cure people's ailments merely by washing and drying feet. Furthermore, they thought it was ludicrous that the store would only be accepting donations and wondered how Ethan and Claire planned to pay the bills. Others, however, saw the beauty of it all and were enthralled by concept of the store and that people were living out their faith in such a concrete manner.

For the first few days, Bill worked vigorously in the store feeling exhilarated that Christ had called him to participate in this momentous project that would have such a profound effect on people's lives. As he worked, he felt honored to be cutting the vine branches that would hang on the ceiling. They would serve as a constant reminder that Ethan and Claire, as well as others who would be doing the healing, were powerless. Rather, they were merely branches through which Christ's power could flow if they were humble and sought to do His will above all else.

Although Bill was thrilled, as he picked up his saw to cut yet another vine branch on the fifth day, he noticed that his enthusiasm and passion were beginning to dwindle. He knew this work had to be done so glorious works could be performed; yet, as he toiled with the branches, somehow the thrill faded Bill grew impatient and was quite eager to press onward and find out what surprises Christ had in store for him.

Because Bill was tired of the redundancy of cutting and pruning the vine branches, he was about to throw up his hands, put down his saw, and stomp out. Just as he was about to do so, he looked up and saw the other men working away. It reminded him of why Christ had sent him there and that if he were to bail out now he would probably regret it for the rest of his life. After taking a deep breath, he stopped, closed his eyes and prayed, "Lord, you have brought me to this place for a reason, and I thank you for the opportunity to be here. The other day you promised me that through this experience you would make the way I was supposed to walk known to me. Father, I do trust you and believe that you will do what you promised. However, so far this feels like just another job. Please grant me the patience I need to persevere and wait for you to show me what the next step is. I surrender everything to you and know that when the time is right you will reveal it to me."

Within moments, Jim looked up and noticed that Bill had quite an unsettled look on his face. "Are you alright?" Jim inquired.

"Yes, yes, of course I am. Why do you ask?" Bill answered as if Jim had caught him off-guard.

Jim was about to answer but never got around to it. For as Bill spoke, he did not pay attention to what he was doing. Rather than cutting the branch, he had his hand in the way and inadvertently cut it in the process. Blood was spewing forth and was going everywhere. Immediately Bill shrieked in panic and pain as he grabbed his hand, "Oh, my God! I'm bleeding, and I know it's deep. Hurry, someone! Get a towel and get me to the emergency room right away!"

Panic and commotion engulfed the room as the men scurried about to gather as many towels as they could to reduce the bleeding. While this was going on, Jim picked up the phone and was about to call 911. However, Claire came forth, placed her finger on the hang up button and calmly announced, "That won't be necessary."

Initially, the men looked at her as if she had lost her mind and began mumbling to themselves, "What in the world is she talking about?" The human part of them wanted to dismiss her actions as irrational. However, when they saw her with a basin and towel in hand, they remembered what had happened to Jim and shortly their murmurings hushed. The men stopped what they were doing instantly. Within seconds, with their eyes were transfixed on Claire, they were eager to see for themselves what would happen.

Claire understood how strange this all was and tried to be patient and give them time to adjust to all of this. She could tell that they had become so engrossed by what she was about to do that they had completely forgotten about Bill. Since time was of the essence, she had to bring their focus back to the problem at hand. "Look, I know you're curious about this; but we simply don't have time to spiritualize right now. In case you forgot, this man is bleeding very badly. Would someone please remove Bill's shoes and socks so I can continue?"

The men quickly removed Bill's shoes and socks while the others wrapped a towel tightly around his hand so blood would not gush everywhere. Once Bill's feet were bare, Claire began. Although she had never done healings in this fashion before, much less in front of an audience, she was still able to tune out the distractions and concentrate her efforts on being a vessel through which Christ could work.

From the moment the water touched Bill's feet, Claire felt a steady current of energy pulsate through her being. However, it was not until she began to use the towel that the energy flowed through her hands into Bill's feet and traveled rapidly until it reached the source of the wound. When it did, exhilarating heat that Bill had never experienced before began repairing the severed artery and healing the torn skin. The true thrill came moments later when the men removed the blood soaked towel and discovered that there was not a scratch on his hand to be seen. It truly was a miracle!

Upon examination, the men, including Bill, were astounded and marveled at this mighty work. Sure, they had heard what happened to Jim when Ethan washed his feet and believed that miracles still occurred on some level. However, once they witnessed the touch of Christ, they saw God in a different way and understood the power of faith. They knew that God was omnipotent and could heal, but it was only after experiencing this miracle that their consciousness was raised to a new level. After basking in the sheer joy of the moment and magnifying God for all the things He had done for them for a time, they opened their eyes and knew it was time to return to work.

Leaving the loving, restful cocoon of Christ's arms and returning to reality took some adjusting as the men who had never experienced this before found out. At first, they tried to talk but were so immersed in the Holy Spirit's presence that they were unable to utter a sound. It would have been easy for them to remain in this state forever. As they looked around and saw the work that the Master had entrusted them to do, they were anxious to return to work.

Just as the men began to disperse, Jim glanced at his clipboard and announced, "Hold up for a second, guys. There has been a change of plans in light of what just happened. Bill, I want you to work with me on staining the walls and let David finish cutting the branches. You did a good job, but let's not test the Lord. One miracle is more than I'm sure everyone can handle in a day." With that, the men laughed and returned to work. Just then, Bill and Jim looked at each other and exchanged a high five as a way of acknowledging that they both were aware that God had kept His word and had set His plan into motion.

For the first few days, the normally garrulous Bill was rather somber as he worked in the store. So many changes had occurred over the past 72 hours that he felt as if his head was spinning and desperately needed time to contemplate it all. Every time he used or looked at his hand, he was reminded of the spectacular miracle God had done for him. The Lord had blessed him greatly, and he wanted everyone to know that God was real. If they simply obeyed

His teachings and tried to do His will, they could ask Him for anything and it would be done for them.

As the days turned into weeks, he noticed that something even more extraordinary was happening. Bill had always been a loving and empathetic individual. However, after the healing whenever he encountered a situation, some unknown force consumed him; he entered an altered state where he was able to discern exactly what was going on simply by listening to his spirit.

When this first occurred, Bill was quite perplexed and couldn't comprehend what was happening. It was without a doubt the strangest thing he had ever experienced. Initially, he wondered if he was hallucinating or if this was merely a coincidence. However, when it persisted, he realized Christ had answered his prayer and had blessed him with this gift so he could help others.

Bill had always hoped that Christ would use him in some capacity but never imagined God would entrust him with such a gift. Some spend their entire lives dreaming and hoping for an opportunity like this. Bill knew God gave him this gift and was amazed that he didn't even have to work for it. He was in awe of God's abounding grace and recognized the grave responsibility that came with the opportunity to serve God.

With a thankful, joyous heart, Bill prayed, "Lord, so many things have happened to me since the healing, and I am grateful to you for opening my eyes and allowing me to see things with such clarity for the first time in my life. Now that you have done this miraculous work in my life, it is my heart's desire to use the insight to help others. Please speak to my heart and show me what to do. I ask all these things in Jesus' precious name and thank you for hearing my prayer."

That evening Christ appeared to Bill in a dream. "My son," Jesus said, "I have allowed these things to happen to you to prepare you for this time. I have called you to help Ethan and Claire in a special way that I have not even told them about yet. They are doing a wonderful job. There will come a day in the not too distant future when Ethan and Claire will not be able to handle the swarms of people who will come for healing by themselves. Just as Ethan and Claire are the vessels through which I heal and empower others, I will anoint you with this same gift.

"I want you to spend the next several weeks in the store healing people in my name. During this time, you will meet many people who will teach you many lessons about what it means to serve. Shortly, people will hear about the healings, and soon you all will be inundated with requests to make appearances. To keep up with the demand, many people will need to be trained to wash feet. This, my son, is where you come in and is the ultimate reason why you were born.

"Training people to wash feet is not an easy task. For this reason, I want you to open a subsidiary of Divine Towels called the Foot-Washing Institute. Because the two will be so closely linked, I want them to be located in the same building. This may sound impossible, but Jim has a large storage room in the back that will suffice nicely, if you do some minor renovations. I will explain more details about the Foot-Washing Institute later. For now, rest assured that I have major plans in store for you. I know how crazy this all sounds, but do not worry about what I am telling you, for I am in control.

"When you wake up, you won't remember much of what I have said to you. There will come a day, in the not too distant future, when you will experience déjà vu, and everything I have told you will come back to you. At that time, tell Ethan and Claire about this dream, and you will see that they are receptive. My son, there are no coincidences in life. I have a purpose for everything I do. Though strands of yarn appear to be separated and unconnected, when I put them on my loom and begin to weave, the strands come together to form a Beautiful tapestry. Peace be with you, my son. Peace be with you."

As the weeks progressed, Claire and Ethan had clearly made a wise choice in selecting Jim and the men to do the job. The men were clean, efficient, and best of all, ahead of schedule. While Claire and Ethan were delighted about this, when they realized that opening day was only a week away, they panicked. Though everything was fine with the store, they had been avoiding the topic of advertising and knew they needed to address it immediately.

Claire who had majored in communications in college was aware of various forms of advertising, including which one would be most effective to use given the situation. Since she wanted to avoid being associated with the television evangelical crowd and wished to reach the intended audience, the task before her was quite difficult and required much thought. Though she had a few ideas about how to proceed, she searched the Internet and talked to several people to help her reach the optimal solution.

Claire grappled with the options for days. Her spirit was deeply troubled, and she still wasn't sure which avenue to pursue. Therefore, she took it to prayer and asked for guidance. At first, it was difficult for Claire to quiet her mind. However, since the matter was of utmost importance, she persisted and before long was able to enter a meditative state.

After a few minutes, Christ appeared to her dressed in a long white robe and said, "Peace be with you, my child. Child, Ethan and you have been faithful in doing what I have asked of you so far, and because of this I am blessing you both in a special way. Do not fear the future because all is in my hands. There is no need to advertise the store or its mission. The right people will be drawn to the store without your saying a word. Once one person has received healing, he will tell another, and this will start a chain reaction. Though you are unaware of it, this ripple has already started with the healing of Jim and Bill. Just have patience, and you shall see that all the things I have told you will come to pass." Having said this, Jesus showed her a vision and she fell on bended knee and rejoiced.

THE MINISTRY BEGINS

After many weeks of preparation, opening day finally arrived. Much to their amazement, every detail had been crafted exactly the way they had intended. The towels were stacked neatly. The awning read "Divine Towels." What a provocative name, if Ethan did not say so himself! Everything was exactly as they imagined, and it was enthralling! Now, all they needed were a few customers. Until lunchtime, the store was dead, and not even one customer peered in the window. This was a bit surprising, but it did give them time to put a few finishing touches on things.

Since Ethan and Claire were new to this field, they viewed the first few days as a learning process and depended on Christ to guide and teach them the best way to serve their customers. This was an ongoing process that required discipline, becoming attuned to others' needs, and learning how to listen with the eyes. Some other techniques that helped in this pursuit included watching a person's body language and facial expressions and interpreting their aura and spirit. In addition to using these techniques, they relied on the Holy Spirit to guide them on the best way to approach and interact with the clientele.

At five minutes past twelve, Claire had just stepped out for a minute and Ethan was about to eat his lunch, when the door opened. It was his first official customer, a young lady who walked with a limp and used a cane. "Welcome. Just let me know if I can be of assistance," Ethan said after watching her for several moments. Ethan wanted to stay, but he forced himself to go in the back and fetch a jug of water. When he returned, her expression indicated that she was both engaged and mystified. Sensing that her intrigue was growing, Ethan decided to spark her curiosity further by adding, "Would you like to see how the towels work?"

She did not answer for a few seconds. When she finally realized Ethan had been speaking to her, she turned abruptly and replied, "Oh, I'm sorry, you startled me. What did you say? I didn't hear you."

"I asked if you would like to see how the towels work," Ethan answered calmly, though he anxiously awaited her response.

"Yes, I would. I'm not sure what it is, but this is the most unusual store I have ever been in. Lately, I have been very uptight because I am in chronic pain in my lower back and have not had a moment's peace. Sometimes the pain is so acute I can't even get out of bed. I have tried everything, but nothing works. I am scheduled to have an operation next week.

"The second I stepped into this store, my anxiety vanished. I'm not sure why it is, but I feel a strong presence of the Holy Spirit in this place. All I know is that for the first time I feel peaceful and am confident that everything will be okay."

Ethan smiled, for this was exactly the reaction he hoped people would have upon entering. "Why don't you sit down, make yourself comfortable, and let me see what God will do to help you? Are you experiencing any pain now?" Ethan asked as he grabbed a towel.

"As a matter of fact I am," the lady said. At that moment, two more customers came in. As soon as this happened, Ethan could feel the lady tense up However, she relaxed again when Ethan said, "I'll be with you shortly. In the meantime, make yourselves comfortable."

The moment of truth had arrived. It was time to explain how the towels worked. Ethan was aware of how illogical it would seem to the lady but prayed that she would be open-minded. "What I'm about to do is quite unconventional and does sound a bit strange. However, you have my word it doesn't hurt and the pain you have now will disappear if you believe with all your heart that it will. I will wash your feet and then dry them with this towel. When they are dry, your backache will be gone, depending on how strongly you believe."

While what Ethan said defied all the rules of logic, there was something about the gentle way he spoke as he looked into her eyes that was so convincing that the lady felt compelled to take off her shoes and socks. She felt that a man like Ethan who was full of tenderness would not lie. The other customers could not help but overhear what was going on. They stared in disbelief as Ethan proceeded to wash the lady's feet.

Once the washing and drying of the feet had been completed, shouts of joy and delight came out of the lady's mouth. Instantly the back pain that had been so intense for so long disappeared, and she could not help shouting about it! "My God, my God, how did you do that? It is a modern day miracle." Then she stood and was free from pain as she had been as a girl. She was overwhelmed as she hugged Ethan and jumped up and down.

Once the lady discovered what powers the towels seemed to possess, she looked at the store differently and felt she had discovered the fountain of youth. Not only did the foot washing rid her of a backache, but she also felt as if her spirits had been rejuvenated in a strange way.

"How much do I owe you for your services?" the lady asked.

"Nothing," Ethan replied. "It's a gift I've been given by God to help people. However, donations are always appreciated."

"Giving a donation is the very least I can do. But before I do, I want to stay here a little longer; just being in here has done wonders for me in ways you cannot even imagine. Go ahead and help the others; I'd like more time to look around."

Meanwhile, an elderly couple saw what the towels had done for the woman and were anxious to see if the towels could help them. They were round-shouldered and had cataracts. When Ethan appeared to be finished with the lady, the couple approached him enthusiastically.

"Wow, that was quite a miracle you performed a minute ago. We have never seen anything quite like it. You hear stories, but when you actually see it for yourself, it changes your perspective. Boy, you have been blessed with an incredible gift!"

"Thank you very much," Ethan replied.

"I'm not sure how it works, but do you think that you might be able to help my wife and me? We have been suffering for a long time with acute arthritis and cataracts. Please help us. We have tried every form of medicine but nothing works, and more than that, it is too costly."

"Well, wish no more, for you have come to the right place. Everyone who asks and truly believes will receive what he desires. Just let me grab a towel, and I'll be right with you. In the meantime, please have a seat and remove your shoes and socks."

As Ethan picked up the next towel, he was thankful that he had stocked up on several basins so he would not have to run back and forth between customers to perform the ritual. When he returned, the wife announced that she wanted to go first. Ethan was obliging and began washing her feet with much love and tenderness. The lady had a hard time seeing when the foot washing began, but by the time it was over she could not only see Ethan's handsome face but could also walk without a bit of pain. "It's a miracle," she shouted as she began dancing around shouting for joy. When she turned around and saw her poor decrepit husband, she immediately sat down again and held his hand as Ethan proceeded to wash his feet as well.

The husband had a similar experience except that his spirit was awakened and he saw things in a glistening new light that he never remembered before. His eyes that had been dull suddenly ignited as he also began dancing about the store laughing with delight chanting, "It's a miracle; look at me, look what I can do." The couple who had been so tired and worn out when they entered now were as energized as two children running in circles around the playground. Ethan stood smiling to himself as he thought about the promises Christ had made and how, after such a long time, they were coming true.

The lady who had been roaming the aisles watched what was going on and wondered how Ethan could do such miracles when doctors who had studied for years couldn't even do these things with modern medicine. She found Ethan, as well as everything about the store, extremely interesting and wanted to know more, but with all the commotion it was hardly the time to break up the joy with an in-depth analysis. She wanted to stay and watch, but she felt guilty for spying. Therefore, she quietly put a check on the counter, took an informational pamphlet and slipped out, vowing to return later.

After some time of marveling over how the towels had rejuvenated them, the couple finally came back and put their socks and shoes back on. "Sir," the gentleman said, "what's in those towels, and why do I feel as young and healthy as when I was a boy?"

"The towel was merely a means by which your healing took place. It was your faith that made you well." Ethan then handed the man one of the informational pamphlets to help clarify the details. After he read the story about the vine and the branches from the Bible, the man was still a bit puzzled, but he knew in his heart that this was what had happened. By this time, the man could not handle any more surprises and quickly changed the subject.

"I cannot begin to understand the power God has bestowed on you, but it is a tremendous gift you have been given. You have changed my life and have done so much to help my wife and me. What can we do to show our gratitude?" the man asked.

"As I told the other lady, I don't charge for this service since it's a gift I've been given by God to help people. However, donations, as well as word-of-mouth advertising, are always appreciated."

"No problem, that's the very least we can do for you," the man said as he stuffed a few pamphlets in his pocket and placed $200 on the counter. Before Ethan had a chance to thank him for his generosity, he and his wife were halfway out the door.

During the first few weeks, Ethan and Claire spent a great deal of time becoming acclimated to their new surroundings and learning how to serve. It was very interesting to watch the various reactions people had upon entering the store. Most entered and were immediately fascinated by the peaceful ambiance. From observing the way the tension disappeared from people's faces, it was obvious to Ethan and Claire that many considered it to be a different world where somehow the rules of society did not apply and where they felt safe to be themselves and let their guard down. Consequently, people were captivated and reluctant to leave the tranquil abode where love enveloped them.

Once people felt safe, the façade of being strong and all together faded away, and their true nature was revealed. Each person's situation was unique; however, basic problems, struggles, and fears turned out to be relatively the same. Most were tired of their daily repetitious routines. They felt disheartened because they did not see a way to get off the merry-go-round and escape their feelings of inferiority, lonesomeness, and restlessness. They wondered if anyone cared or knew that they even existed.

Despite how people choose to handle these issues, until they accept the fact that they are powerless and hand their problems to God without reservation, the problems will haunt them in one way or another until the day they die. This is one of those things that people know; yet, it is difficult to do it in daily life because they want everything on their own terms. Does it mean sitting back and passively waiting for God to intervene? Should we adopt that old philosophy, "God helps those who help themselves" or would it be best to do something somewhere between the two extremes? These are difficult questions and sometimes people feel that no matter where they turn, they are trapped and cannot escape.

Some may outright dismiss the fact that they even have such feelings and use it as a defense mechanism because they have spent much time searching for answers, but have come up empty-handed. Having failed, they are perplexed and resign themselves to the fact that there is no more to life than this. Though they go through life the best they can, secretly they hold out a glimmer of hope that someday they will find a way to unlock the door of their hearts. However, it was not until they entered Divine Towels, that many sensed that the wait was over and their dream was about to come true.

Others, however, were quite skeptical and asked many questions even after reading the informational pamphlet. They thought it was most peculiar that people who had common sense were falling for this sham. They were interested in knowing how miracles of such proportion could occur when doctors, who had received years of medical training, could not cure their ailments. Many of these people did have their feet washed. However, because they entered the store with an ulterior motive, viewing it as an experiment to see what would happen, rather than with a pure, humble, and believing heart, they were not healed.

These people were not surprised and used it as a way to strengthen their position that there was nothing miraculous about the store. They reasoned that the people were very vulnerable and susceptible to the power of suggestion. When it came time to explain this phenomenon, they argued that these people had strong determination and that it was just a matter of time before their will drove them to get better. It is very easy for someone with limited knowledge to make sweeping bold judgments based on how things appear. Yet, if they understood the situation these people were in and the way they suffered on a daily basis, they would have never made such hurtful statements.

The most difficult people to serve were those who came in, browsed, and quickly left. Although these people usually appeared to have a macho, invincible air about them, a veil of sadness and brokenness hovered over them. They seemed to be screaming out for help. However, since they were too proud to ask for help, they were uncomfortable and ended up walking out of the store.

Once they witnessed what the towels could do and understood that faith in Christ was the driving principle behind the towels, most people responded favorably. Not only were they willing to open their minds, but they were willing to step out on faith and try something new in order to receive relief from their ailments. Many came in recounting stories of how they had gone to various doctors and specialists and how they had tried many remedies but that nothing did the trick. Consequently, they were sick of doctors and all the self-help books. It was not so much that these things didn't help, but sometimes it felt like only a temporary fix.

Taking all this into account and recognizing that they had been called to an extraordinary ministry, Ethan and Claire vowed to go to whatever lengths necessary to help a person - within reason. Sometimes this would require spending 10 minutes with a person and other times an hour. Providing quality service for the spirit was the most critical factor in their business and would ultimately determine if people would return or tell others about the store. Therefore, they considered the time it took to serve others to be a worthwhile investment as long as a person was open-minded and willing to listen.

Ever since Bill could remember, church had been an integral part of his life. His parents were God-fearing people who made sure he was brought up properly. It was not a big surprise to find him in church every Sunday morning when he was a boy. Unlike other boys, Bill attended church even when he went to college because it nourished his soul in some way and gave him a reason to go on living day after day. Church always seemed to energize and make him feel that he could take on the world. Yet, within hours, the great sense of empowerment that had been so strong always dwindled, and life returned to normal.

While Bill always liked going to church, as he drove up and saw the tall, white steeple, he was overcome with much elation that God had done a mighty act, and he was eager for everyone to know. Though Bill was a devout member of the congregation and was outgoing when it came to participating in church activities, he was a quiet type and people did not know him that well. That day, when the pastor issued the call for anyone to come forward and bear witness to how God was working in their lives, the congregation was a bit surprised when Bill came up and began to speak.

"Hi. My name is Bill. Many of you know me. Boy, this is hard. Please help me, Lord. Okay, I'm here today to testify that God isn't a far off being, but a real force that is alive and cares for all of His children very much. I have proof of it, for a miracle has happened to me. A few weeks ago, I was feeling low and wondered if there was a way to live out the Great Commission in daily life. Sure, we do many projects in the community and at church, but are we truly living out the Great Commission and bringing people to know Christ? Let's face it. It's difficult enough to get through the day, let alone to find the time to do anything else.

"I'm sure I'm not the only one who is overwhelmed by the cares of life. However, sometimes I become so frustrated at the mere thought of having to do my routine again just to survive, especially when there are so many people who need help and important things that need to be done, that I want to scream. I know things are what they are and it's best to keep focused on the blessings I have in life, but this doesn't help solve the underlying problem. Though I try my best to be positive, when I read about how exciting it was when Jesus sent his disciples out to proclaim the good news and perform works of mercy, I become jealous because that's what I want to do with all my heart and soul.

"I love church; don't get me wrong. However, I have difficulty keeping the wonderful feeling I get here alive. It's like taking drugs and getting the ultimate spiritual high to come here I become empowered and am eager to go out and spread the Gospel message. Yet, within a few hours, the great sense of empowerment that had been so strong fades and life returns to normal. It's depressing, and I hate it!

"Though it may appear that there's no way to stop this vicious cycle, if you step back and take the frustration out in the form of ceaseless prayer, an answer will come. Some of you are probably saying to yourselves, 'Man, is this guy crazy or is he smoking something? How dare he come in here and tell me I'm not praying!'

"I understand this attitude you may have because I've had the same reaction at times. However, the other day at the height of my frustration, I cried out for mercy and told Jesus that I felt as if I was going over the edge and needed help. I have been a Christian all my life and was well versed in the scriptures. Yet, it wasn't until I found myself in this crisis that I understood what the scriptures actually mean and knew that Christ is the only one who can get me out of my predicament.

"It's not easy to quiet your soul and wait patiently for God to guide the way. However, when you do so in the right spirit without a hidden agenda, the benefits are tremendous. When I prayed and asked Christ to help me, the horrible anxiety that I felt vanished and was replaced by tranquility. Though I still had to face the same daily routine, I knew Christ was with me and that He would make a way out.

"It's funny how God works and whom He sends to help His people get to the path they are destined to take. My former boss, Jim, a friend whom I hadn't heard from in a while, invited me to help him on an outreach program in the community. When he first described it, I was reluctant and expected it to be just another ordinary community service project. Boy, did I turn out to be wrong! Jim told me about Divine Towels, a new store he was helping to build, had the potential to change life in forever. It's a place devoted to healing and empowering people; it turned out to be the answer to my prayer.

"When I began, I was thrilled to be working at the store. However, as time went on, the thrill faded and I began to tire of doing the same repetitious task. I was cutting vine branches at the time and inadvertently gashed my hand. I screamed, and the men were about to call 911. Claire, a co-owner of the store, heard me and washed my feet with the towel. When she did, I felt a current of energy flow from my feet to my hand where the gash was. When it reached my hand, the energy welded the artery and skin that had been severed back together. When the blood-soaked towel was removed, my hand was as good as new.

"Needless to say, when I saw that there was not even a scratch on my hand, I was ecstatic. It's one thing to see other people being healed, yet when it happens to you, you can't help but see life in a whole new way. Within a few hours, my initial astonishment gave way, and I discovered I had been filled with a new type of fervor. For the first time in my life, I could see life clearly and breathe fresh air into my lungs. It was as if I had been totally rewired and had the type of passion for life I had when I was a little boy. Now that my batteries were fully charged, I was fired up and was ready to go out and empower others, helping to liberate them from the barriers in their lives that oppressed and prevented them from realizing their dreams.

"My friends in Christ, God has not abandoned us, but society is in a crisis. Life has become overwhelming, and people don't know how to help themselves. Jesus saw how tired people were of being oppressed and how they longed to be freed from the source of their strife. Many today are fully aware of the problems that keep them from realizing their dreams, but they feel like victims because they lack the power to implement the solutions.

"This is definitely a sad reality. However, what appalls me is that this attitude has infected the Christian community. Jesus said not to hide our lights but to expose them and let them burn brightly for the world to see. Hearing the good news does lift the spirit, but if we don't put the Gospel into practice and use it as a tool to empower ourselves and others, what type of lights are we? Slavery was a crime that was abolished. However, we are just as enslaved to the situation we are in today as the men and women who spent their days in those cotton fields. We say we are Christians and believe that through the name of Jesus we have the power to cast out demons and evil spirits. Folks, please wake up! We have a demonic plague hanging over us that is sucking us dry. Many feel victimized and don't know how to help themselves. Would someone please be kind enough to tell me what is wrong with this picture?

"The question we should be asking is, "How do we acquire the power to do these mighty acts that seem to be so out of our reach?" Well, Jesus says that if we seek Him and do His will in all things, we can ask Him for whatever we want and it will be done for us, However, many ask in the wrong spirit and become upset with God for not waving His magic wand and granting their requests. God gives gifts to His people not so they can coast down easy street but so they will be in a better position to help and do good for other people.

"Since my visit to Divine Towels, my life has changed dramatically. No longer do I feel that I am floundering. I know, without a doubt, that I need to take the fervor I have inside me and spread it to as many people as I possibly can. Life is not easy, but if we wish to be liberated, we must find a way to rise up against the forces that oppress us. Believe it or not, Jesus has given our community a unique resource in Divine Towels. Not only does Jesus use the owners as instruments to heal physical ailments but also to revive weary spirits just as the disciples did after Jesus ascended into heaven.

"I realize what I'm saying is strange. However, it's true. If you're tired of the same old thing and desire to be freed from the monotony of everyday life, come to the store and be energized by Christ as you have never been before. I believe that we can change the world, but we must start living out the verse, 'I can do all things through Christ who strengthens me.'"

When Bill finished, the room was silent. This testimony was very challenging to say the least. It was evident that the Holy Spirit had anointed Bill and had given him the words to show that there was a way to become empowered and move ahead. The source of the power was Jesus and if they did things His way, He would give them the power to bring about positive change in the world.

———————

Throughout history, many activists have seen the grave injustices and have made it their mission to do everything in their power to promote social justice. While pursuing this endeavor, they met many people who were oppressed and longed to be freed from the bondage that prevented them from fulfilling their dreams. Although these people knew what the problem was and what it would take to get out of the situation they were currently in, many were simply too worn out from their lives and lacked the resources necessary to dig out of it. Today, many live their lives in frustration, wading through the swamp hoping someone someday will come along and liberate them from bondage.

Driven by faith and the desire to set the human spirit free, activists throughout the ages have heard the desperate cries of these people and have responded. After examining the source of the problem and observing how the key players operate, they have formulated an action plan and determined the most effective way to obtain results. Filled with passion for the issue, they have stepped up to the plate, formed coalitions, and challenged people vigorously to open their minds and hearts and to think in new ways. Because of their ability to articulate their vision, they inspired people and laid out an action plan on how it could be accomplished. They also realized that the vision would never be fulfilled unless people were united and worked together to achieve the common goal.

Many look at the great accomplishments leaders have made throughout the ages and marvel at their passionate ability to stir people and get results. They often look at the state of affairs today and wish they had the charisma and passion needed to inspire and empower people the way great leaders did in the past. Many today still desire to be agents of change and to make the world a better place to live, but they are unable to rally the necessary enthusiasm needed to pull it off. What starts out as a fireball in their soul, ends up being another unfulfilled dream.

Like others, Ethan and Claire admired such people and longed for an opportunity to lead a crusade and liberate people from the psychological strongholds that oppressed them and kept them from being whole. They were tired of talking about the steps that needed to be done to bring a solution to fruition and were anxious to undertake action to make it reality. However, until now, this had all just been an idealistic fantasy.

When Christ graced them with the opportunity of a lifetime, they were ecstatic; it was a chance to lead people on the ultimate spiritual crusade. Though the idea of serving humanity was their ultimate dream come true, once everything was set and ready to go, they discovered that while the adventure they were about to undertake would be exciting, they would also encounter many challenges along the way.

While it is challenging and exciting to explore unfamiliar territory, it is also nice to become acclimated and develop a routine, so you know what to do in a crisis. Divine Towels had only been open for a few weeks, yet Ethan and Claire were already comfortable. At this time, word was getting out about what was happening at the store.

One day everything changed when Ethan and Claire arrived at work and were greeted by throngs of people who were standing outside their store. At first, they wondered if the community was hosting an event they were not aware of. However, before long, they realized that the people had found out what was happening and were there to be healed of their ailments. Hence, it was obvious that they had a serious problem. While they were delighted to see such a large turnout, from a logistical standpoint the task before them seemed arduous.

They recalled that the Lord had said it would be a success but never did they imagine it would be so successful in such a short amount of time. Ethan and Claire panicked. Since they weren't quite sure what to do, they went in the back door and prayed for help. "Lord, we did everything you said, and we are grateful for the opportunity you gave us to serve and heal others. The line outside our door is so long, and we are only two people. We are willing to help as many people as we can, but we desperately need some extra help right about now."

Just then, the phone rang "Good morning, Divine Towels, may I help you," Claire said sweetly, as if nothing was wrong.

"Good morning, Claire, It's Bill I just wanted to tell you that you should be expecting some business. At church yesterday I gave testimony to what happened when I cut myself and how my whole life has changed since that time. I wish you were there to see the faces when I told them that Christ was working miracles again the way He did when He left the earth long ago. I mean it was just so delightful," Bill said.

Claire was elated by this and could see that the Holy Spirit had kept its promise to Ethan. Though she was very interested to hear the details, she did not have time for this. People were banging on the windows waiting for the store to open and it was making her nervous.

"Bill," Claire interrupted, "I'm happy for you. But this is not a particularly good time to talk about this. We have a large crowd of people lined up outside waiting for us to heal them."

Recalling the first part of his dream, Bill was filled with great joy, and sensed that his hour to serve had come. "Wait," he shouted with great excitement. "Before you hang up, there's something I must tell you. A few weeks ago, after I had been healed, I had a dream and was told by Christ that you would encounter this very situation. He proceeded to show me that . . . ."

Bill was about to tell Claire about the dream he had, but she was unable to concentrate on what he was saying. Before Bill could even get a sentence out of his mouth, Claire interrupted him. "Bill," she said, "I really am interested in what you have to say. Unfortunately, right now I'm trying to do so many things simultaneously that I can't really think about what you're saying. However, if you think you can help us in some way, don't be bashful. Come on down and we'll put you to work. Oh, and by the way, when you do come, be sure you come in the back door so you don't have to fight your way through the crowds."

He headed for the door. He had waited for this moment all his life, and he was anxious to begin harvesting fruit for the Lord. When he reached the door, he thought he should call Jim and to let him know what was happening at the store. Perhaps Jim might be interested in tagging along and helping as well.

———————————

Claire and Ethan lined up several basins, filled the holders with informational pamphlets and several vessels with water, and turned on the soft music to create a warm, inviting atmosphere amidst the confusion. Now it was time to unlock the door. The scene reminded them of opening the doors at Kmart on the morning of Black Friday and seeing floods of people pour in. On one hand, they dreaded this, yet they felt blessed that Christ had called them to this ministry and would not have wanted it any other way. As they opened the door, they prayed again that the Holy Spirit would reside with them as they healed people.

Some did rush in, but many entered with much reverence as if it were a sanctuary. For a few minutes, Ethan and Claire were so amazed by the masses of people who entered that they just stood there as if they were watching a movie. However, the daze was broken when Carol handed Claire a towel and asked her if she would heal her from cerebral palsy.

When Claire realized what was happening, she snapped out of it and asked Carol, a devout Catholic, to follow her. Carol could walk and talk but had slurred speech and lacked fine-motor skills. Consequently, she required assistance taking care of herself throughout the day. Despite her disability, she was active in her community and worked full-time.

In college, Carol had been eager to participate in community service activities; however, she was unable to do so because of her disability. This frustrated Carol to no end. She yearned to make a difference, yet she was trapped in a body that would not cooperate with her. She was tired of always needing help and wanted to help others instead.

Despite her limitations, Carol had been blessed with a special gift of being able to write with such clarity and insight that it often made people see life in a different way. Carol knew she had been given a tremendous gift with which to inspire people in wonderful ways, yet she had hit a dry spell and felt as if she was spinning her wheels. At one time, she thought she knew what she wanted to do with her life, but now she wasn't sure. Carol was ambitious and eager to help change the world, but she had no idea where to begin. Thus, Carol was here because she sought wisdom on what to do next.

Claire did not know Carol but sensed that there was something very special about her. Claire could see that though she was bright and had much going for her. Carol was lonely and felt like an outsider.

"What is it that you seek?" Claire asked.

"Good question," Carol answered. "I have been asking myself that question a lot lately. I guess someone in my situation would naturally want to be cured of his physical affliction. However, there are things I want more than that."

Claire heard this and was amazed. The girl who could not have been more than 19 years old had an old soul and it was clear that she understood there was more to life than merely having a physical body that worked properly.

After a brief pause, Carol continued, "I guess my mind is the problem. I want to do so much. I seek the wisdom and clarity of mind to know what role I am to play. I'm convinced we are all here for a reason, other than just to do our daily routines. God might not have given me a body that works as well as others, but He did bless me with an ability to write and to contemplate what is important in life. Like you, I want to help people and give them hope. Right now I can't seem to get out of my rut no matter what I do. I have prayed about this matter fervently, asking God to show me what He wants me to do for Him, but thus far, an answer hasn't come. I've come because I've heard that Christ has performed miracles through you. Please help me; I don't want to end up being another person who wastes the talent he has been blessed with."

Hearing Carol's story, Claire knew Christ had special plans for her. Since Carol had been so matter of fact in what she sought, Claire was eager to get started. Thus, she placed the towel between her hands and prayed that Christ would pour His healing on her however He saw fit. After sitting like this for a few minutes, Claire now felt energy flowing in her body and began washing Carol's feet. Carol could tell a force was present that was trying to prevent this healing from happening. Claire suddenly felt dizzy and had tremors in her hands as Carol did.

When one truly comes into union with his maker and tries to live a righteous life, obstacles will come up and try to pull him away from Christ. Claire knew this on an intellectual level. Yet, when she encountered it first hand, she was not sure what was happening. At first, Claire ignored this thinking that it would only last a minute. However, when she picked up the towel to dry Carol's feet off, the dizziness intensified to the point where Claire wondered if she was going to pass out. Claire did her best to focus her attention on being a channel of healing, but she knew that within seconds that she would pass out and be defeated if she did not act immediately. Though Claire was tired, she looked at Ethan and bellowed, "In the name of Jesus Christ, Satan be gone!"

After she uttered these words, the negative force that had tried to prevent the healing was replaced by an abundance of warm flowing energy. The dizziness that had plagued Claire also left and she felt revived and energized to help as many people as would come through the door that day.

"Sorry about that outburst, Carol," Claire said. "Something special is about to happen and though I'm not sure what it is, I know a force tried to prevent it. However, it's gone and will not return. I don't want to talk about it anymore. Besides, we have work to do so that you can work for the Lord."

When Claire resumed drying Carol's feet off, Carol felt a strange sensation in her mouth and jaw. It was as if the nerves in her brain were being rewired so she could speak without the speech impediment. Since she had never experienced this tingly sensation before, Carol wasn't sure whether to laugh or cry. Yes, something definitely was happening, but what? Without warning, the Holy Spirit filled Carol with words and she began to sing with great joy. When Carol opened her mouth, the sweetest sound came out and filled the air. When the song was over, Carol heard a voice say, "Daughter, someday soon you will speak with the clarity of the wind."

At times God permits people to have downtime to give the body and mind a chance to rest so they have the energy to face the next challenge. As a young man, Jim had been the busy type who never stopped moving and was always involved in projects of one sort or another. Yet, after the accident, he underwent a period of adjustment and had to figure out how to do things in a new way. Though he managed to learn how to function again, Jim had a difficult time adjusting to not being able to do the things he always enjoyed, such as working with Habitat for Humanity.

Jim's life changed when he met Ethan and returned to working with his hands. Although he always enjoyed doing renovations, when it came time for him and his crew to work on the store, Jim experienced an exhilarating rush in his soul that he had never felt before. The peace that resided in the store was medicinal and made him feel alive. Jim looked forward to going to help out, but when it was time to leave he always felt a bit sad, like a piece of him was missing.

Once the renovations were complete and it was time for the store to open, Jim was joyful yet depressed at the same time. Jim was ecstatic that the store would be used to help people and revive their tired, restless spirits. Yet, since he had devoted so much time to designing and building the store, he had trouble with the idea of separating himself from it. He found the work Christ had called them to be so enchanting that his soul yearned to be part of it in some way.

For weeks Jim had prayed that Christ would somehow open up an opportunity so he could work at the store. When Bill called Jim to tell him that Ethan and Claire needed help, Jim knew God had answered his prayer. It was quite an honor to help build the store, but it was nothing compared to the elation he felt at the prospect of helping Ethan and Claire heal others. Knowing how difficult it could be on a busy day to find a parking place around there, Jim suggested that Bill pick him up on the way over.

It is one thing to hear about a problem, yet it is another to experience it firsthand. Jim and Bill thought they knew what to expect when they arrived. However, when they saw the swarms of people who had come to be made whole, they were moved. Unlike revivals where people were invited up to recommit their lives to Christ, people were not just being healed of their physical ailments, but they left to see life and its problems with amazing clarity as well as with a renewed sense of purpose--not simply to do their routines but also to perform works of mercy. The sight of this was truly amazing and made them want to participate all the more.

Once they had recovered from the initial shock, they remembered Ethan and Claire were inside and no doubt inundated and needed help immediately. They were eager to be of assistance in any way they could. Yet, upon entering the store, they felt useless and wondered if they had done the wrong thing in going there, for they realized all the people were waiting to see Ethan and Claire and that they could not help them at all.

With the steady stream of people, Ethan and Claire were in their glory. The ministry Christ had called them to was not only up and running, but was a flourishing success. While they were doing what they loved, they soon realized that they were only two people and could not possibly handle the people by themselves. If their business was to succeed, they would need other people to help them.

This was a wise idea but at the moment not very practical. After all, people were still waiting to be healed, and they could not just get up, walk out, and begin looking for helpers. Though they felt overwhelmed and frazzled, they could not afford to become upset but needed to stay focused. While they wanted to stay and heal more people, they knew if they did not take a break to throw some towels in the wash and pray over some of the basins filled with blackened water that their supply would shortly be gone. Thus, they sprang into action scurrying about the store and gathering up the used towels and basins.

Until this point, Ethan and Claire had remained relatively calm. However, upon searching the room and finding only two dirty basins, they panicked and could not imagine what was going on. They had been washing feet for four hours without a break; there was no way that many basins could get up and walk out all by themselves. Just when they were starting to panic, they saw Jim pass by and drop off a few of the remaining clean basins along with vessels of fresh water and proceed to take the dirty basins with him.

Ethan and Claire were not quite sure what to think. While they were grateful to God for interceding and sending them much needed help, when they thought about what he might have been doing with the dirty water, they panicked. They remembered God had asked them to perform a ritual when they disposed of the dirty water and were afraid of what might happen if the instructions were not followed. Until they talked to Jim and found out exactly what he had been doing, they would not have a moment's peace.

"Hi, Jim," Ethan said in an effort to sound cheerful. "Boy, it's certainly a surprise to see you. When did you get here, and more importantly, how did you manage to fight your way through that crowd?"

"Oh, Bill and I have been here for hours. We came in through the back door as Claire said."

Claire then remembered that Bill had called. "I'm sorry that we didn't see you come in and that we didn't even have a chance to say hello. Ethan and I have been inundated. It's amazing to see how God is moving and the numbers of people who are being healed. At first, I thought the healing was merely physical, but now I'm convinced, from observation, that once their feet have been dried, a force enters people's body and alters their entire outlook on life. Consequently, they go on to perform amazing acts to empower and end the suffering of others. Anyway, enough about me. What have you and Bill been up to for the last few hours?" Claire asked.

"Man, oh man, do we have a story or two to tell you," Bill said enthusiastically. "I know you both are extremely busy, but I think you'll want to hear what we have to say; it's equally compelling as what you just finished telling me and will reduce your stress load tremendously."

Ethan and Claire knew that Christ had been working miracles behind the scenes and were eager to hear what Jim and Bill had to say. Ethan said, "Come on, Mom, let's go in the back and hear all this good news! The people can wait; this takes priority."

When they saw what was going on in the back, they were amazed. All the basins they had used with the dirty water were sitting there in a line waiting for them. Because Bill saw that their eyes immediately went to the basins, he began, "It's obvious to us that it is becoming too much for you two to handle all the duties in the store by yourselves. We were both honored to help build the store, but when I heard you were overwhelmed with people, I remembered a dream I had about a month ago. Jesus told me what to do.

"When we arrived at the store, we were revved up to roll up our sleeves and begin helping. However, people were waiting to see you and we realized that we couldn't help them at all. We felt useless and wondered if we had made a mistake in coming here. When a man named Paul approached me and told his problem, my heart ached and I felt compelled to do something to relieve his suffering. At first, I tried to get you, but you were busy. Then I relayed my frustration to Jim who suggested that we go in the back and ask Jesus how He wanted us to serve.

"When we prayed, Jesus reminded me of my dream. Again, He told me that for several weeks I was supposed to apprentice under you and would be washing feet and healing people with you. Once I learn how to serve, I am supposed to open and run a spin-off of Divine Towels called the Foot-Washing Institute. The purpose of the institute will be to teach people how to wash feet. Once people are properly trained, they will help out in the store and go to other places and wash feet. In this way, the ministry at Divine Towels will expand.

"When I heard this, I was shocked and thought Christ must have been mistaken. Of course, I was elated. I had no idea why He had chosen me to do this for Him. After all, I had no power. However, Jesus assured me that if I was humble and trusted Him completely, He would use me to do miraculous things. Although I had never done a healing before, I surrendered my will and trusted that Christ would do the rest. I washed one man's feet, and he was healed. After him, another and another came, until I was out of basins.

"While I'm grateful for this gift, it's humbling to know that unless I'm one with Christ and allow him to use me as He wills, healing will not occur. This is a great store, and it is an invaluable source of hope for the community. You are doing a wonderful service for the community. However, you are only two people and can heal only so many. If you want to help as many as possible and want to bring light to the darkness, please allow more workers to come and heal with you. I am happy to train those who are called to minister in this way."

Ethan and Claire realized they needed help, but it was not until they heard Bill's story that they saw how other people could be used to support their ministry. They always knew they were called to this ministry but were surprised others would feel compelled to follow in their footsteps and, in essence, be their disciples. Things were powerful before, but when they saw how everything was unfolding, they were in awe. Of course, this was the next logical step.

"Wow!" Claire laughed. "Just when I thought everything was about to turn chaotic, God came along and gave us the answer we needed. Talk about perfect timing. It's truly amazing to see how God works, and the way He makes His will known. You are not only our friend but a messenger who was sent to show us how we are supposed to expand this ministry. The ministry God has called you to is a mighty one, and I am grateful that God has given us the opportunity to serve others together. I can't possibly think of a better person for the job than you, Bill."

Claire embraced Bill. While she still had more that she wanted to say to Bill, at the moment she was overwhelmed and unable to think clearly.

Once Claire had finished with Bill, Ethan was eager to hear what Christ had in store for Jim to do.

"Bill, I must admit you're a hard act to follow, but I'll give it my best shot," Jim said.

Sensing that Jim was a tad down on himself, Ethan said, "Don't say that. Christ has blessed us all with special talents, and they all are equally valuable. So do me a favor and lighten up on yourself. We're your friends, and whatever God told you must be valuable. We need as much help as we can possibly get. Please share, buddy, and don't be afraid."

Jim smiled and began, "I too had no idea what I was supposed to do when I got here. However, when I opened my heart, Christ showed me that I also was going to alleviate your burden by becoming the store manager and taking care of the day-to-day activities that you two really don't have the time for. My duties, as Christ told me, will include managing daily operations, answering the phone, scheduling special events, and keeping the books. Some may think taking this job is below them; however, I am honored that Christ has selected me, a lowly unworthy servant, to play such an important role in this wondrous ministry. You are meeting a critical need in the community, and I feel privileged to play a supportive role in your ministry."

Once again, Christ was working behind the scenes and met Ethan and Claire's needs before they even asked. Filled with the spirit of gratitude, Claire prayed, "Thank you so much, Lord, for this incredible ministry you have called us to and for blessing each one of us with unique talents. You have brought us together so we can serve others. Please pour your Holy Spirit on us and use us however You wish. We pray these things in your name. Amen."

Upon opening their eyes, they knew the Holy Spirit was with them and that it was time to get back to work. Just as Ethan was about to leave, he remembered that he still needed to teach them about the dirty water. "Before I go back to work, I must show you both the procedure Christ taught me for handling the dirty water. As you pour the dirty water down the drain, use hot water and pray for Christ to come and destroy the evil. Remember, it was Christ who said He is the light of the world, and thus He kills all darkness. If this routine is not followed each and every time, unclean spirits will infiltrate the water supply and hurt people. So it is of the utmost importance to pray for Christ's spirit to descend." Once Ethan and Claire were sure that Bill and Jim understood the significance of this ritual, they returned to work.

It is said that if you work hard enough, you can have anything you want. Sure, it might take time, but if you make up your mind and refuse to give up, anything is possible. Just look at how Ethan and Claire started out. Yes, they encountered many hardships and obstacles along the way. However, because they depended on Christ's constant help and friendship, they were able to do what seemed to be impossible: opening a thriving store and living the life many Christians would surely envy.

Over the years, people marveled at the tremendous obstacles Ethan and Claire had to endure and often wondered how they beat the odds and triumphed no matter what circumstances they faced. Whenever people posed this question to them, they simply answered that they trusted totally in God. To this people scoffed and said okay, not really understanding what they truly meant.

If you were to look at Ethan and Claire's lives, it would seem safe to assume that their lives were perfect and that they were very popular. After all, God had blessed them with an extraordinary gift. However, looks are deceiving! When you help people in a unique way, you would think people would go to any lengths to repay your kindness. Some people were indeed grateful, lavished Ethan and Claire with gifts of appreciation and told them to call if they needed anything. While they appeared to care, it was short-lived. Once the newness of it all wore off, life returned to normal, people resumed their own lives and Ethan and Claire found themselves alone.

Initially, this was quite hurtful; however, after a while, they got used to it. The truth was they had been through this their entire lives and had learned not to permit the actions of others to affect them. They knew Christ had put them on earth to do a special mission and getting mad at others was not only unproductive, but was a trick Satan used to get people to take their focus off Christ.

Ethan and Claire did not always have this attitude, especially in tough times. Intellectually, they knew God loved them and would always be with them and keep them safe no matter what. Yet, there were times when they resented God for giving them such grueling lives. Furthermore, they didn't understand why God seemed to be absent when they faced agonizing situations and needed His comfort and support most. This feeling of abandonment was exacerbated when others would talk about how their friends and family provided support in whatever way they needed. People cared about them and were friendly up to a point. However, Ethan and Claire's friends had their own lives and didn't want to get overly involved.

Becoming a beautiful flower does not happen overnight. Rather, it is a slow process that requires going through a lot of dirt. Indeed, Ethan and Claire found themselves in the dirt. Nonetheless, they were grateful. From reading the Bible, they knew that when the Lord selects a person to be His instrument, the Lord becomes like a drill sergeant who puts His children through rigorous basic training to prepare them for their ultimate mission.

In theory, it sounds logical that the Lord sends people into exile and strips them of all earthly comforts for a time so He can teach them to be humble and to depend on Him. Yet, there are times when this training can be so grueling that it becomes more than even the toughest people can withstand. Ethan and Claire understood such training was necessary and that they belonged to the Lord. Although they knew that being separated from the world was part of the test, at times they took it personally and were devastated when they found that their family and friends had forsaken them. Learning lessons was one thing; it was another to have the people who were supposed to care abandon you when you needed them most.

During this precarious predicament, Ethan and Claire experienced a wide range of emotions. At times, their souls were filled with hopelessness and total despair. At other times, they felt invisible as if no one cared if they lived or died. There were days they did not want to get out of their beds. It blew their minds that the people they had helped repeatedly over the years (who claimed to love them so much) could just reject them in their hour of need. Although they knew that they were being tested, there was a time when they felt God was pushing them beyond human endurance. At this time, they would have done anything to alleviate the anguish; but there was simply nowhere to escape. Often they wanted to scream, "HELP ME!" but it was as futile as yelling at the wall. Ultimately, they were trapped and there was no one to listen or care. Despite how they felt, the situation was out of their control, and there was not a thing they could do to change it.

Ethan and Claire found themselves in a quandary. On one hand, they felt privileged that God had called them into exile so He could train them for their ultimate mission. They also knew they belonged to Christ and as long as He was with them, nothing could harm them. At the same time, however, they were so frustrated and angry at their friends and family for abandoning them that it was all they could think about. It was also upsetting to know that they did not have any earthly support system to fall back on. They wanted to let it go, but could not—no matter how hard they tried.

It is easy when everything is going smoothly to believe in God and to pledge to be faithful to the ends of eternity. However, when you do not sense God's presence and you find your life in shambles, what do you do? Do you allow yourself to get down, wallow in pity, and fall for the snares Satan uses to try to lure you away from fulfilling your purpose on earth or do you trudge forward and use it as a time to get closer to God and to learn to trust even more?

Like the Israelites, there was a time when Ethan and Claire griped about the endless struggles they endured and were bitter why other people seemed to have easy lives. However, it wasn't long before they realized they weren't making any progress and were doing something wrong. Consequently, they decided to step back and find out what God would have them do by reading the Bible. From reading the story of Moses, they learned that there was no way to escape the wilderness. If they wanted to get out of exile, they had to change their attitudes and trust God like little children.

Everyone dreams about what it would be like to fight heroically for a noble cause to banish evil and to see justice prevail. While we may do our best to fight injustices and to set the captives free, in an age where everything is so difficult to get done, we often feel powerless to make life better and as if our efforts are futile. Often we see injustices happen every day to innocent people and wish there was something we could do to make the situation better instead of sitting idly by in utter frustration.

God has indeed given us access to an arsenal of spiritual weapons. However, unless we are trained in how to use the weapons effectively, they are useless to us. It may be useful to learn the theory about when to use weapons; God puts us in difficult situations so we can gain practical experience on how to use weapons. Until this time, Ethan and Claire had often wondered why God had put them in a desperate situation; however, it became clear that if they wanted to help people, they had to gain practical experience.

Through this experience, Ethan and Claire discovered just as the devil has tactics to make Christians feel hopeless and despondent, biblical heroes had a cache of weapons at their disposal. They learned strongholds could be broken if they were willing to become disciplined and persistently use spiritual weapons to wage war against Satan himself. In that moment, Ethan and Claire had a profound insight and realized why Jesus had put them in this situation. If they truly wanted the Lord to use them, they not only had to learn how to use the weapons. They had to become specialists.

This was nice to say in theory, but from a practical standpoint, Ethan and Claire were bewildered and did not know what to do to get out of their slump. Consequently, they turned to the Bible and were surprised by the answers they found. It was wonderful to read about how biblical heroes triumphed over evil and won souls for Christ. But, it was even more helpful to read how they overcame adversity. Like us, they were tempted to wallow in pity when faced insurmountable obstacles. Instead, they refused to succumb and despite what they felt like doing, they praised and thanked God for putting them in the situation.

The idea of praising God in times of great hardship seemed foreign to them; they simply could not relate. In their experience during moments of extreme distress when they needed God most and cried out for help, they were utterly confused why God did not answer them, hid His face, and seemed to be absent. What added to their confusion was that Jesus was the one who said to come to Him when they were heavy laden that He would give them rest. Consequently, the idea of praising and thanking God for withholding His help when they needed it most seemed preposterous!

The more they thought about this, the more exasperated they became. Sure they were tempted to walk away and forget about it for a while. However, even if they cleared their heads for a time, they knew it would not help and would just delay the inevitable. Somehow they had to find a way to solve this problem, for until they did, they would have no peace. Despite being frustrated, they once again found themselves on their knees.

Suddenly, they had an insight or a vision so to speak and it altered their whole way of thinking. They pictured themselves being in the boat with the disciples during the storm when Jesus fell asleep. Like the disciples, they were tempted to wake Jesus up when they saw the giant waves wanting to devour them. However, just when they were starting to become frantic with fear, they heard a voice that said, "Peace be with you. Be still, for I am with you and will help you. Keep your eyes fixed on me, and you will never fail!" Intellectually they knew this was true; yet because they were overwrought with anxiety, it was easy for them to forget about the still, small voice that was always inside of them.

Just then, Claire saw herself as an agitated, screaming baby who was having a temper tantrum. Despite all the efforts to appease her, nothing helped. In the end, it was only when God spoke peace that her troubled soul was comforted and calmed. These words may have been simple; yet, they had such a powerful, transforming effect that they altered Claire's life forever.

Once Claire had calmed down, Jesus told her she had nothing to fear because He walked beside her down those long, lonesome roads. He went on to explain that He surrounded those who obeyed Him with a bubble of protection, and nothing could penetrate it. While evil forces would surely do all in their power to destroy her peace, in the end their attempts were like an annoying flee trying to attack a heavily guarded fortress. When Claire saw this, she was amazed and it altered the course of her life forever. It gave her peace and reassured her that as long as Jesus was at the boat's helm and she kept her eyes on Him, it did not matter what she had to go through.

For a time, it seemed as if Ethan and Claire had cleared this hurdle and were starting to have everything the way they wanted them. To this end, they relished being the vessels God had chosen to work through to heal people, spending their days washing feet, and doing speaking engagements at night, but it was a grueling schedule that took tremendous stamina. The demands of their job were challenging and required them to live as Jesus did: healing and helping people in the community while spending much time in their own little world so they could remain in constant communication with their Father.

Just when it seemed that Ethan and Claire had gotten into a groove and were cruising down life's highway at a nice clip, they hit an unforeseen detour in the road. The detour God gave them tested the strength of their convictions by making them confront an unpleasant incident from their past. When they hit the detour, they realized it was easy to allow God to use them to heal strangers, especially when an emotional connection isn't involved. However, just add emotional connection and hurt feelings, and the task of remaining obedient to God becomes very challenging.

The shakeup happened when a woman wearing a head scarf entered the store. As soon as she did, tension permeated the room. Because this had never happened before, Ethan and Claire spent several minutes trying to find out who the woman was and what had caused the air to be filled with negativity. Initially, nothing came to mind. However, after studying her face for a few minutes, they finally dawned on them who it was. When it did, they were flabbergasted and filled with a torrent of emotion!

As they stood looking at Gail, they remembered the hurtful things she had done years ago and wondered why she was here. Gail had started out so sweet. Like many, she got swept up by the lure of fame and fortune and had permitted it to cloud her judgments. Yes, the sting of the past was hurtful. However, that was years ago and Ethan and Claire decided it was best for all to forget the past and move on.

As Ethan and Claire looked at Gail, they wondered what catastrophic event could have caused her to come to their store. Certainly intrigue alone would not have caused her to come, especially considering all the things Gail had put them through. Long ago they had made it a practice not to make assumptions. However, judging from her body language and the sheer terror in her eyes, it was obvious something tragic had happened; she was here because she was in a desperate situation and had no other options.

The awkward moments that followed felt like eternity. The tension in the room was made worse by the silence as they glared at one another. For years, Ethan and Claire imagined what they would say to Gail if they ever saw her again. However, now that Gail was staring them in the face, they did not know what to say.

Had this happened a few months back, Ethan and Claire surely would have reacted differently. They would have been angry and told Gail to leave immediately and never return! However, their time alone in the wilderness with God had altered their outlook on life dramatically. Although they were a bit irritated that she was here, they shut their eyes, remembered that Jesus was with them and knew that the Holy Spirit would direct them what to say.

After taking a deep breath, Claire broke the silence when she held up her right hand and said, "Peace be with you. What can we do to help you today, Gail?" In that moment, the animosity that had been so prominent vanished instantly. Suddenly, the emotion Gail had held inside her for years came unleashed.

"Wow! I've been debating whether to come here for weeks for several reasons. But no matter how hard it was to do it, when it came right down to it, I really didn't have much choice."

Gail paused for a moment and then continued. "The trouble began the day Tim issued me that horrible ultimatum: either have children for me anyway you can or we are getting divorced. When he said this to me, I was shocked and didn't know what to do. Yes, I also wanted children since they are truly a joy. But when he threatened me, I was very angry. When he gave me that ultimatum, my feelings for him changed. It was as if a switch inside me flipped, and I saw him for who he truly was. The joy that I was looking forward to more than anything became a chore.

"In the weeks that followed, I spent much time thinking, trying to decide what to do. I contemplated leaving, but the mere thought of leaving and not having life on my terms was too much for me to bear. I had grown accustomed to my lifestyle and had invested too much time into the relationship to call it quits. While I did not like the way he treated me, I decided to stay and have his children.

"The decision to stay turned out to be a bad move, for it nearly cost me my life! And so I tried unsuccessfully for years to become pregnant the natural way, but I was forced to consider alternatives. Initially, we toyed with the idea of adoption; however, Tim made it abundantly clear that he didn't have any intention of adopting but expected a full-fledged heir.

"Because I had no other options and my marriage depended on it, I was forced to consider in vitro fertilization. Ordinarily, this would not have been a problem except that when I was younger I had a precancerous cyst on an ovary. The doctor told me I had a predisposition for cancerous cells to grow and that I needed to be monitored closely. After investigating the process, I knew there were potential risks to having in vitro fertilization. I know I should've told Tim about it, but I was afraid of how he might react. While everything inside me told me not to do this, because I was in a desperate situation, I kept it to myself and hoped for the best. Despite my positive attitude, things were rocky right from the start.

"Becoming pregnant was difficult. Nothing worked. Not only was it depressing, but extremely frustrating and stressful as well. Although I wanted to give up, I stuck at it for fear that he would divorce me. After 14 months of trying and having a few miscarriages, it finally worked. I should've been happy, but I was sick the whole time from the massive number of hormones injected into my system. Consequently, I spent the majority of nine months either in bed or over the toilet. While my pregnancy was laborious, as soon as the twins were born, all the trouble went away. Life returned to normal and life was indeed glorious, at least for the next five years.

"Then on June 2, 2003, my life changed forever when I woke up with a dull, throbbing pain in my stomach. If I had been smart, I would have listened to what my body was trying to tell me and had it checked right away. But I did not. I went on with my normal routine, hoping the pain would go away. I believed I would be fine. Despite my attempts to be positive, the pain persisted for months. When the pain became so unbearable, I just couldn't take it anymore. I was forced to break down and to go to the doctor.

"It wasn't until I got in the car and began driving to the doctors that I realized there were two reasons why I had been putting it off. First, I dreaded telling Tim I was sick. Although he could be very kind, whenever he knew I was sick, he turned into a wild person. It was one of his quirks that when he knew I was suffering in any way, he became so frightened that he acted viciously angry towards me. Being sick was hard enough, but I couldn't stand to be screamed at in the process.

"It was distressing enough to deal with Tim, but I was even more terrified to go to the doctor and find out what was happening. As I walked into the doctor's office, I knew I had no one to blame for this except myself. I had used all of my get-of-out jail free cards, and there was no way to skate by this one unscathed.

"The life I once knew changed forever a week after the doctors ran tests and the results came back. After hearing the words, 'Well, you really did it this time! Deciding to wait until now really hurt you. I'm sorry to tell you, but you have stage-4 inoperable terminal ovarian cancer, and there's nothing I can do.' The rest of the day was a blank. Getting this news was worse than being punched in the gut. It was as if a wave crashed over me and as it retreated, I could feel my whole life and dreams being sucked away. Once it retreated, I stood naked, stripped of all that I was and wondered who I was and what I would become.

"These past few months have been horrendous for me because I have been virtually incapacitated, as I was during my pregnancy and because I have had too much time to think. Naturally, I am terrified and can't even fathom what will happen to the twins when I am no longer around," Gail said, pausing for a moment to wipe the tears from her eyes and to regain enough composure so she would have the strength to continue.

"I had stage-4 inoperable terminal ovarian cancer and that I probably did wait too long. Upon learning that I had cancer and that there wasn't any hope for me, I considered all my options. I have spent all my time looking for ways to fight the cancer, going to the best doctors, and exploring many treatment options. However, so far, nothing has worked! While racking my brains looking for help, I remembered that at one time you both were into alternative healing. Despite our history, I thought about calling you but chickened out when I picked up the phone.

"Then the other day I was talking to someone who suggested that I go to Divine Towels because people were being healed and lives were being drastically changed for the better. Although this sounded a bit strange and because there was such an influx of people being healed, I figured there was no harm in trying it. I mean, I didn't exactly have much to lose!

"It's not like me to act spontaneously. Usually, I am very methodical and research things so I know what I'm getting into. I had no idea that this was your store. I must admit it is extremely awkward for me to be here. Part of me wants to run far away, for I am humiliated and ashamed of myself for the way I treated you both who were my true friends. At the same time, however, there's also a part of me that believes it was not an accident that I ended up here. I desperately need your help because this is the only option I have. As I stand before you both, I am not quite sure if I should stay or go or even if I am welcome."

Divine Towels was definitely a refreshing, inspirational, and most needed place people could go amidst the storms of life for peace and solace. However, creating this peaceful environment was quite challenging and required much discipline. The key ingredient that made the store a sanctuary was Ethan and Claire's unwavering commitment to carrying out Christ's instructions explicitly and to ensuring that the environment was stress free.

Preparing the store was one thing; however, remaining in constant union with Christ so He could work through them proved most challenging. Ethan and Claire had spent a considerable amount of time alone with God in the wilderness and had become quite adept at getting through whatever challenges came their way. The encounter with Gail was far different, however. It threw them completely off-guard.

For years, Ethan and Claire fervently prayed that true reconciliation would occur and that someday Gail would come to know Christ as her Lord and Savior. However, now that Jesus had answered their prayer, they felt intense, conflicting emotions. Ethan and Claire knew in their hearts they needed to have mercy on Gail. They knew they had to forgive as Jesus did and push the delete key and instantly erase the many years of hurt, sorrow, and resentment.

They yearned to do the right thing. When they saw Gail and heard her story, suddenly a torrent of horrible emotions and memories that had lain dormant for years erupted. Soon the feelings of love and forgiveness vanished, giving way to rage, bitterness, and resentment. Instantly, Ethan and Claire felt an overwhelming urge to unleash their anger and tell Gail exactly how they felt. Ethan and Claire understood there was a difference between praying and wishing someone well and truly forgiving Gail to the point where they could have a relationship with her without harboring any resentment or animosity.

While they were about to snap, they closed their eyes, and had a vision that they were being given the ultimate spiritual test. Now that their store was established and they were doing the Master's work, they had to decide what they to do. Would they let God use them as instruments to help Gail or would they let the animosity they felt towards Gail consume them?

As they stood there with their eyes closed, they pictured Gail as a distressed soul on the side of the road pleading for help. Many so-called friends passed by, uttered a few kind words, and continued on their way. Within minutes of their departure, a familiar face pulled up, got out, and began tending to Gail's needs. Seeing this action unfold, Jesus said, "Peace be with you, my precious children. You are here simply to serve others, not to be served. I know you are angry and hurt. But let it go and let me carry the load. Your job is not to judge but rather to allow me to use you as I deem fit. Do not be afraid to help and have mercy on Gail. I will be with you and will help you every step of the way. Remember, I came to give mercy to those who need it most."

After Jesus said this, He breathed on them and filled them with His spirit. Now that Claire was peaceful, she said, "Peace be with you. Don't be afraid, we are here and want to help you. I don't deny that things have been strained between us for years. But that was years ago. Jesus said we need to let the past go and love one another as He loves us. So let's just put the past behind us and move on."

THE MINISTRY EXPANDS

At times in life, it is easy to focus so much on our current task that we lose sight of where God is leading us. When this happens, God tries to get our attention by putting things in our path to open our eyes so we see the broader strokes of His paintbrush.

Ethan and Claire were quite content to work in Divine Towels, knowing that with Christ's help they were planting seeds of hope and giving people the tools to win the spiritual battle against the enemy. This feeling was confirmed when people who had been healed often stopped in and told stories about what they were doing to revitalize their communities. Hearing these stories was wonderful and certainly motivated Ethan and Claire to continue their work.

Yet, when they stepped back, they realized they were healing only a small percentage of the population and yearned for a way to touch more people. The feeling was substantiated in the following weeks when Jim received numerous calls from hospitals, nursing homes, homeless shelters, and other establishments asking if someone from Divine Towels would pay them a visit. Ethan and Claire wanted desperately to go help these people but could not because they were two people and could only do but so much.

When Bill initially told them about the Foot-Washing Institute, Ethan and Claire were glad. However, it was not until they considered it for a while that they saw the how the Foot-Washing Institute was an answer to their prayer. Once others were trained in the art of foot washing, they could work in the store. This would free Ethan and Claire so they could concentrate on expanding their ministry into the community. It was essential to get the Foot-Washing Institute up and running.

Bill was thrilled that God had called him to establish the institute. Yet, he did not know how he could possibly teach others how to wash feet. After all, healing others was not something that could be taught on an intellectual level. Rather, it was a gift the Holy Spirit bestowed on the humble, those who sought to be Christ's hands and feet on the earth.

When Bill realized this, he was deeply troubled. He was quite anxious to teach others how to wash feet so more people could be healed; nevertheless, he obsessed about what to teach or even how to attract people to the institute. Bill prayed about the situation, but the harder he tried to come up with an answer, the more distressed he became. He even tried bouncing some ideas off Jim, but nothing helped. The problem was that the institute was based on an abstract concept and nothing concrete could be taught.

Bill found himself in a dilemma. Finally, he surrendered and sat in a secluded place and read the Bible, hoping it would provide an answer to this problem. He read in Exodus that Moses served as a judge for the people of Israel and informed them of God's laws and decrees. While reading the story and hearing that Moses' father-in-law told Moses he needed to appoint men of God to help him, Bill began to get a vague idea as to what his next step should be. He took the matter to prayer and sought clarification about the matter.

"Lord, thank you for the story you had me read in your Word. I sense that you want me to appoint people of God to help me; yet, I am not sure if I'm reading too much into this or how this applies to the situation I am in. Please send your Holy Spirit and show me what I am to do. I surrender all that I am to you. It is my desire to be your instrument and for you to use me in whatever way you see fit. I pray these things in your name. Amen."

At this point, Bill quieted his body and focused on Christ. Soon, Christ came to him as He had done before. "Peace be with you, my son. Because you have listened to me carefully thus far and have proven yourself trustworthy, I am blessing you and will show you the next step of your journey. You're right; you can't teach others the art of foot washing. It is a gift of the Spirit I bestow upon my disciples who keep my commandments and seek to do my will above all else. Don't worry about what you are to teach the people who attend the institute. My hand is on you, and I will tell you what to say.

"I know you're anxious to get the institute running, and so am I. However, before the institute can officially open, you need to understand that the institute is more than a place where people learn to wash feet. Just as Divine Towels has been able to impact the local community, the Foot-Washing Institute will be the umbrella under which this exhilaration will happen on a larger scale. Think of the institute as the accelerant that will illuminate the darkness in the world by lighting an onslaught of candles that, in turn, will light other candles. Just as a forest fire burns out of control, the Foot-Washing Institute will instigate a raging fire that will extinguish darkness forever.

"Because I have allowed the institute to be the initial candle that will trigger this event, I charge the institute with the responsibility to oversee what the other candles are doing. Before long, the institute will have many attendees who will be anointed with the gift to heal. As Claire taught you, you also must instruct those who will be given this gift to remain humble and never develop an arrogant attitude. Remember healing and empowerment comes from me and no one else. People understand this in theory and have the best intentions; however, humans are tempted and can easily fall from grace. While I can't stop this altogether, to ensure that the people live holy lives beyond reproach as much as possible, I want you to create a council of elders to mentor people and remind them that they are simply my instruments.

"At the Foot-Washing Institute, people will definitely learn sound biblical teachings about how to be my instruments. However, as you know, just because they receive training on how to wash feet and can apply the principles they are taught, does not mean that everyone will be able to do it. Because foot washers must be humble and pure in heart, they will need to be mentored regularly.

"Since you cannot possibly mentor all people in this way, I want you to create a council to help you with this task. This council will be comprised of special people who will hear about Divine Towels and the institute and will be eager to help in any way they can because they have devoted their lives to serving me. Through this mentoring board, many wonderful things will come about.

"Until this council of elders is established, the institute will not officially open. I know you want to continue working in Divine Towels, but I want you to devote your full attention to establishing the Foot-Washing Institute. Don't feel guilty about leaving Ethan and Claire in the lurch.

"Your first task in developing the Foot-Washing Institute will start immediately. First, train an apprentice to take your place at Divine Towels. By doing this, you will gain first-hand experience on what it takes to wash feet as well as what needs to be taught at the institute. Once you have learned this, I want you to post a letter on the store's Website and send a copy to all Christian churches issuing a call to action. The purpose of this letter will be to call the Christian community to live out my Great Commission the way I intended - through service. Explain the type of work the store is doing, the current situation the store is in, and need for people to help expand its ministry. Invite those who feel disconnected to the world and long to serve me to become students at the Foot-Washing Institute.

"I have much more to tell you, but you cannot grasp it now. Please understand I do not expect you to do all of this by yourself. Just as you helped Ethan and Claire make their dream of opening Divine Towels a reality, when you explain all that I have told you, they will be eager to help you make this dream a reality and will see this as a natural extension of their ministry. If you listen to me and continue to seek me above all else, you will do much to further my kingdom. Go, my child, and share this with others. Peace be with you, my son, peace be with you."

Bill sat in silence for several moments in wonder at all that Christ had revealed to him. Christ truly had plans for him, and Bill realized that if he had not been obedient, perhaps this day would have never come to pass. The task would definitely be quite challenging. Yet, Bill was confident that if the four of them stuck together as a team, and allowed Christ to be their captain, they would be able to accomplish whatever they had to.

When Bill had collected himself, he announced to everyone that he had received a very important message from Christ about the Foot-Washing Institute and wished to discuss it over coffee when the store closed. Seeing the joy in Bill's eyes, the group knew that the Lord had spoken and that everything would be all right. They were very eager for the day to end and for coffee time to begin.

When five o'clock rolled around, everyone was quite anxious to lock up and put the coffee on so that the meeting could begin. Normally, it took everyone half an hour to finish chores; however, since they were anxious to hear the news, they moved more quickly than usual.

By 5:20, everyone gathered around the table ready to take notes. Bill was excited to relay this message to his beloved teammates. Yet, since he was still digesting all of it himself, he began the meeting by asking the Holy Spirit to help him and to guide the discussion that would follow. Bill then recited everything that Christ had told him. As the group listened to the message, they sat with their eyes shut and basked in the glorious image he was painting with his words. They marveled at how God had taken a simple idea two people had for serving others and was transforming the concept into something that had the potential to affect the whole world.

The words Bill spoke were so profound that for a time no one said a word. "Well," Claire finally said after much contemplation and a big sigh, "it certainly does sound as if Christ has much work planned for all of us. I'm sure we are all overwhelmed by this; however, we can definitely pull this off if we do this one step at a time and decide who is going to do what."

"Yes, you're right," Ethan said. "If we just break this down and see what needs to be done, we will be able to handle this. There is a lot of work to do. Yet, I am confident that if we continue to work as a team and rely on God for strength, we can do whatever we set our minds to! I have never done this before, but I think the best way to begin is to focus on the Foot-Washing Institute. From first glance, it seems obvious that we will need more people to help us. We will also need some renovation. Yet, before we get ahead of ourselves, let's brainstorm and do this in a logical, orderly fashion."

As Ethan said this, he got the easel, the pad of paper and a few markers to write with. Just as he was about to uncap the red marker, Ethan looked at Bill and said with remorse, "I am so sorry, Bill. You should be the one who is up here. After all, you are the one who will be running this project. I want to help you in any way I can; however, I don't want to take over. Please forgive me; I just got carried away."

"That's okay, Ethan," Bill said. "Please continue. You are handling this well, and frankly, you would be doing me a favor. I am not a territorial person who is offended if someone helps me.

We are all here because we seek to serve Christ and to further His kingdom. We also each have gifts, and if your gift will help organize this project, I would be a fool not to let you continue. If I don't agree with something, I won't be afraid to let you know."

Ethan smiled. It was obvious that the good of the project took precedence over personality issues. Now that they had dealt with this issue, Ethan continued. "Now," Ethan said after he wrote Foot-Washing Institute across the top of the page, "from what I gather, the Lord wants the institute to focus on two main tasks: teaching others how to wash feet and managing an accountability board to oversee the efforts of newly taught foot washers. This is fine, and it's certainly a grand idea. Yet, before we implement it, let's break down each task and clearly establish what each job will entail.

"The first task we need to address, and the more straightforward of the two, is teaching others how to wash feet. Whenever I think about the gift the Lord has given me, I view myself as an instrument that sits on a shelf unable to do anything worthwhile unless I allow Christ to work through me. Just as a craftsman uses his tools to produce a beautiful product, when I allow the Lord to use me as He wills, He always does wondrous things. However, when I am demanding, I become a clog and prevent the Lord from doing His work. Self-interests prevent us from being instruments that the Lord can use. It is easy for people to comprehend this intellectually; yet, despite our good intentions, we are creatures who like things our way. If we truly desire to be Christ's instruments, we will need to learn to die to self and allow Christ to use us in whatever way He sees fit. Those who desire to be Christ's instruments must be obedient and turn away from their wicked ways.

"Another lesson we will need to teach is that when God entrusts people with a particular gift, they become His hands and feet on the earth and are expected to act accordingly. People will need to understand that this sacred gift is not their own, but a gift Christ has given them so they can actively heal and empower others. Sure, healing others is cool, but the trouble comes when people lose their humility and somehow think they are powerful and no longer need God."

After a brief pause, Ethan continued. "It is also critical that we create an accountability board to oversee newly taught foot washers. I'm not sure how to design such a board or how it would function. However, it just seems to me that unless people are held accountable for their actions they tend to stray and, before long, things turn chaotic. We don't have to discuss it now, but it is definitely a critical component."

When Ethan finished, Bill had a good idea of what he would need to teach. They grasped the concepts but wondered how they could convey them to those who would come to the institute. They knew what Ethan had said was right. Yet, by now, their brains were overloaded and they were unable to think. The group decided to reconvene once Bill and Jim had a chance to work on what they had discussed already.

Ethan and Claire were very excited about the institute and were committed to doing whatever it took to ensure that Divine Towels was a success. Yet, they had mixed feelings about it as well. They had gotten into this line of work because they wanted to spend their time healing people, not training others how to heal people. They realized the Foot-Washing Institute was definitely a means to an end and would ultimately free them up so they could help more people. It was just that they were not looking forward to having additional work.

In Ethan and Claire's opinion, Christ had given everyone a specified job to do. They already had enough to do and did not want to micromanage affairs. They trusted Bill and knew God had selected him to lead this effort for them. Nevertheless, because the Foot-Washing Institute was connected to Divine Towels and would have a definite impact on it and because they wanted everything to go smoothly, they felt they would have to keep a close eye on how things were progressing.

Once Bill had a general idea of the direction to head in, it was time to get down to work. However, even with all the help, they still were not sure what to do. Most people would come to the institute for sincere reasons. Yet, a few would come because they were curious or to spy on what was happening. How could they possibly discern who was for real and who was fake? Until he had resolved this question as well as how would he teach people a new mindset that was contrary to the ways of the world, Bill felt they would not be able to proceed.

Since Bill had a good rapport with Jim, Bill decided to bounce some ideas off him. They could have gone around in circles forever but decided just to ask Jesus what He wanted done. Hence, they prayed again. "Thank you, Lord, for the work you have called us to do. We are honored that you have called us to do this for you. We are happy to set this up for you so people will be able to penetrate the darkened corners of the world with your holy light, but we don't know what to do. Just as you have guided your servants throughout the ages, we ask you to be with us and instruct us on how we are to teach others to wash feet. We turn this over to you and thank you in advance for your help. We ask this in Jesus' name. Amen."

Bill's prayer was answered that night when he was visited in a dream. "Peace be with you, my faithful child. I have waited until now because you were not ready to hear what I had to say. Ethan and Claire have taught you how to wash feet. However, if you plan to teach others, you must understand fully what happens during the foot-washing process. When people wash feet, they become the vessel I use to transform the person whose feet are being washed. If healing is to occur at all, it is vital for my vessel and me to be of one mind."

Suddenly, Bill found that Jesus had taken him back to the place where Jim and he had been praying earlier that day. Initially, Bill wondered why he was reliving this scene until he looked up and saw that Jesus had walked into the room. "My sons," Jesus said as he tapped them on their shoulders, "please rise. I have something important to show you both."

Once both men were on their feet, Jesus put his hand on Bill's heart and breathed on him saying, "Be ye transformed." Bill saw that his spirit had left his body, and he felt spirals of energy enter his head. While he looked the same on the outside, Bill was filled with Christ's spirit; he was no longer the same person. In that moment of transformation, Bill understood on a deeper level what it meant to be Christ's hands and feet on the earth.

"Now that I have transformed you and you understand what I actually do when a person has his feet washed," Jesus said after a moment, "I want to show you how to teach others how to wash feet. Listen carefully. After you see this, you will wake up. Please write the instructions down immediately exactly as I describe. The technique I am about to show you consists of four steps. Each step is comprised of two components - one physical and one spiritual. If you teach it at the institute and tell how I came to you in this dream and taught you this technique, those who come for the right reasons will learn everything they need to know.

"When you teach this technique, it is important to stress that those who desire this gift must rely on me for everything. Many will come and will be eager to serve, but once you explain these things to them, few will remain. Because this is a gift that I will bestow on those who truly seek to do my will, I expect them to use the gift to help people and not to edify their egos. Woe to anyone who tries to wash someone's feet with the wrong attitude; they will wish they never touched the towel. I'm being adamant about this because I'm sick of people disregarding me and turning what I have deemed sacred into a mockery."

At this time, Jesus took Bill into the living room of Juan who was in his last stages of his fight with terminal cancer. Normally, Juan stayed in bed because of the severe pain. However, because he was going for a checkup, he was sitting in his recliner waiting for his wife to drive him to the hospital.

Without a word, Jesus knelt beside Juan's recliner where a vessel of water, a basin, and a towel had been set out and began teaching Bill the technique. "First, wash the feet. When you do, all that separates a person from me (including any afflictions he has) will be transferred from him into the water in the basin. Next, rinse the feet so they are free from any dirty water in the basin. Dry the feet with a clean towel. When you do this, I will enter his body through you, and it will become the temple on earth where I will dwell. Finally, anoint his feet with oil and give him the towel to serve as a reminder of this experience."

When Jesus finished speaking, Bill woke up. Initially, he was awestruck by everything that Christ had just revealed to him and wanted to sing Christ's praises. Yet, Bill remembered what Jesus said about writing the technique down, and so he did it immediately. At first, Bill was afraid he would not remember all of the details. However, as he wrote, he recalled everything and knew Christ was beside him guiding him every step along the way. When Bill finished writing, he tried to go back to sleep, but he could not. Bill just could not stop thinking about his wondrous dream and the marvels that would soon unfold because of it.

Bill could hardly wait to get to the store the next morning to tell everyone about his dream. There was no way of knowing if they would have a break during the day. Yet based on the short time he had been there, he knew the store would not get busy until 9:30 a. m. He planned to tell everyone the news around nine, once they had finished their morning routines, which consisted of prayer, committing the day into the Lord's hands, and getting the store ready for the morning's first customers.

It is never a good idea to go into a situation with a preconceived notion of how things will turn out because they rarely go the way you would expect. Just as Bill was getting ready to tell about his dream, a few customers came in. There weren't many, but just enough to cause them to stop and help the people.

Everyone was glad that people came in but wished that they had had a break, so they could hear the good news.

The staff anxiously awaited the end of the day. Throughout the day, the group tried to assemble to hear the good news, but they were interrupted either by the phone or by more customers who came in to be healed.

By 4:50, everyone was glad the day was over and eager to get everything cleaned up. Unfortunately, just as Bill was about to lock the door, Kathy walked in. Initially, Bill was going to tell the woman that they were closed and to come back in the morning. However, he refrained, sensing that God had sent her to the store for some reason. He felt compelled to attend to her himself.

Like many, Kathy was tired and worn out from her routine. She was not physically sick, but she was very depressed and felt trapped in a holding pattern with no way out. Years before, she lived in a vibrant community where people genuinely cared and looked out for one another. People did everything together and shared whatever they had. In those glorious days, Kathy did not work but spent her time ministering and caring for others. Life was never the same after she moved to help her husband take care of his elderly parents.

While Kathy did not really want to leave her friends, she decided to make the best of the situation and use it as an opportunity to spread joy and do good things in her new community. She tried her best to fit in and be friendly, but she felt as if she was in a time warp where she did not belong. People took offense with everything she said. Usually, Kathy was a good-natured person who did not let anything get to her, but after being ostracized for some time, it started to really get on her nerves. She was not only homesick and longed to be back in her safe environment but could not understand why God had taken her from the place she loved and put her into a land of barrenness. Did God hate her and want to ruin her life? There had to be a reason why God had sent her here, but she did not have a clue what it was.

Like others, Kathy prayed for deliverance and to be shown what to do. For years, she persevered trudging through the day, being thankful but all the while hoping for an end to the monotony. Then, one day it happened. God spoke to her heart when she was praying. "Dearest child, I know how much you have longed to serve me and to bring people to know me. The joy and oneness you had with me years ago is about to return. Arise, child, and have your feet washed at Divine Towels. There your spirit will be renewed, and you will discover why I have sent you here."

It had been such a long time since she had heard God's voice that she wondered if she was dreaming. When she went online and discovered that Divine Towels was only 20 minutes from her house, she was thrilled for it was exactly what she had been looking for. Not only was she excited about the miracles that the Holy Spirit was doing at the store, but she could hardly wait to get to the store and have her feet washed.

The drive to the store may have only been 20 minutes, but it felt like an eternity. As she drove, she wondered what would happen once she arrived. Was she up to whatever challenge God had for her? For years, Kathy had beseeched God to use her in whatever way He saw fit. However, now that God had answered her prayer and was putting her to the test, she prayed for the courage to follow willingly and that God's will would be done. Kathy arrived at the store, took a deep breath, walked in, and trusted that God would take her in the direction she was to go.

Within minutes, Bill greeted Kathy. "Hi, my name is Bill. You look like you might need some assistance, so how can I be of service to you today, ma'am?"

"That's a good question; however, right now I don't know myself. Perhaps you might be able to help."

"I'll certainly try my best."

Kathy explained her life in a caring environment and the change she experienced when she moved to this community. "Since the day I moved here, I have felt very restless and have yearned to do something to help. I have asked Christ for guidance and to put me in a position where I can truly serve Him. It may sound strange, but Christ came to me today and told me to come here. He also said that if I came here and had my feet washed that I would know how I was supposed to serve others. I read about the store online and am moved by the work that Christ has called you to do. I hope I am not being too forward, but I just feel that Christ has sent me here to help you in some way."

In that moment, Bill was overwhelmed by what was happening. From the first moment Bill laid eyes on her, he was intrigued; however, he didn't know why. As Kathy told her story, Bill was fascinated by how well she expressed herself. Additionally, he was mesmerized by her eyes and felt he could see into the depths of her soul. Kathy might have been a stranger; yet, he sensed that they were kindred spirits and had known each other before.

Because of this special bond, Bill was eager to tell Kathy about his plans to open the Foot-Washing Institute and to ask her if she wanted to be his apprentice. However, after thinking it over for a moment, he decided to wait and see what would happen once she had feet her washed.

"Well," Bill said after a brief pause, "you have come to the right place. Those who come asking with pure hearts so they can achieve a higher good are given their heart's desire. So if you're ready, let's get started."

Washing feet all day may seem trite after a while, yet it was always thrilling to witness a person's reaction once he became enlightened and was transformed. Once Bill began drying Kathy's feet, she shut her eyes and felt disoriented. Soon she found herself in a room where she saw a sad carpenter looking at an elaborate blueprint he wanted to work on and a gigantic tool chest filled with tools. Unfortunately, he could not work on the project because the tools he needed to complete his work were lying in his tool chest in a state of disarray. There had been a time when the carpenter worked on his masterpiece and had made much progress. However, because the tools he needed had worn out and were irreplaceable, he was unable to finish his work.

At the end of the story, Christ appeared and explained what this meant. "Precious daughter, I am the carpenter and have an elaborate plan to bring the world back into union with me. I have much work to do; however, if I am to carry out my work, I need hardy tools that I can depend on. You may think I have forgotten about you and that I haven't heard your prayers. The truth is I have a very special job that I need you to do for me. I have been planning this surprise for a long time. However, I waited until now to tell you because I needed to teach you many lessons to prepare you for the job.

"Daughter, the tools in my toolbox may look identical, but I use each tool for a very special purpose. For example, you are a very highly valued tool that I need to complete my work. There are many tools that I want to use; but they are not in mint condition. I am frustrated by this; but, Bill, Ethan, and Claire are helping me refurbish my tool set. Through them, I am not only healing believers of their ailments but am revealing how I want to use them. Those who have been healed are learning that if they obey and follow my lead, I will give them the power to transform the world. Because people have committed themselves and have asked me to use them to heal others, the store is a success. The problem is there simply are not enough people to heal the crowds.

"You are here because you are humble and always ask me for direction before taking any action. I have selected you to help the people at Divine Towels open the Foot-Washing Institute, which is dedicated to teaching others how to wash feet. I have given Bill the task of opening the institute, and I want you to help him. Once the institute is operational, people who graduate will be able to run the store. This will free up the owners to spend time bringing the ministry into the community where it is desperately needed.

"While this is a good idea that will help in the long term, right now Bill doesn't know where to begin. Don't worry about money. Because you will be working for me, I will provide whatever you will require to pay your bills, as I do for the rest of the team. I realize what I am saying is exciting, yet disconcerting; however, do not be afraid. I am with you and will guide you. Bill is a great man and will be your mentor. Listen to him. He will guide you well."

Kathy knelt and praised Christ fervently. She may not have known what was in store for her, but she was more than glad to do whatever her Savior asked of her.

When Bill saw what was happening, he was not quite sure what to make of it. He had performed many foot washings but had never seen someone who seemed to have such an intimate and passionate relationship with her Lord. Bill might not have known what was happening, but he was determined that he was going to find out before she left.

After watching Kathy for about ten minutes, Bill got up enough nerve to talk to her again. "Miss, I was just wondering if you are okay."

"First off, my name is Kathy, and I have never had such an incredible experience. Thank you so much for giving me the time I needed. After you finished washing my feet, Christ told me He had sent me here to help you. He told me that you are in the process of opening a school to teach people how to wash feet and that I am to help you in any way you need. I can't believe I actually am saying this, especially when I am a nobody. All I can say is I'm merely doing what I have been told."

Bill was sure the feeling he had gotten when Kathy first walked in had been from the Holy Spirit. While he marveled at this, he was equally amazed by Kathy's candor. After a brief pause, Bill began, "Wow, sometimes it just amazes me how Christ works, and the strange ways He answers prayers. A little while ago, this place was swarming with people who wanted healing.

Because there were only three people to wash feet, we felt as inundated as apostles did when Jesus asked them to feed the five thousand, and we wondered how we could possibly heal all the people waiting in line. The experience made us all feel powerless; hence, we asked Christ to send us some more help. Within the hour, you entered. I feel Christ has brought us all together so we can all do great things under His direction."

When Bill thought about the individual events of the previous few weeks as well as what had just transpired, his soul was so elated with joy that he shouted, "Halleluiah." Within moments, Claire yelled from the backroom, "Bill, are you okay? What's going on out there? We're eager to get on with our meeting and find out about your dream."

"Yes, Claire, I'm fine. Would you all please come out here? There has been a slight change of plans. There is someone very special out here that I would like you all to meet."

No one on the team had ever met Kathy. However, when they saw the sparkle in her brown eyes, they sensed that they had been long-time friends and knew she was here for a special reason. Hence, they were eager to see what kind of surprise Christ had in store for them.

"Hello," Claire said eagerly. "I'm glad to meet you. I'm Claire, and this is my son Ethan. We are the founders of Divine Towels."

"The pleasure is all mine. As I was just telling Bill, I love this store and see that it is having a positive effect on the community. I've been praying for a long time that someone would have enough faith to undertake a bold initiative and allow God once again to work wonders on earth as He did in ages past. When I read your pamphlet, I was overjoyed. I know you probably hear this story a million times a day, but for the first time in my life I feel fulfilled and know why I was born. After I had my feet washed, Christ came and told me that I was supposed to help Bill open the Foot-Washing Institute."

When the group heard the sincere, gentle-hearted way this woman spoke, they instantly felt a strong connection with Kathy and knew Christ had sent her to fill a special role on the team. Initially, everyone was so overwhelmed by what she had just said that they found themselves staring at Kathy with amazement.

At the moment, there was an eerie stillness in the room. They felt Christ's presence encircle them, and they knew He had brought them together for a reason. It was apparent to Bill that Kathy had all the qualities he was seeking in an apprentice. However, since he was feeling very emotionally charged, he wasn't sure if his judgment was clouded and felt it was best not to make a hasty decision. Hence, he decided to consult everyone and see if they concurred.

"Kathy," Bill finally managed to say, "would you please excuse us for a few minutes? We definitely want you to stay and talk with us; however, I need to talk to my teammates. Please wait here; I promise we will be back shortly."

Kathy agreed to wait while everyone went in the back. "I don't know about you," Bill said, "but something extraordinary has been happening around here for the past few days. Whatever we ask for seems to happen without a lot of work. I have a burning desire to ask Kathy to be my apprentice and feel she would be perfect. Yet, I'm not sure if it's me who wants this or if the Holy Spirit is talking to me. Please help me."

The team chuckled when they heard these words. Somehow Bill had articulated what all of them had been asking as they listened to Kathy speak. Once the group told Bill that they were feeling the same thing, Bill laughed at the coincidence and took it as a sign that God wanted Kathy to be his apprentice. Once the team decided that Kathy should be a member of their team, they were eager to go out front and watch Bill offer her the job.

Much to Kathy's amazement, Bill and the others returned within five minutes. "Kathy," Bill said, "forgive me if I appear forward. As soon as I saw you, I felt we had a special connection and that your presence here was an answer to my prayer. When you spoke, the feeling I initially had intensified, and I felt compelled to make you my apprentice immediately. Yet, since this team makes the decisions that affect everyone as a group, I needed to consult my teammates.

"They agreed, and I knew the Holy Spirit was at work. On behalf of the team, I welcome you and know you will be a great asset." Kathy was filled with joy. God was allowing her to serve with the team in this special way.

"We are all happy you are here, but we don't have time to celebrate for there is work that needs to be done immediately. As you know, Jim and I are starting the Foot-Washing Institute to teach people how to be vessels that Christ can use as He sees fit. While the institute is a logical next step in expanding this ministry, Jim and I are having a hard time figuring out how to teach others how to wash feet.

"Just as you were walking in the door, I was preparing to tell the team that last night Christ appeared to me in a dream and told me what to do. I had tried to tell them the news all day; however, we were constantly interrupted. I must admit, it was frustrating. Yet, when you walked in and we talked, I finally saw why God in His wisdom had delayed the discussion.

"Kathy, Christ told me to teach all students a ritual. This ritual may seem simple; yet, if it is not done by someone who seeks to do the will of Christ, the person will not be healed, and the person performing the ritual will suffer great turmoil. I want to teach you the ritual for a few reasons: so you will have the gift to heal others, so you can make suggestions on how to make the instructions clearer, and so you can get a feel for what I am thinking. I have never performed this ritual before and am not sure what I am doing or if I am even doing it right. The one thing I know for sure is to do what Christ directed me to do and trust Him to do the rest.

Bill filled a basin with fresh water and continued. "Being an instrument is not an easy job. It requires one to realize he is useless unless he is manipulated by the operator. Therefore, when performing this ritual, remember you are merely the vehicle through which Christ's miracle-working power flows."

As Bill performed the ritual, Kathy watched closely and imagined that Christ was washing her feet. She always believed she understood what it meant to be the hands and feet of Christ. However, when she watched Bill tenderly touch her feet, the words took on new meaning. Not only did Kathy receive the gift of being able to heal others, but she also knew that everything she had gone through in her life up until this point had occurred to prepare her for this experience.

"Now that you have received the gift of healing others and know what I plan to do at the Foot-Washing Institute, it is time for me to tell you how I want you to help me. Ultimately, I want you to help me run the institute. However, before we open, to ensure that we don't waste time training people who come simply because they find the idea amusing, I feel it is critical that we find a way to discern who comes for the right reasons. I have been praying about this matter for several weeks and have asked the Holy Spirit for direction. But so far, an answer hasn't come; perhaps I have gotten too close to it."

"I see your problem," Kathy said. "It seems to me that solving this problem should be simple enough. All we need to do is discuss how Jesus called disciples to lay down their lives and serve one another. We then explain that the first thing that all disciples need to do is to have humility and to serve one another. This can only be learned through hands-on experience. There are many examples we can use to see if a person is willing to be humble. We can find some situations or try different scenarios to see if a person is willing to help another.

Once Bill and Kathy figured out how they would teach students how to wash feet, they drafted a letter to send to the different churches to recruit students to attend the Foot-Washing

Institute. Jim had been the vice-president of the local chapter of Habitat for Humanity for many years and had done a fair amount of writing to get people to help out on various projects. As they thought about how they would compose this letter, Jim thought he could apply the thinking he used at Habitat.

Soon they found that this approach was useless. They weren't asking people to donate a few days of their lives to help others. Rather, they were challenging people to live out Christ's call in a proactive way. To entice people to come to the institute, they would need to write a letter that spoke to people's hearts. The Foot-Washing Institute would not only prepare people to serve and empower others but would satisfy a longing many had in their hearts. The only thing Bill and Kathy needed to figure out was the best way to do this.

Initially, it was quite difficult to come up with the right wording. However, when they reflected on how Jesus spoke the truth, they were inspired and knew if they just wrote from their hearts that everything would work out as it was supposed to. After praying and asking for guidance, they found these words and used them in the letter.

Dearest Child,

How many times have you come home after a long day at work, looked at yourself in the mirror, and wondered if this is what life had come down to? Yes, I am talking to you. You go to church, are energized by the Spirit and inspired to carry out the Great Commission. Yet, within hours, the surge of passion dwindles, and you settle back into your old routines for another week. You think I do not notice, but I do. Why does this happen and how do we kindle the passion we hear at church or reading the Bible and inject this idealism into our daily lives?

For centuries, people have searched their souls for answers to this question, and some have even found ways to achieve this. Yet, many still can't seem to find a way to fill the void that lies deep within their souls. Just when it may appear that all is lost and we are locked into our routines, Divine Towels, a new store located in the heart of Coppertown, is providing people with hope.

Divine Towels is quite an extraordinary store devoted to empowering people and to freeing them from their afflictions, so they can pursue their dreams. People who have visited this store and had their feet washed, believing that they have been touched by Christ, have not only been healed of their afflictions but experienced a radical shift in their consciousness. As a result, they have gone forth to live as a new creation and have left with the wisdom to offer solutions to problems. They have replaced the gloomy corners of their world with joy and invigoration. Rather than living cautiously within their safe environments, these people have become activists and are demanding social change to promote equality for all.

While many positive things are happening around Coppertown, the staff at Divine Towels is inundated with an influx of people and is desperately looking for help to meet the needs of the people. If you have ever yearned for an opportunity to be like Jesus' first disciples and carry out the Great Commission, perhaps God is calling you to attend the Foot-Washing Institute, a subsidiary of Divine Towels. Some might read this, find that pursuing an opportunity like this to be just what they have been looking for all their lives, and may respond to this call immediately. However, after pondering it for a while, others might hesitate and wonder how they could possibly contribute to this cause.

Some might wonder how the people who work at Divine Towels acquired the power to heal, since healing seems to happen instantaneously. In fact, there are scientists who will try to point to this as just another example of how the mind reacts to the power of suggestion. However, if this was as the medical community labels this, 'the power of suggestion,' then why do so many well-educated people fall for this old trick?

What may seem to be a phenomenon is actually the result of an intimate bond between Christ and the person performing the healing. The healer realizes that healing occurs when he allows himself to be a vehicle through which Christ's power flows. Hence, to be a channel the person must be humble, live in accord with the commandments, and seek to do Christ's will. If you feel that Christ is calling you to participate and you desire to help further the Kingdom of Heaven, come to the Foot-Washing Institute and let the staff train you to serve others.

Love always,

Your Lord, friend, and Savior, Jesus

Until now, things had gone relatively smoothly at Divine Towels. However, the letter challenging Christians to put their faith into action helped them realize that they were taking their ministry to a new level. They were also raising the bar. Opening the store and healing people was one thing, but now that they were calling people to action, they had crossed a delicate line. Posting a want ad to fill a position was considered acceptable. Yet, when people read the letter, shock waves rippled through the community. Divine Towels was more than just a store; it was a force to be reckoned with.

While there wasn't anything wrong with trying to give people hope, some were quite disturbed that people who had received healing were disrupting the flow of society. People not only believed in Christ, but they came to understand that, if they wanted things to get better, they had to use the talents that God had given them and become active ambassadors who made change happen. Consequently, their attitudes were transformed. Suddenly people who had been known as the quiet type who minded their own business became outspoken activists. They were determined to reform a system that lacked passion and was apathetic to the needs of others.

It has been said that people are entitled to their beliefs as long as they do not impose them on others. This is a nice supposition; yet, if society operated under this motto, it would lead to total anarchy and chaos. Thus, to ensure a harmonic society, each civilization must to hold its people to some standard. This is all well and good, but the problem people were having with this letter was that Ethan and Claire had challenged people to ditch the status quo and adopt a higher moral standard.

Unlike evangelical crusades that merely built up one's spirit, Divine Towels capitalized on people's enthusiasm offering them pragmatic ways to live out the Great Commission. Now that the letter was written and the challenge issued, people found themselves at a crossroad and had to examine their convictions. Would they be willing to take a risk and allow Christ to use them to further the Gospel, or would they decline the invitation for fear that they were not up to the challenge? Whatever decision people made would not only alter their lives but say much about the strength of their convictions and character.

THE SOUL STATION

Reading the Gospels and the Acts of the Apostles is electrifying and excites people to carry out the Great Commission. We love hearing about heroic people who stood up to the injustices that plagued society and undertook bold actions to better society. Hearing such stories tends to inspire us to venture from our safe surroundings and to be Christ's hands and feet to a broken world.

In an ideal world, it would be wonderful to do these things; yet, it is very difficult to interject Christian values into a society where people act differently depending on the situation they are in. We understand this; still, we become frustrated because we do not know how to live out Christ's mandate in this type of environment. Many try their best to make the situation better, but doing the right thing is a constant battle that wears down the most spirited warrior. Some may say that the problem lies with a person's outlook, and it would be better if they had fun, enjoyed life, and didn't get worked up over every little thing. This is nice to say; but the fact is we are our brothers' keepers and must act accordingly.

The people of Coppertown were typical of folks living in any small town. Many worked, socialized, and attended church together. By all accounts, the Coppertown Community Church was much like other churches in that it held worship services, Bible studies, weekly prayer meetings, and community outreach events. Sure, all had dreams they had always wished to pursue; however, many felt trapped by the circumstances of their lives. Despite trying to make the best of it, they were frustrated and hated what was happening. The worst part was that they felt as if they were watching a horror movie and could not do anything to make it stop.

In their despair, many spent countless hours in prayer asking God what they would do if they were liberated from their oppression. However, once God finally granted them the deepest desire of their hearts, they were stunned and unsure about what to do. Certainly many were grateful, but now that God had granted their requests what would they actually do?

From the first day the doors of Divine Towels opened, life in Coppertown changed dramatically. The strange part was that it happened so naturally and unexpectedly that no one was quite sure what had occurred. When people had their feet washed, it was the first time in their lives many experienced freedom from their afflictions and they were slow to talk. People were transformed as if a force had entered their bodies and released the toxins that held them captive. They were revitalized, like a plant that had just been pruned and repotted in fertilized soil.

There was also a significant shift in how they viewed their relationship with the world and with others. No longer did people walk around with attitudes of self-importance and indifference. Rather, they were humble and asked what they could do to be part of the solution and make life better for others. Their lives changed in so many ways, but they needed time to find out what they wanted to do with their lives. From spending many years watching, they knew what needed to be done to improve the situation. Now that the cage was unlocked, they were empowered to go forth unafraid and carry out the Gospel! It was as if a switch went on in their hearts and they were changed forever.

Ethan and Claire found the Acts of the Apostles inspirational. To them, the book clearly demonstrated that anything is possible under the Holy Spirit's power. They still believed the Holy Spirit's power is as alive today it was in biblical times. Yet, as they looked at events in the world, it was obvious why things had deteriorated so much. People focused so much on getting through the day that they no longer saw the need to ask the Holy Spirit for guidance. It was only when they opened Divine Towels and had to depend totally on the Holy Spirit for help that they once again felt His mighty power at work.

Indeed, it was exhilarating for Ethan and Claire to feel the positive energy in the air and see what was happening to people because the Holy Spirit had breathed new life into their souls. It pleased them to know that these things were happening because they obeyed God and opened Divine Towels. Yet reflecting on where their ministry was going, they realized there was a gap that had to be filled. They found that a few weeks after having their feet washed, people longed to recharge their spiritual batteries. They needed a place to acquire the strength and support they needed to carry out their mission.

Ethan and Claire understood and often wished such a place existed. Despite how much they wanted to build such a place and knew how badly it was needed, the fact was they were working to capacity and could not possibly do anymore. Consequently, they decided to give it to the Lord and wait for Him to make a way.

When Claire woke the following morning and began her day with prayer and meditation, she was astounded by what Jesus told her. In her meditation, she saw beyond people's façades; she sensed how people felt on a much deeper level.

Claire knew Jesus came to liberate the oppressed and set captives free. Yet, when she saw the total hopelessness and despair, she wondered if there truly was a way to reach and deliver them from their mental prisons. Just when it seemed people would spend their lives in utter despair, Jesus stretched out his hands and calmed the raging sea. At that moment, Claire saw a brilliant light and heard Jesus say, "Come to me, all you who labor and are burdened, and I will give you rest. Take my yoke upon you and learn from me, for I am gentle and humble in heart, and you will find rest for your souls. For my yoke is easy and my burden is light." (Matthew 11:28) When Jesus spoke these words, the oppressive wall that blocked people from receiving mercy and comfort vanished instantly.

She knew that Divine Towels was helping people in extraordinary ways and was grateful that God had put Ethan and her in a position to do much good. Still, she recognized that more needed to be done.

Claire asked Jesus to show her what to do. Within moments, Jesus appeared in his white robe and began. "Claire, my beloved daughter, I started you at Divine Towels to see how you would manage it and if I could depend on you. Because you relied on me at every juncture, we have worked as a team and Divine Towels has thrived. Now I see that I can depend on you and I am ready to give you a greater challenge.

"Divine Towels is certainly a wonderful place that is energizing and empowering people by my spirit to take on the world. With the surge of energy they receive, many feel renewed and are anxious to carry out the Gospel. They undertake bold initiatives, help others, and perform many works of mercy in my name. I applaud their efforts; yet after a few weeks of working relentlessly, people will grow tired and will need to recharge their spiritual batteries.

"I became weary while I was on earth. At such times, I retreated to the mountaintop to be alone with my Father so I could gain the strength I needed to continue with my mission. People today also desperately need a quiet place where they can go to hear God's voice, rejuvenate their weary souls, and acquire the zeal needed to carry out their missions with passion.

"When I was on earth, I told my disciples, 'Come to me, all you who are weary and burdened, and I will give you rest.' People may know on some level that I am there and want to help them.

However, it is obvious that people are so weary, but they don't come to me for help. Instead they turn to counterfeit substitutions (drugs, watching TV, drinking, etc.) as a way to drown out their problems. These may mask the problem temporarily, but in the end the problem still exists.

"I want your help to show my people that if they come to me, I will help them with their problems. I want you to create a place that I call the Soul Station to be a local retreat, a quiet, tranquil place where people can retreat from the grind of their daily lives and be nearer to the heart of God. The goal of the Soul Station will be to stoke the embers in a person's soul, ignite passion in him, bring him closer to Christ, and remind him what is truly important in life. It is God's ultimate desire for us to have a personal relationship and to be in union with Him.

"Like Divine Towels, the Soul Station will begin as a small venture, but once people see and understand the benefits of having such a place in their community, it will grow. I long for people to come close to me, but I stir their hearts in different ways. I always want it to center around three basic types of ministries: individuals, healing, and group. I realize this is all new to you, but do not fear, for I am with you and will help you.

"Jesus went on. 'The first ministry is designed so individuals can rest their bodies and focus on drawing closer and having a meaningful relationship with Christ. The second environment is designed for people who need healing and help. Finally, the third environment is a community setting, where people could participate in guided meditations and reflections.'"

"As you can see, I have designed the Soul Station to be a unique, much-needed resting place where people may go to be comforted and refreshed. People who visit the Soul Station will find that it satisfies a deep, inner hunger, like nothing they experienced before. I want the Soul Station to be a nonprofit entity that accepts only donations so that all my children can experience this sense of abounding peace.

"I know you're wondering how I expect you to accomplish this daunting task. However, do not fear. There's no doubt that Ethan and you could easily open the Soul Station, but the Soul Station should open under the auspices of my church. This will show people that the church does care about their intimate needs.

"I know you love working in Divine Towels, but for a few weeks I want you to take a break and develop the content for the three ministries and work out the logistics for the Soul Station. Once you have done this, a wonderful man of the cloth will come ask you for help opening a Soul Station. When this happens, I want you to share this with him and work with him to implement the vision of the Soul Station that I just laid out for you. I realize I'm asking a lot and that you are overwhelmed by all that I have told you. But if you trust me and do what I ask, you will do much to further my kingdom."

From hearing about the plans that Jesus had for her, Claire knew that Jesus had His hand on her and had blessed her immensely. Developing the three ministries was going to be a full-time job. She also realized that God had given her an incredible opportunity. As a result, not only was her heart singing with joy, but she was also eager to get started, for she knew it would help many people.

It was extraordinary to think about what God wanted her to do, the ideas behind the Soul Station and the wonderful things that would result. Yet as Claire drafted a list of what needed to be done and investigated, the awe of it all faded. Most tasks could be handled rather easily. However, there were a few major concerns that had to be addressed. Where would they build the Soul Station and how would they finance it?

Many challenges lay ahead of her, but Claire remained calm. Throughout her life, she faced tremendous obstacles that seemed impossible. During such times, when she was inconsolable, she imagined she was in Jesus' arms, talking the problem over with her beloved son Ethan. Ethan was a wonderful sounding board, and he had a way of helping her see things from a different perspective. She could hardly wait to tell Ethan everything that happened and get his thoughts on what to do next.

Ethan and Claire customarily went out for dinner after they finished working at the store. It gave them a chance to unwind and discuss anything significant that had occurred throughout the day. Sometimes they were so emotionally drained from healing people all day that they did not say much. As they drove to the restaurant, Ethan knew by the look of sheer delight on his mother's face that something wondrous had happened. He was tempted to press her for details, but he knew it was just a matter of time before she told him. Since he rarely saw her with such a gleeful look in her eye, he decided to see where it would lead.

After Claire parked the car and began gathering her work gear, Ethan knew that tonight was not going to be a leisurely dinner. Ethan had no idea what his mother was going to tell him. Yet it was clear from reading all the signs that tonight was going to be memorable and life changing in some way.

Once they ordered their main course, Claire could not hold back any longer. "Ethan, my dear boy, I am so happy to be working alongside you at Divine Towels. Without a doubt, the last few months have been the most exciting and wondrous time I have had in my entire life. Truly we are fulfilling our purpose on earth and seeing lives transformed before our eyes. Many people who have been healed leave Divine Towels with a new sense of purpose and are doing amazing things under the Holy Spirit's power. This is exciting, but after a while, these people grow weary and their enthusiasm dwindles. Many people love fulfilling their mission but have also indicated that they long for a place where they could go for renewal and to recharge their spiritual batteries. Because this has been weighing on my mind for several weeks, I decided to pray about it and see what type of guidance Jesus would give me.

For a few days, He did not say anything. However, this morning I was given implicit directions."

Claire pulled out her preliminary notes and told Ethan about the three ministries of the Soul Station. As she described each ministry, Ethan closed his eyes and tried to imagine what it would look and feel like. Ethan loved the whole concept. God had created each ministry in such a simple, Beautiful way to help people quiet their minds so they could draw closer to Him. Each ministry was amazing enough, but Ethan became ecstatic when he thought about the combination of the three and that God had asked his mother to take these ideas and develop them.

Claire was quiet for a time. She had said a lot and knew Ethan needed time to think. Typically, Ethan was not impulsive; he thought matters like these over very carefully before reaching a decision. However, this was definitely not one of those times. The fact was Ethan was thrilled with the news and saw it as a wonderful extension of Divine Towels. Consequently, he didn't feel any need to think or spiritualize over the matter. He loved the whole idea of the Soul Station and was quite eager to do whatever he could to help it become a reality.

"Mom, this idea is wonderful and exciting," Ethan said after only a few minutes. "I am so delighted that God asked you to do this for Him that I can't even put it in words! You have done an amazing job sketching out what needs to be done. As you described the Soul Station, I could I see myself there and feel what it must be like to be there in that tranquil place.

"The concerns you have raised are valid, and to tell you the truth I share some of your apprehension. However, we have nothing to fear, for God has a plan and has promised to supply us with whatever we need. Having said that, I know if we talk these issues out, as we always do, and work as a team, there's nothing we can't do. Just look at everything we have been through together. Ah, this is a breeze!"

When Ethan said this, Claire smiled. "Come here, my sweet boy. You just have this knack of knowing just what to say to make your mother feel better."

Ethan responded, "Before we discuss these issues, I have some exciting news to tell you regarding operational matters first. You may wonder what one thing has to do with the other, but if you bear with me for a few minutes, you will soon see. We've both been very focused on being instruments that the Lord can use to heal people. This is good; however, sometimes we do not always know all the things our volunteers do behind the scenes to ensure that things flow smoothly. Jim has been briefing me weekly on significant operational and financial matters. We are so lucky to have him!

"Among the things Jim has worked on since we've opened is to create a searchable, categorized database of people with various talents whom we can call if we ever need help. As people leave the store, they often hand their business cards to Jim so he can contact them if we ever need help. This database will help us find people to help us develop the Soul Station. I realize people get caught up in the moment and often say to call them anytime. However, given the fact that we helped them in such a profound way, who knows, perhaps a few might actually help us. You know what Jesus said, 'Ask and you shall receive.'

"Jim has also been keeping a close eye on our finances. Even after salaries and monthly bills are paid, something inexplicable has happened month after month. Not only are the coffers full, but they are overflowing! It's astounding and reminds me of how Jesus multiplied the loaves and fishes and fed the 5,000. The more people we help, the more Jesus rewards us. Jim has been meaning to ask us what we wanted to do, but we've been so busy that it has been difficult to find time to have meetings. Because Jim is so conscientious and dedicated to helping us, he put the money in an escrow account."

Claire could not believe what was happening. She had become so engrossed in her own work that she had not noticed what her coworkers were doing. In that moment, Claire awoke and asked, "How much money are we talking about?"

"Close to $125,000. This is more than enough to build a store and design it anyway we want."

Claire was astounded and wondered if she was dreaming. Suddenly Claire realized what was happening. God had not only given her this wonderful dream to fulfill, but He had ensured that all the details fell into place. Within seconds, euphoria enveloped the room. It was clear that the Holy Spirit was directing their every move. Therefore, nothing more needed to be said.

After a brief pause, Ethan changed subjects. "For some reason I keep thinking about the first ministry and can't get it out of my mind. I suppose it's because it tries to help people connect with God on a much deeper level than they are used to." Ethan was about to say something else but stopped suddenly and closed his eyes, for Jesus had suddenly put a brilliant idea in his head. It took the whole concept to an entirely new level.

"Just now the Holy Spirit gave me incredible insight on how to make it even better! The premise behind the ministry is extraordinary, and I do like the idea of having individual prayer closets. However, if we design it the way you suggest, it will only serve a handful of people who desperately need it. If we want this ministry to have a profound impact on people, we must make the ministry available so people can take advantage of it in a timely, convenient way that suits them. For this reason, we need to make this contemplative ministry available to people via a Website."

As Ethan said this, the strangest sensation came over him. Words came from his mouth, but Ethan wasn't aware of what he was saying. Rather, the Holy Spirit had taken over and it wasn't until he finished and saw his mother's reaction that he realized what had just happened.

Ethan was exhausted as if someone had just knocked the wind out of him. The concept behind Divine Towels and the Soul Station was amazing enough, but this exceeded their wildest dreams. For several moments, Ethan and Claire looked at each other in sheer wonder.

"Look," Claire said. "This is a good idea, and I know we will eventually put the Soul Station online. For now, however, I have a lot of work to do."

"I totally understand how you feel and I realize how much God has given you to do," Ethan said as he chuckled. "However, you know how the saying goes, 'God never gives us more than we can handle.' Come to think of it, why don't you call my old computer teacher from high school, Joe Tish? He knows a lot about computers and would be perfect for the job. I heard he retired recently. You know he is very active in the community and loves a good challenge. I know it kills you to ask people for help; however, I bet if you show him the plans that you have, I'm sure he would be willing to help, or could at least recommend someone who could help us."

"Ethan, thank you so much. You've given me so many ideas and helped me figure out where to start. You're right, I'll call Joe and use many of the suggestions you gave me. As you can see, the Lord wants me to do a lot of work for Him. The Lord has also told me to cease doing my regular duties at Divine Towels for a short time so I can devote all my time to developing the Soul Station. Although I will not be with you every day, I will always help you if you get in a bind. I am sorry to leave you on your own at Divine Towels, but I'm confident that you will have enough people from the Foot-Washing Institute to help you in my absence."

Claire had been excited when God told her to develop the Soul Station. However, after discussing the idea with Ethan, resolving some critical issues, and seeing the mysterious way God worked to ensure that everything would go smoothly; she could hardly wait to get started. Claire's work would revolve around developing the three ministries. She understood that the Soul Station would provide people with the ultimate spiritual experience and would at last satisfy the longings of their hearts, as nothing else could.

Creating Divine Towels had been a daunting challenge; however, it was easier than developing the Soul Station. The two were similar, but she realized the Soul Station would prove more challenging to develop. After all, it sought to help people tune out the distractions of the world, open their hearts, and discover God in a new way. Claire realized it would have an impact on people's lives.

At the same time, Claire realized she had to stay focused if she wanted the Soul Station to become a reality. Yes, great works would be done, but ultimately everything was dependent on Claire completing her work.

Claire had a knack for breaking large projects into manageable tasks. For several minutes, she paced the room, trying to find the best way to proceed. She had been so consumed with trying to open the Soul Station that she forgot she had taken copious notes during dinner the night before. She pulled out her notes and read them over, realizing that if she simply followed them, God would do the rest. With this in mind, Claire took the notes and began to break them down into tasks.

Once Claire had a list of tasks, she wondered where she would get the people to do the work. Of course the database of people Jim had created would be a great starting point. She trusted that Christ was guiding her all of the way; yet, several issues troubled her. Even if she got the right people and told them what Christ wanted her to do, would they actually help her build the Soul Station? Where would they build the Soul Station and who would run it?

After working on this for several hours, Claire was at a standstill. She had accomplished a lot but knew that she could not go any further until Christ answered some of these questions.

While Claire was eager for Him to answer her, she learned it was best not to fret, to tell God what she needed, and to leave it at that.

That night Jesus came to her in a dream and said, "I know you're eager to open the Soul Station, but the time has not come yet. There is still much work that needs to be done first. I also want you to develop the content for the three environments. Again, remember that the purpose of the three environments is to help people quiet their minds so they can draw close to me and hear the still, small voice inside of them. Achieving this will take a lot of work and will challenge you to the max. This is difficult because people do not know how to still their minds.

"Once you have done this, I also want you to make a video and show it to two groups of people: the builders of the Soul Station so they understand the concept and the visitors of the Soul Station to give them an introduction so they understand the purpose and the centers."

Claire was amazed and humbled that she was being asked to do this. The video would be the ideal way to show people what the Soul Station and its three ministries were about and to discuss the types of activities that would fall under each of the three ministries. It would also help people see that the Soul Station was truly a place where the weary and broken could go to escape the madness of everyday life and be refreshed and renewed. Once they saw the video, they would be in a better position to determine which ministry would best fulfill their needs.

At this point, Claire typed the principles and provided a short explanation of what each meant. As she read it over, she realized it sounded like a rehearsed litany and certainly did not help people know how to penetrate the world of the unknown. She deleted it immediately and vowed to try again.

Claire contemplated the video. She knew that people would be drawn to the Soul Station because of the ambiance and would surely find the three environments helpful, regardless of knowing the basic principles. This was good on one level, but if people wanted to get the most out of their experience, it was essential for them to learn to penetrate the world of the unknown. Claire knew how challenging and unnatural this was since it would require people to turn inward, tune out the noise of the world and become conscious of the still, small voice in their souls.

Claire spent the next several weeks in prayer, reading the Bible, talking to others, and searching the Internet to find techniques to help people learn to be quiet so they could discover that God truly does reside in a hidden world deep within their souls. Through this process, Claire learned that truly the kingdom of God resides within. People are very good at exploring the external world. Yet, there is an internal world that many have never explored. Even if they have, many have only scratched the surface.

Claire liked this; nevertheless, to make it more meaningful, she felt she had to take it one step further. Jesus' words came back to her, "Come unto me all ye who are heavy laden and I will give you rest." Claire realized how much people needed a place to go to rest from their labor. The problem was people were so used to the busyness of their daily lives that the idea of resting was a foreign concept.

As Claire contemplated this, she knew that the video needed to teach people how to tune out the external stimuli and still themselves so they could be one with God. Still, the question remained. How? She asked the Holy Spirit for guidance and she decided to start with her own story. Once Claire knew what to do, it was time to write the script. The following is the introductory narration of the video as the narration plays, the video will show a roaring ocean along the seashore.

My Soul Station

Whatever mood I am in
Happy, sad, joyful, depressed
I go to a place deep within my soul
To find my friend
Waiting to greet me with open arms.

My thoughts, successes, and failures are all known by you.
Yet, you stand welcoming me,
Inviting me to sit and feast.
Your spirit descends and fills me.
I become one with you wanting for nothing.

I want to stay in this state of ecstasy.
Yet, when I have been filled,
You bid me to return to work
Spreading love, bearing fruit,
Harvesting and saving souls.

I want to go and do the work
You have planned for me
For it will bring you much glory.
Yet upon returning to the earth,
I feel so empty and long for your tender embrace.

Help me remember whenever I ache for you
That I am never alone.
For when I shut my eyes and become still
You enter and breathe
Love and light into my soul.

"We live in a fast-paced, pressured world, and it's easy to feel
inundated with responsibilities of daily life. Most people have

adjusted to their hectic schedules but still are weary from their never-ending routines and often wish they could stop and rest.

"People can certainly unwind to an extent in their own way, but it is merely a temporary fix and fails to address the underlying problem. If people want true rest and to be refreshed, they must take time out to be with God. Some are listening to what I'm saying and are scoffing. They will no doubt say, 'Gee that's a good idea, but you don't understand. I don't have time now to do all my chores! It's a nice thought, but I don't have a good fairy who will take over and do the work for me.' I understand this reaction because I've been there. It may be hard to find time, but rest assured that unless you make time, sooner or later you will suffer burn out and will not be able to continue serving others the way you currently do. You may not want to admit it, but you know on some level that what I am saying is true.

"Jesus retreated to the mountaintop to be alone with His Father to gain the strength He needed to accomplish His mission. We are mere humans; surely we must do the same. If we want to revive our weary souls, become empowered to do the work of Christ, and acquire the zeal needed to carry out our missions with passion, we must find a quiet place so we can hear God's voice. Even when you commit to make a holy time, it can be difficult to know how to still your mind. Yes, we need to open our hearts and let God know what is happening in our lives. However, merely getting things off your chest and holding a one-way conversation with God is not enough.

"The Bible says that God longs to be part of our lives and wants to comfort and help us. This is true; yet, often it feels as if there is an imaginary wall between us and God that prevents us from being blessed. In times of need, when we cry out to God and our pleas seem to go unanswered, it is natural to become frustrated and to want to walk away in exasperation. During such times, we wonder if God hears us and why a God who claims to love us so much doesn't answer us instantly in the manner we want.

"I spent several months contemplating this age-old dilemma. I did everything I could to find an answer to this question, including reading the Bible and other spiritual books, praying, listening to tapes, and attending seminars; however, nothing seemed to help. At the end of this time, I felt angry and frustrated and couldn't understand why God was making this so difficult. To get myself out of this horrendous quagmire that was going nowhere, I did the one thing I knew: pray about the matter, relinquish control, go about my business, and let God handle it in His time and way.

"Soon the Holy Spirit explained the problem to me. I'd been so hell-bent on having my needs met instantly and wanting to be comforted that I never stopped to listen or consider how God saw the situation. God showed me two distinct images that helped me see things from His point of view. The first was during the storm when the disciples were in the boat and Jesus was asleep. The second was of a baby screaming, throwing a tantrum and despite the mother trying to hold the baby, the baby refused to be calmed. The message that I took away from this was we make things harder for ourselves because we refuse to stop crying and wait for God to comfort us. We want what we want now. If we don't get what we want, we become exasperated and get in a dither, just as the disciples did when Jesus fell asleep.

"Seeing this helped me realize that if I wanted God to help me, I needed to try a different approach. God wants us to come to Him in all situations and be the ultimate source of calm for the storms of our lives. However, after we have told God our needs, we need to let it go and wait for Him to answer us. We may know this intellectually; yet, when we get in a tough situation, our faith goes by the wayside and our natural instinct is to panic.

"When the Holy Spirit revealed this, I was truly amazed and couldn't believe how it changed my life. The more I thought about it, the more I knew that the Holy Spirit had given me this insight for a reason. I know that churches do their best to encourage people whenever they are in need to take time and wait upon the Lord. Some hold retreats or quiet days throughout the year, and such events do give people the spiritual fortitude required to get through their lives. Such events are enriching. Still, I have found from my own experience, there are times when they are not enough. Retreats do give people a spiritual lift and empower them to live the Gospel and be lights to a darkened world. Yet at times, life can be overwhelming, and we simply need a place where we can clear our minds and regroup.

"Normally whenever someone has a wonderful, pie-in-the-sky, grandiose idea, he is quick to run to his pastor, ask to form a committee, implement the idea, and meet spiritual needs. This is a nice thought; but, in actuality, this is not feasible. Pastors might be the head of the church, but they can't possibly be expected to be all things to all people. God doesn't ask just church leaders to serve Him. Rather, God blesses all of His children with talents and expects them to spend their lives doing all in their power to help one another, even if it isn't in their job description.

"At that moment, I closed my eyes and God showed me my new assignment, which was absolutely spellbinding! God wanted me to take a leap of faith and cause a stir in the community by opening a new spiritual haven. Just as Jesus came to the disciples in the midst of the storm and calmed the sea, He wanted people to see the Soul Station as a place of refuge when the storms of their lives became unbearable.

"When Jesus said this to me, I was rendered speechless and couldn't believe Jesus wanted me to do this for Him. Jesus went on. 'Now that I have given you a general idea about the Soul Station, I now want to give you some specifics. First, the Soul Station should be a local retreat center where people can go in times of need to receive comfort, be spiritually renewed, and learn to hear my voice. As you know, I speak to people in different ways. Consequently, I want the Soul Station to be designed so it will never grow stale but will always satisfy the specific spiritual longings that a person has. Although I am giving you all the flexibility you need, I always want whatever exercise you create to meet two criteria: be a means to help people experience my presence and be centered around three basic types of ministries: individuals, healing, and group.

The first ministry is the most important and is designed for individuals. When people come to the Soul Station, they should go into a private dimly lit prayer closet, lie on a couch, put on a pair of headphones, and select from an online menu of contemplative material, such as soaking prayer, sermons, meditations, reflections, and Bible stories. The second ministry is designed to help people who are in need of healing. In this ministry, people could have their feet washed, have a massage, or take part in a stress management class. Finally, there are ministries that can be carried out in a group setting, such as meditations, reflections, and prayer/healing/communion services. Each of the three distinct ministries is designed to help people quiet their minds so they can hear my voice. While the Soul Station is a wonderful way to help people grow closer to me, in no way should it ever be a substitute for going to church.

After Claire made an initial video, it was time for her to help people understand how different their lives would be if they took God at His word and abided in His presence. Claire knew God does not merely want his people to view Him as some distant being who wants to be obeyed. Rather, He wants to be a constant companion and the one to turn to first in everything.

As Claire deliberated this task, she thought about several people she knew who were having a hard time and needed the Soul Station. She understood their daily struggles and how desperately they needed help. It became clear that she could not simply go online, select contemplative videos, post them on a Webpage, and hope they would meet people's spiritual needs. If she really wanted to help others, she needed to show them that Christ was in control of everything and was the only one that could deliver us from all of their predicaments.

People may know this is the truth on a deep level. Yet, when crisis hits, we become fearful because our lives seem to be spiraling out of control and we wonder why a God of love does not intervene and save us from the situation. During such times of great despair and anguish when we do not know if we can endure any more, we cry out to God for help. However, when God does not provide the comfort and solace we desperately need or answer us in the way we want instantly, we panic and quickly run to our friends and family, cry on their shoulders, and seek their advice on how to get out of our predicaments. While this may temporarily relieve our distress, ultimately God is the only one who can quiet our souls and give us peace.

Claire understood that Jesus wanted the Soul Station to be committed to helping people be one with God and to assuring them that the king of the universe would guide and protect them every step of the way. This was definitely the goal. Still, from studying the problem and her own experience, she knew there were several mental obstacles that prevented people from obtaining peace of mind and knowing that all was well. To help people get the most from their experience at the Soul Station, she decided make a video called "How to Be at Home," which would teach people how to shut out the noise in their minds. The following is the narration for the video.

"At times people reach a point where they become so disgusted with the way life is that they yearn to do anything to escape. We run ourselves ragged and realize, despite our fervent attempts, that we are exhausted and cannot do anything on our own. Some see it as a wake-up call and resolve to do whatever it takes to get closer to God, including repenting, reforming their lives, and vowing to follow God wherever He leads.

"We may want to follow Jesus; yet, it's not so easy. Some may begin each day by giving the day to the Lord and asking Him to direct their steps. Still, often we feel as if we are living in dichotomous worlds, and we find it difficult to operate in two mutually exclusive environments: a world that is loving and one that is not. We may long to be in God's presence and experience a world of acceptance and love. We are so accustomed to the way things are on earth that we have difficulty tuning out the world, letting go, and allowing Him to love us. Jesus himself understood how difficult this was for us. This is why He reminds us that we are supposed to 'be in the world not of the world.'

"The situation people face when trying to communicate with God is similar to the mindset soldiers must have to survive the battlefield and the difficulty they have relinquishing it when they return home. Many people have so many concerns and want a quick way to escape from their problems. Of course we know that Jesus said, 'Come unto me, all ye that labor and are heavy laden, and I will give you rest.' Yet, when we cry out to God and God doesn't answer us immediately the way we want it, we become frustrated, assume He isn't listening and doesn't care. Because we want instant gratification, we often turn to substitutions to drown out the internal noise. These may mask the problem temporarily; in the end the problem remains.

"We know that God loves us and will always take care of us. The problem, however, is that there is a serious disconnect between what we know and what we do. For when we are in a tough situation, we become frenzied and turn from the small, inner voice of wisdom in our hearts. When we end up in a horrible predicament because we didn't listen to our hearts, we vow never to do it again. Paul answered this question well when he said, 'I do not understand what I do. For what I want to do I do not do, but what I hate I do.' If we want to grow closer to God, we must tune out the constant noise of the world and quiet our minds so we can truly acquire the peace and rest that God wants to give us.

"This cannot be learned intellectually; it can be accomplished only by developing childlike faith and trusting Jesus completely. All of us long on some level to put our heads down and let God refresh our wearied souls. However, many cannot acquire the peace we desperately desire because we have so many fears that plague our minds, and we don't know how to rid ourselves of them. Many times these thoughts enslave us and actually prevent us from having peace of mind. We know that we can do all things through Christ who strengthens us. If we want to have peace of mind and be filled with God's power, we must learn to control and guard our thoughts.

"It's easy to pledge our full-fledged devotion to God, and to ask Him to put in our path what He wants us to do. Yet, when God does what we ask and we don't like the direction He is leading us, why do we kick and scream every step of the way instead of going along willingly? The answer is that we must learn why God has put us in our current situation and learn not to allow ourselves to become emotionally charged when life doesn't go our way.

"The Soul Station will be a quiet, nurturing haven where the weary can find the refuge they so desperately desire for the next leg of the journey and learn how to hear the still, small voice inside of them. Although God wants to help us, often we can't hear Him because we are so used to the relentless pace of everyday life that we don't know how to quell the ceaseless rhetoric in our heads. The Soul Station provides three sacred environments as a means to help people slow down, quiet themselves, and enter a contemplative state where they are able to feel and be in God's presence."

THE CONFERENCE

The annual evangelical conference at the Coppertown Community Church had always been the event the congregation looked forward to and spent much time planning. In addition to the choir's special music program, participants could attend various events throughout the week. Every year the conference focused on a central theme that the evangelism committee had selected.

Ordinarily, coming up with a theme was not that difficult. However, this year was different. Perhaps it was because the conference had been held for 12 years, and frankly, they were tired of the same old thing. They knew the Gospel and what they were supposed to do as Christians but had difficulty applying it to their everyday lives. The congregation loved hearing about the work the missionaries were doing in foreign countries. Yet, what they really needed were some practical strategies for how to spread the Gospel in their backyards. After a short discussion, it was obvious they had selected a pertinent topic that people would find useful. All they had to do now was to develop appropriate content.

To help them with this task, the committee turned to their well-loved pastor of 12 years, Dr. Eugene Bees. Dr. Bees had been with the church ever since his ordination and was usually very happy to do whatever he could to make this annual event a success.

However, when he heard what the committee wanted him to speak on, he was somewhat doubtful. He was not avoiding the topic. Rather, he was shocked that they had selected a topic he had been contemplating and wrestling with for several weeks.

Dr. Bees was a good pastor, and he had performed many good acts for the church and community throughout the years. The church held events weekly for members to participate in, sponsored missionaries who were living overseas, and had several outreach ministries. These events were uplifting; yet, whenever he read the Acts of the Apostles, he felt they were missing the mark. If the evangelical conference was to be successful, he had to put a mechanism in place that would help his congregation implement the Gospel.

For several weeks before hearing about this topic, Dr. Bees spent much time thinking and talking with close friends about this. In these conversations, it was clear that church was God's house conceptually but not practically. Dr. Bees knew that just as a parent cared for his child, God cared for His people and church. Hence, the question became how could the church, starting with his own, create a nurturing environment to help and empower weary and burdened travelers?

Dr. Bees yearned to lead his congregation in a new direction; yet, he wasn't sure how God wanted to use him, and this was very frustrating. Dr. Bees read the Bible and prayed for guidance, but nothing helped. Finally, he realized the answer might come easier if he put the matter in God's hands.

Mrs. Bees had a honey-do list for him that he had been putting off for quite a while. Dr. Bees decided it was a good day to knock a few things off that never-ending list. Dr. Bees was going to pick up a few gallons of paint; he remembered he had a gift certificate at the hardware store in town and decided he should use it before it expired.

Dr. Bees hadn't been in town for a few months and was quite surprised to find the hardware store where he had shopped for nearly 20 years was gone. However, he was even more surprised by what had replaced it. "Divine Towels," he said to himself, "that's quite an unusual name. I wonder why are so many people standing in line just to buy an ordinary towel." Dr. Bees knew he ought to be getting on with his errands. Yet, he could not help but wonder what all the commotion was about regarding the new store, and he decided to investigate.

Because Dr. Bees didn't know anything about the store, he stood in line like the others and observed what was happening. The first five minutes were rather boring; however, as he moved up the line, his curiosity was piqued when he peered in the window and saw people having their feet washed. He took a pamphlet from the stand and read it while he stood in line. He laughed aloud when he sensed that Christ was answering his prayer.

When it was time for Dr. Bees to have his feet washed, he did not sit down right away. Rather, he stood in awe and gawked at Kathy for the longest time as if he were in some kind of trance. There just was something about Kathy's demeanor and the way she washed people's feet that was beautiful to watch. Since Kathy was accustomed to various reactions, it did not bother her that he was staring. Finally, after several moments, she said, "Hi, my name is Kathy. Can I help you?"

"Yes, you can," Dr. Bees said. "I'm a pastor at a local church. A few days ago, the evangelical committee at my church asked me to speak on ways to apply the Gospel in everyday life. I had been thinking about the same topic for several weeks. The reason I am here is that I do not know what to say. I seek wisdom from the Good Shepherd on how to shepherd my flock and help them apply my homilies to their lives in a concrete way. My desire is to be used by Christ, yet I don't know what He wants me to do. I'm not sure if I'm making any sense, but I do hope you can help me."

Dr. Bees' words amazed Kathy, for they seemed to be in keeping with what Claire had said prior to writing the letter. Kathy knew people would respond to the letter but was surprised that

Jesus had sent a pastor who had so much humility. Kathy often felt a connection with the people whose feet she washed but sensed she was supposed to work with this pastor in a special way. Perhaps God wanted the pastor to be involved with the Foot-Washing Institute in some way. Only time would tell. For now Kathy had to focus on the task at hand.

"You have come to the right place," Kathy said as she smiled. "Please have a seat and take off your shoes and socks. I know you don't know me, but trust me. I know how you feel because I felt exactly as you do before I came here and had my feet washed. Don't be afraid. Jesus will help you and give you the wisdom you need to carry out His will. By the way, what is your name?" Kathy asked, as she poured the water into the basin.

"My name is Dr. Bees."

"Are you familiar with how this works?"

"Well, I read the pamphlet on how healing happens, and I do believe that God works miracles."

Initially, nothing happened when Kathy washed Dr. Bees' feet. Yet, when Kathy dried his feet, he felt a surge of energy enter his head, which made him euphoric and lightheaded. Dr. Bees had never experienced anything like this before and felt as if his body was being rewired. As a reverend, he read about people who had experienced such miracles, and he knew that people still had personal encounters with Christ. However, now that he was having an encounter, the concept became real.

While sitting with his eyes closed, Dr. Bees heard a familiar voice and knew it was the Lord. "Peace, my son, be still. There was a time when my word ignited a raging spiritual forest fire in people's souls that could be felt throughout the nations. This explosion of goodwill caused people to become zealous and passionately committed to helping one another and to stop at nothing to carry out the Gospel. Because people aspired to do my will above all else, I gave my people whatever they needed. No one wanted for anything. Soon it seemed that my devoted disciples were a dominating force and were successful wherever they went.

"When people saw how successful my devoted disciples were and that they were as tenacious and vigilant on living the Gospel as athletes who train for the Olympics, some were quite disturbed and wished they weren't as intense. After all, while everyone is entitled to his own beliefs, he does not have the right to impose his beliefs on others. Because people were complaining, my disciples decided it was best to tone things down a bit. Soon their fervor began to ebb. It started subtly, but over time, people were compromising to the point where my disciples were no longer doing what I asked them to do.

"At one time, souls were ablaze with passion; it was inconceivable that anything could stomp it out. Much to my distress, people do whatever they want and disregard my commandments because they no longer suit their lifestyles. This has caused the fires to smolder. Today, many people no longer have a passionate sparkle in their eyes; rather, they walk around as if they were in a daze and have no life in them.

"Believe it or not, I came to liberate people from their oppression so they could have life abundantly. I also came to earth to set an example of how to live and to show people that truly being free begins and ends by seeking to do my will above all else and obeying my commandments. Time after time, when people have strayed from my path, I have forgiven and reminded them that they are special to me and that earth is not their real home. My people are here merely to fulfill a mission and should look only to me for comfort, not to the counterfeit substitutions of the world. I long to awaken my people and to make the world a vibrant place where great things happen again!

"It may not seem obvious to you, but I created all creatures so they would serve a unique purpose. Despite what people may think, people are not on earth so they can have fun, rather because

I want to teach lessons and because I have work that I want them to do for me.

"People need to think of their lives in a new way, as a tour, an exciting adventure. My people do not know everything I have planned. However, before I send them, I assure them that they will have quite an adventure of a lifetime; they will be safe as long as they stay by my side because I know every twist and turn.

"Although I have designed the tours and have promised to guide my people every step of the way, the tours are quite difficult at times and often break my most devoted disciples. There will be times along the way, when they will not like the places where I lead them and will wander off in search of an easier way. In their hearts they may realize that if they truly want me to use them then I must put them through rigorous training to test their endurance so they learn to be totally dependent on me. It is easy for a person to say he will depend on me for everything, but it is only when he faces trials and he has nowhere else to turn for help or comfort that will determine the strength of his character.

"There are difficult times when even the strongest people, who know the testing won't last forever, reach a point where they will do anything to escape the misery. They will look for a shortcut; but in most cases after a brief time, my people will wake up, realize what they have done, feel distressed, wonder why they ever went astray, and long to return to the intimacy they once had with me. Of course, people are ashamed of themselves for going astray, but the fact is I know everything even before it happens. My children often forget I love them unconditionally and long for them to return to me so we can finish the tour together.

"People know I am always there to help them. However, at the same time, people also need a support system to keep them from straying. I never envisioned my church merely as a place for people to go to attend a worship service, attend meetings, and chitchat over a cup of coffee. Rather, I wanted it to be a place where people find rest, have their needs met, and receive the strength and support they need to carry on. I also wanted it to be a force that is focused on putting love into action in the community. There are many agencies that serve the needs of the community; yet, people still feel lonely, scared, and unloved. The world sends the message to be tough and independent, but people long for an alternative.

"The world has turned into a cold place where many feel as if they have endless responsibilities. Many are worn out and wonder if I put them on earth for any other reason except to keep this pace up. Because of the way society is now, by the time people are finished a day of work, they are exhausted and do not have the energy to do any more." As Jesus spoke, Dr. Bees was filled with awe and hung on His every word.

"Some feel life has deteriorated so much that they can't be fixed. This is a lie, and opening Divine Towels has been the initial domino that will once again change the course of history and help bring things back into balance. Just as revivals stir people's souls and make them eager to serve, when people have their feet washed, they are invigorated and see life with a new purpose. I enjoy firing people's souls up. But unless the newly rekindled spirit is nurtured and immediately given a worthwhile task to do, people's enthusiasm will dwindle and will begin to stagnate again.

"To prevent this, I want you to create a nurturing environment that will plant seeds of hope, love, and compassion into people's hungry souls. This place will be extraordinary in that it will meet people's needs and, given enough time, will cause them to see life in a new way. Consequently, there will be a renewed commitment to social activism towards ending the needless suffering people experience daily. Such a place is no doubt a fantasy people love to think about turning into reality. Throughout the years, many have tried to create such a place. Some have been successful; however, I want more than anything for my church to work towards making this transformation a reality.

"To accomplish this task, I need someone who is willing to take a risk and stir people to action. Just as I asked Moses to lead the Israelites out of Egypt into the promised land, I want you to lead my church. This cannot be done simply by preaching a 20-minute sermon to your congregation once a week or holding a few weekly activities. Leading requires action, getting your hands dirty, and showing people by example how to live the Gospel.

"While some still are dedicating their lives to helping others, somehow the enthusiasm is dwindling and this makes me very sad. My church is dying, and I want you to help resurrect it. I never intended Christianity to be a philosophy but rather a way of life. It is time for people to put the Gospel into action and for my church to become a center that empowers and gives people the tools they need to go out into the world to perform acts of mercy.

"You are at Divine Towels to have your feet washed, but then you are to hold a foot service at your church. The staff at Divine Towels is quite eager to expand their ministry and will help you.

"I promise that if you step out in faith, do as I am asking, and allow me to guide you, you will do much to further my kingdom and transform the mentality of society forever. When other pastors see the faith you have and the great works those who have had their feet washed are doing, many will be eager to imitate your effort. Hence, the foot-washing ministry will be the mechanism I will use to make my church an invincible force that will not be dismissed. Now go, my child, and work tirelessly toward achieving this end."

When Jesus finished speaking, Dr. Bees opened his eyes and grinned with delight. He was overwhelmed that Jesus had chosen him for this task and eager to work with Kathy and the rest of the staff at Divine Towels. There was much to do, and he did not want to wait any longer.

"I never experienced anything like that before in my life," Dr. Bees said once he had re-acclimated himself with his surroundings. "I'm not sure what happened, but my life has changed drastically and I feel transformed. It's hard to describe but until I came and had my feet washed, I always felt as if I've been living life with a veil over my eyes. However, when you washed my feet, Christ came to me and gave me a mission. I'm amazed and can't believe what He has asked me to do for Him.

"Jesus told me that it was not enough to commission people to go out and live the Gospel. I must find ways to help my congregation respond to the needs of others. He also said that as part of the upcoming evangelical conference at my church I am supposed to hold a foot-washing service and that the staff at Divine Towels will help me."

At first, Kathy was quiet. Then she spoke to Dr. Bees with admiration. "You are a blessed man. I know it took courage to say that aloud, but you are a loved man whom Christ chose do this. The staff at Divine Towels and I have wondered when Jesus would ask a pastor to hold a foot-washing service at his church. I know how suddenly this all happened and how overwhelmed you must feel by what God asked you to do."

Dr. Bees was stunned by Kathy's reaction. Not only was he confident that everything Christ had said to him was true, but he was also quite anxious to get started. "Okay, I'm here and I'm committed to doing whatever it takes to accomplish the goal. Now what do I do?" Dr. Bees asked.

Kathy was delighted by Dr. Bees' attitude. She knew that the upcoming conference would be quite different from others. There was such a feeling of optimism in the air; it was easy to tell that the Holy Spirit was at work.

Winning an Olympic gold medal is definitely the ultimate goal of any serious athlete. In an effort to obtain this one moment of fame, all dedicate countless hours of their lives training their bodies, perfecting techniques, and disciplining their minds. They are so focused on becoming the very best that they have little time for anything else in life. If an outsider were to look at this, he would marvel at the discipline but would also wonder if the endless hours of dedication were worth it for the opportunity to win gold. Such people often utter clichés like, "Life is too short to spend your days in this way. After all, life is meant to be enjoyed."

Dr. Bees liked sports and felt athletes had much to teach Christians. In his mind, the two were similar but approached pursuing their prize differently. Christ calls us to dedicate our lives to seeking and preparing for the ultimate prize, Christ's return. When we attend church, we are reminded of this duty and energized to recommit our lives to pursuing this endeavor. Unlike athletes who are relentless in pursuing their goal, our enthusiasm often dies within hours of leaving the walls of the church, and we return to our old ways.

The sermon Dr. Bees planned to preach would be different from any other he had ever preached and would alter the dynamics in his church forever. Some would surely be infuriated and leave because they did not like being proactively challenged. He knew the battle he was about to undertake would not be easy and that satanic forces would do everything they could to stop him from moving forward. Although Dr. Bees was not looking forward to this battle, he was determined not just to wage war, but to win.

With this in mind, Dr. Bees began writing a compelling sermon titled, "Call to Action" as the introduction for this year's evangelical conference. From working with Kathy the last few weeks, he had a good handle on what he wanted to say to his congregation. If the foot-washing ministry was to have a chance of growing, he had to present the idea in a nonthreatening way so he could reach as many people as possible. Normally, it took Dr. Bees a while to write a sermon. However, because Christ was guiding his thoughts, the words flowed naturally.

"Welcome to yet another annual evangelism conference," Dr. Bees said once people were settled. "Normally, the evangelism committee helps me plan this. However, when they told me that they wanted me to discuss how to apply the teachings of Christ to their daily lives, I knew this was going to be an extraordinary conference. The topic is very relevant and one that desperately needs to be addressed. Not only does it address evangelism, but it cuts to what our mission as Christians should be. For years, I have preached on the need to take Jesus' message and spread it. People know what they ought to do intellectually; however, many are not good at knowing how to apply the teachings of Christ to their daily lives.

"When people raise this question, we always say the best way to talk about the Gospel is by the way we live our lives. I agree with this, but what does this mean? Sometimes I wonder if we are actually living out the Gospel and how we will account for ourselves on judgment day. Will we be able to answer Jesus' questions knowing we did all we could to feed the poor, clothe the naked, and ease the suffering of others? Or will we stand there stuttering, offering lame excuses as to why we didn't apply His commandments?

"Jesus does not ask us simply to live in the world but to respond to situations the way He would. Because we belong to Christ, we are called to do more than daily routines. Rather, we are called to be His hands and feet on earth and to do all in our power to correct injustices and create a better society. This requires that we become activists and undertake bold initiatives that will lift the human spirit. This is certainly an admirable goal that we should strive to achieve; however, is it possible to do this in the chaotic world we live in today?

"I stand before you today and tell you it is not only possible, but it is our duty as Christians to be a people at odds with the world. In preparing for the conference, I wanted topics to be uplifting and inspirational. If this annual conference is to help us, it must address whatever we struggle with. For this reason, I want to focus on ways we can apply the teachings of Christ to our daily lives."

Dr. Bees could tell he had his congregation's attention and that they quite eager to see where he was going. While he was pleased by their reaction, he knew the next portion of his sermon would be controversial and cause the traditionalist to become outraged. Cognizant of the effect the next portion of his sermon would have, Dr. Bees took a deep breath and continued.

"Indeed, this is a good topic. However, doing this was not easy and I spent much time in prayer asking Jesus for help. Unfortunately, since I was revved up and expected an answer immediately, I didn't get what I wanted and became frustrated. I had become so obsessed in wanting to do this that it had taken priority over serving my Lord. I knew this and, thus I just surrendered the situation to God and asked Him to put on my heart what I was to say.

"It always amazes me the way God answer prayers. I'm not sure how or why it happened, but I ended up at a new store in town called Divine Towels. This store is devoted to healing and empowering people through the washing of feet. When I had my feet washed, Christ answered my prayer and told me what to do. Until then, God had spoken to me only through scripture. However, when my feet washed were washed, I actually heard His voice as clearly as you hear me right now.

"He explained that while the church was successfully helping the community in some areas, much more had to be done. I could spend hours speaking on what needs to be done; however, at the moment, it is irrelevant. For until we can identify the barriers in our lives that are keeping us from carrying out the Gospel and find a way to remove them, they will continue to impede us from doing God's work. Many of you understand what I am saying. Although it may be your heart's desire to remove the barriers, sometimes crushing them seems impossible.

"Divine Towels has helped me discover how to live life more abundantly. My brothers and sisters, I know life is a constant struggle, but it doesn't have to be. Often we wonder why we don't have the power the early disciples had. There is a way to break free from the chains that prevent you from moving ahead. If you are tired of running in circles and want a new way of looking at life, please come to the events of the week."

Judging from the positive feeling in the room when he finished, Dr. Bees was certain the conference was off to a wonderful start. The sermon created a feeling that there would be a second Exodus and that God was going to deliver them from their anguish. There were others, however, who felt that Dr. Bees was aggressive. They did not like the direction he was heading. However, they decided to wait until he finished what he had to say before making a final judgment. Despite people's personal opinions on the sermon, two things were clear: Dr. Bees' sermon was unlike any he had delivered before and that the Holy Spirit was speaking through him.

Usually, people were in great rush to be first out the door when the service ended; however, the sermon touched their souls. Many were moved and sat thinking about what they had heard. If this sermon was any indication to the week ahead, the conference would surely be a success.

Dr. Bees was delving into a topic he did not have much experience with and had every right to be fearful. Yet, from spending much time with Kathy and in prayer, he had received clear guidance on how to proceed and had confidence that he would be successful. Dr. Bees had planned to address important precepts during his initial sermon but decided it was best to use the time to set the tone and get people thinking. So far, everything had gone as planned, and he was pleased. However, tomorrow evening would be a different story. He would take the next step, stoke the fire, and set the embers ablaze.

A TRANSFORMED LIFE

Dr. Bees had been known for his charisma and his ability to deliver well-crafted, thought-provoking sermons. However, the introduction he had given at this year's conference was extraordinarily powerful and unlike any the congregation had heard before. Many were convinced that the Holy Spirit was speaking directly to them through Dr. Bees. There was something compelling about the message that convinced people, stopping them dead in their tracks and forcing them to take a hard look at where they were going.

Many believed God had put them where they were for a reason and until they mastered what they were supposed to do, God would not allow them to take on anymore challenges. Although they knew the best way to get through the daily grind was to be cheerful, at times they still grew weary from the monotony of their lives and prayed for deliverance. As they left the conference that evening, many were elated and full of hope; they felt the sermon was an answer to their prayers. Not only were they eager for the conference to resume the next evening, but they could hardly wait to invite their friends to the conference as well.

That night, many people lay in bed bursting with excitement and felt as if they were children again awaiting Santa. They just could not stop thinking about Dr. Bees' compelling sermon. What's more, they were filled with wonder and anticipation as they thought about what awaited them the following night and the miraculous plans God had for their future. Because of all of the excitement, people made it a point to arrive early to ensure that they would get a good seat.

Judging from the attendance of prior years, Dr. Bees had a good idea that the same people would attend the conference. However, when he walked into the sanctuary the next day and saw many new faces, he was pleased and took it as another sign that this was indeed the direction God wanted him to go in.

"Good evening," he said. "Good to see that most of you are back tonight. Originally, I was just going to pick up where we ended last night. However, because I see so many new faces, I will briefly recap. I believe we are all here in one way or another to prepare for Jesus' return. Some of you already know why you are here. Yet others haven't quite figured it out and are waiting for God to give you marching orders. You can think of this week as a down-and-dirty spiritual boot camp that is designed to give you the tools needed to empower others.

"When Jesus sent His disciples out to preach the Gospel to the nations, he authorized them. 'I have given you authority to trample on snakes and scorpions and to overcome all the power of the enemy; nothing will harm you.' (Luke 10:19) Whenever I hear that scripture, I feel emboldened to use my talents to work for good and create a just and equitable society. And so I step out earnestly in faith, trusting that God will put me in a position where I can do His will. At times, I am victorious; yet, at other times I do not take the higher ground but act like a turtle that retreats into its shell when the road is difficult. Satan loves us to dwell on our shortcomings, wallow in guilt, and take roads that lead to dead ends. As Christians, we must focus on our mission and not be enticed to taste the poisonous, delectable eye candy that lines the road of paradise.

"Have you ever thought about what judgment day might be like? Of course, some people who have not lived good, upright lives will no doubt be frightened. Others are confident they will go to heaven because they believe in Jesus Christ and believe they are saved by His blood. While this is my belief, I often wonder how we will answer when Jesus asks us if we did everything in our power to help mankind.

"The Christian walk can often seem impossible. Christ calls us to be a unique people and take bold action to correct unjust situations. I am sure many of us have no doubt worked tirelessly to correct problems. Sometimes our efforts prove worthwhile and yield positive change. However, I often walk away from a situation exasperated with a sense of failure because I accomplished nothing. I firmly believe there is a solution to every problem. Yet, the likelihood of the solution being implemented is slim because the people involved are only looking out for their own interest.

"As a child, I always hated when mama cooked something for dinner that I didn't like. I still remember her rule that I wasn't allowed to leave the table until I finished my dinner. Like most children, I threw a temper tantrum, hoping that if I acted up enough mama would give in. However, she never did. After sitting in front of my plate for several nights, I learned it was easier to eat my dinner and to get it over with than to sit there for hours.

"Brothers and sisters, it is time for a reality check. We are here not simply to carry out our daily routines but rather to fulfill a specific destiny. God planned for us the moment we were conceived. You are the only person in the world who can do the job God sent you here to do. No one else. There are no shortcuts. The fact is, whether you like it or not, until you complete the work God has sent you here to do, you are not going anywhere. Many here are eager for God to use you as tools and to reveal what He wants you to do.

"We read in the Gospel, 'Ask and it will be given to you; seek and you will find; knock and the door will be opened to you.'

(Matthew 7:7) Like you, I have often asked but become frustrated when I was not answered. Nevertheless, I believe God does answer us, but He does it in His time and in His way. I have found that He often answers prayer by putting circumstances in our path as a way to get us where we need to go.

"Many here are certainly involved in various church ministries and know you are helping the church. However, have you ever felt that God is calling you to do more for Him that you simply are unable to identify? If I am describing you, perhaps God has called you here so you can retreat from the world and listen to His voice.

"I know how frustrating it is to feel that God wants you to do something for Him and not have a clue what it is. I too have felt this way and have found that it is best to give the situation over to the Lord. I then ask the Holy Spirit to show me how I can best utilize the talents He gave me to accomplish His will for the day.

"In preparing for tonight, I reread a book I read in seminary called *In His Steps*, a Christian novel that asks the question 'What would Jesus do?' We know intellectually that Jesus is always with us and sees everything; yet, sometimes our behavior would be radically different if we actually believed this. We all want to do the ideal thing. Yet, we are weak people. St. Paul put it this way, 'I do not understand what I do. For what I want to do I do not do, but what I hate I do.' (Romans 7:15) If we ever hope to stop this vicious cycle, we must rely totally on Jesus to help us and show us what to do.

"From time to time, we do fail. However, it does not help to lament past mistakes. We must move on. Much work needs to be done to prepare for Jesus' return. Just as soldiers in an infantry perform various tasks when they are engaged in warfare, Jesus has blessed us all with talents and expects us to use them to win the war against injustice and to win hearts and minds for Him. Such a war cannot be won by relying on intellect but rather by following the orders of their ultimate commander, who already knows what it will take to win the war.

"Once you make up your mind to fight the battle, forces that you never knew existed will do everything to stop you from marching forward. Hence, to win the battle you will need much stamina, a strong character, and the armor of Christ. Christ has promised that He will not let us fail, but we must rely on the Holy Spirit to guide our every move.

"Many here know what I'm saying is right and earnestly pray for guidance to get past the roadblocks in their lives. We ask God to show us what He wants us to do; yet, when we go about our day and see that nothing has changed, we tend to become discouraged and question why wonders are not unfolding before our eyes. We have faith, but sometimes we wonder if we are really doing anything to help the Lord. We become frustrated and long for Christ to take the veil from our eyes and show us what is going on.

"If I have just described your predicament and if you want God to show you what He wants you to do, then perhaps God sent you here tonight. As I mentioned last night, Divine Towels is an amazing new place that is committed to empowering believers to do the work of Christ. When people of faith have their feet washed at Divine Towels, they are not only healed of their physical ailments, but they are also transformed and given the power and wisdom to know how to bulldoze the barriers of their lives. Consequently, people are living life in a new way, confronting the forces that oppress them, holding people accountable for their actions and seeing results.

"Many read the Bible and marvel at the works of the disciples that are recorded in the Acts of the Apostles and want to serve in the same way. If you are tired of the monotony of your routine and long to serve Christ more, come forward and have your feet washed. You don't have to walk through life alone. Jesus will help you. Simply place yourself in the Master's hands, and He will use you as a tool to accomplish His work on earth.

"My mother taught me as a boy that it is not what you say that counts but rather what you do to help others. With this in mind, if we want people to know Christ, we must show people what it means to be a Christian. We can and must actively tear down the barriers that oppress people. If we are truly Christians, we cannot sit back and watch our brothers and sisters suffer. Rather, we must send the world the message that any behavior that injures the human spirit will no longer be tolerated. We must stop using the word *can't* and remember that we can do all things through Christ who strengthens us.

"When my feet were washed at Divine Towels, Jesus explained that while my sermons were inspiring, He wanted me to mobilize people to put the Gospel into action. He said that just as He had given the disciples the power to cast out demons, heal the sick, and be lights to a darkened world, He has blessed us also with this same power.

"This statement is quite baffling, especially if you listen to the news and think about the situations in your lives that you don't seem to have any control over. However, Jesus has a plan for each of our lives and wants us to use the spiritual gifts He has given us to rid the world of evil.

"When I learned about the miraculous things that the people who had had their feet washed at Divine Towels were doing, I knew that the Holy Spirit was at work empowering them. I imagined a vast city that had experienced a power outage and saw flames of fire that were dispersed throughout the city illuminating corners of the darkness. At this time, Jesus explained that people who had been healed at Divine Towels were making a difference.

"I asked myself several questions. Is this a dream or is this really happening? If I did this, would it work or would everyone walk out and say I had gone mad? In this moment, I had a better appreciation of the questions Mary must have had when Gabriel asked her to be Jesus' mother. Yet, when it got right down to it, only one of these questions ultimately mattered: Was I going to trust and obey or was I going to allow fear to keep me from obeying the Lord?

"As you can see, I decided to do whatever Jesus wants and to step out in faith. Although I have no idea what's going to happen or how the foot-washing ministry will turn out, I know it honestly doesn't matter. Jesus is in control and will guide me every step of the way.

"Some of you are probably wondering what has happened to me and why I'm speaking in this way. After all, I have never addressed anyone, much less the congregation, in such a manner before, and, frankly, it does seem quite out of character. The truth is that when I had my feet washed at Divine Towels, the Holy Spirit touched my heart, and my entire outlook on life changed. I love being the pastor of this church. However, since I had my feet washed, I see everything very clearly, and I feel compelled to take this church in a new direction.

"I spent much time in prayer and in the Bible studying what worked. I was struck that those who helped humanity most stood firmly by their convictions. When I look at the violence of today's society, I see that the world is in great chaos. I believe the world has reached this state because we live in a society where anything goes and moral standards no longer exist. There once was a time in history when Christians were powerful people who stood up for what was right and just. If we ever plan to win people to Christ, we must take a stand and reestablish a moral authority.

"Some may believe the decay has gone too far. Perhaps they are right. Yet, I believe Christ longs to end the suffering of the world and to restore it to a state of peace and harmony, but He can't do it without our help. It is analogous to an orchestra playing a symphony without a conductor. Under a good conductor, music can come alive and speak to the heart. Yet, if the orchestra plays without leadership, there is discord. God is our conductor, and He has blessed us all with unique gifts. If He is to produce a harmonious world, we must use the gifts He has given us in the manner He directs.

"If we really want to be a healing force in this cold, broken world, we must be plugged into the source and allow the Holy Spirit to direct our every move. It is not too late to fix the world; however, we must amend our lives, put our faith into action, take a stand for what is right, and fight vigorously against the forces that seek to harm the human spirit.

"If you want God to show you how to help crush the enemy, come forward boldly with a humble heart and allow Jesus to use you as He wills. The people from Divine Towels are here and are willing to wash our feet. Jesus has blessed each one of us with a unique gift. He has promised to use us if we come like children and seek to do His will above all else. What we ultimately must decide is whether we want to help Him do His work or would rather be a liability."

Dr. Bees sat down and allowed five minutes for silent meditation and reflection. When the hymn "Softly and Tenderly" had finished playing, Dr. Bees began again. "Let us pray. Father, we are like lost sheep that have wandered far. It is our hearts' desire to come home and be nurtured and fed by you. You have a special plan for each one of us, and you have told us that if we ask for help that you will show us what to do. Lord, we come and tell you we want this conference to be different. As your children come forward to have their feet washed tonight, please transform them into holy instruments that you can use to accomplish your work on earth. We pray these things in Jesus' name. Amen."

As people had their feet washed, Dr. Bees realized this conference was profoundly different; people were impacted at the core of their being. The service set the tone for the conference and no doubt opened people's eyes and breathed new life into people's souls. Dr. Bees was pleased with the response thus far and felt it had the potential to be the initial domino that would change people's lives forever. He realized that having one's feet washed was not just a one-time thrilling event. Instead, it marked the start of a lifelong journey in which one was aware that he would no longer walk alone but that the Holy Spirit was with him and would lead him step by step.

As Dr. Bees watched the service, he realized that his primary purpose was to be a shepherd: provide spiritual leadership, help people overcome the obstacles of their daily lives that oppressed them, and spur their enthusiasm by showing them how to apply the Gospel to their daily lives.

Customarily, Dr. Bees received a number of calls during the week of the annual evangelism conference. However, it was clear that this annual conference was unlike any they attended before. Many indicated that the conference spoke to their spirits in a unique, compelling way. Not only did the conference rekindle a passion and helped them step back and see what was truly the central priority in life, but people seemed different, as if a surge of positive energy had been breathed into their soul. Consequently, they could not wait to return each night to see what was going to happen.

Based on such sentiments, Dr. Bees could tell the Holy Spirit was at work and that this conference was truly transformational. Although Dr. Bees was pleased by the response, he knew that people became preoccupied with their everyday lives and after a few days tended to forget what they learned about at conferences such as these. To help people remember, it was imperative to set up a mechanism to help and encourage people. Stepping out in faith and living differently is hard enough; without a support system, it is impossible. While Dr. Bees felt that the Holy Spirit was guiding him to do something, he wasn't quite sure exactly what God had in mind.

A lot was weighing on Dr. Bees' mind that night, and he wondered what he could possibly say the following night to conclude the conference. Also, the committee had scheduled a special meeting at the conclusion of the service to wrap things up and discuss what to do next. So much depended on the outcome of the conference. Dr. Bees turned to Jesus and asked for guidance. Jesus came to him in a dream and said, "Peace be with you, my son. Do not worry about what you are supposed to say to your congregation tomorrow night. Meet with Ethan and Claire in the morning and tell them exactly how you are feeling. At the end, say 'Soul Station.'

"This will remind them of a project they have wanted for a while. As of late, they have wondered why it has not gotten off the ground. Once they tell you everything, not only will you understand your role in bringing my plan to fruition, but you will also know what to say to your congregation tomorrow night. Do not fear, my son, for I am with you."

Hearing this guidance, Dr. Bees reflected on how much his life had changed over the past few weeks. Yes, he knew God had called him to be a pastor and had great plans for him. Yet, what God had done over the past few weeks was miraculous. Now that Dr. Bees had his marching orders, he could hardly wait to tell Ethan and Claire what the Holy Spirit had laid on his heart.

From the day that Divine Towels opened, Ethan and Claire's lives changed radically. Truly, it was an extraordinary gift to get up every day, partner with Christ, and see countless miracles happen before their eyes. Every day was a new adventure. While the work Christ asked them to do was extraordinary, they were aware that if they wanted to continue, they had to remain humble above all else. Because they were in this for the long haul, they began each day by asking Christ to show them what He wanted them to do.

Ethan and Claire were delighted with serving Christ. They had become so immersed in doing Christ's work that nothing else seemed to matter. When Dr. Bees met with them the next day and told them about his dream, they were amazed at what was unfolding before their eyes. God was taking the Soul Station to the next level.

"It never ceases to amaze me how God works and how He allows people to meet for a distinct reason," Ethan said with much exhilaration. "You are not aware of this, but mom has spent the last several months seeking the Holy Spirit's help about how to do exactly what you just described. Do you think it's a coincidence that you're here and are saying these things to us? You're right, it's one thing to fire people up about the Gospel, it's another to empower people and give them the tools required to carry out their mission. With the help of the Holy Spirit, mom has designed a program to help people recharge their spiritual batteries and receive the nourishment they desperately need to carry out their mission. I could easily sit here and tell you about the Soul Station. However, to help you to better understand what the Soul Station and its programs are all about, I want to show you a video that mom made."

Dr. Bees closed his eyes and tried to visualize what the Soul Station might look like. He loved the conceptual idea of the Soul Station but found it almost ironic for he had been toying with a similar concept himself. Dr. Bees watched the video and saw how the concepts fit together. Then he understood why everything had happened as it did. He just could not believe the wondrous opportunity God had afforded him.

"I was just thinking of an adage I tell my parishioners when someone comes to me for advice, 'Be careful what you ask God for because you might just get it.' I am confident that God has answered my prayer, and I have no doubts whatsoever that God wants me to do this. I finally have a topic for tonight's sermon, but my concern has shifted. The idea of the Soul Station as a local retreat is great. It is a new concept that dares to put Jesus' words into action. Some may flat out reject it because it falls outside the boundaries of what they consider 'normal.'

"I understand that people are very comfortable in their traditions. If I can show people that the idea of the Soul Station is a direct response to the verse, 'Come unto me all you who are heavy laden and I will give you rest,' they might be willing to accept it.

Taking a two-tiered approach might work best. First, I'll show the video and then discuss why the ideas are indeed biblically sound."

He added, "I know this is short notice, and you probably have a lot to do today. However, since all this happened last minute and because you have already done much of the leg work, could you possibly help me prepare tonight's sermon?"

Ethan and Claire smiled and agreed to do whatever they could to help. For the next few hours, Claire sat with her notes and Bible in hand and gave Dr. Bees background on how the three distinct ministries of the Soul Station were created to coincide with biblical principles.

When the meeting was about to start, a flurry of positive energy filled the room. Rejuvenated, everyone was anxious to hear what Dr. Bees was going to speak about. It was obvious that the Holy Spirit was working through the pastor, and something spectacular was about to happen.

Dr. Bees tapped the microphone and began, "Welcome back. It is good to see so many people are here again. Before we begin, I admit I do not have all the answers. I am the pastor of this church, but that does not make me an expert. I do not know about you, but so far this conference has been amazing. We have discussed and learned many things. Tonight I want us to consider where we go from here.

"After the spiritual high of last night, I must admit that I wasn't sure what I was going to talk about tonight. It seemed impossible that anything could top having God touch and heal His people in such an intimate and profound way. I knew we needed to move forward, but I did not know how. Of course, we could conduct the customary church activities like prayer groups, small groups, Bible studies, and missions. All of these are good. I am not discounting them. However, they do not seem to set one's soul on fire, especially given the kind of week we just had.

"I'm just going to say this and lay it all on the line. I have been here for 12 years, and we have experienced some wonderful things together. As many of you indicated, this conference has truly been a transformational experience and it is obvious that the Holy Spirit is starting something new!

"Last night, I was so enthusiastic and I found myself praising God in a new way for all the blessings He has bestowed on us. Besides an overwhelming sense of wonder and awe, I also spent many hours praying over what I could possibly say tonight. Although many compelling things came to mind, nothing extraordinary jumped out at me. I ended up leveling with Jesus. I explained my predicament, asked for guidance and went to bed.

"The one thing I have learned about God over the years is never to presume to know what He is going to do. I know this, but I was still surprised when Christ came to me last night in a dream. He told me that He had great plans for the church and wanted me to meet with Ethan and Claire to get some ideas on where to go from here.

"This morning I told Ethan and Claire how I felt a conference such as this inspires us to serve our fellow man. After returning to our daily routines, we experience a spiritual letdown and try to rekindle the passion. Despite trying to keep an altruistic outlook, being a light in a darkened world wears us out. It's essential then to have a quiet place to go to recharge our spiritual batteries if we want the stamina to run the race to the finish line.

"People may realize they need such a place to go. The problem is that such a place is not readily available, but unless we create such a place in our community, life will return to normal, and this entire experience will have been in vain!

"After I voiced my concern, Ethan and Claire laughed and told me not to worry. Before I could say another word, they told me about an idea the Holy Spirit gave them called the Soul Station. What they told me was exactly what I had heard from Jesus the night before. They have spent several months fleshing out the concept. Before I share what they told me, by way of introduction I want to set the stage by showing you a video. So without further ado, will someone dim the lights?"

Many were completely entranced by what Dr. Bees was saying and hoped he would deliver a sermon as powerful as the one they heard the night before. However, many were touched by the message of the video. They had spent years praying that they would have the foresight and courage to develop a place of spiritual renewal. When people heard Dr. Bees speak, they were reminded of Jesus' words, "Come to me, all you who labor and are heavy laden, and I will give you rest."

Despite the anticipation and joy in the room, there was a small pharisaical faction in the congregation, disparagingly referred to at the 'pharies,' who tried to undermine the evening. They were disgruntled people who enjoyed nothing better than saying no. As Dr. Bees delivered his introduction, he could tell from the glares the pharies gave him and the way they murmured that they were not pleased. They were downright skeptical and felt Dr. Bees was taking an idea too far. They were traditionalists who saw no need to change how they worshipped God. Because of this, they were tempted to show their opposition by getting up and stomping out. However, because Dr. Bees had served them well for years, they gave him the benefit of the doubt waited for him to finish before rendering final judgment.

Dr. Bees' introduction was dramatic. It stirred people's souls and caused them to think about God in a way nothing had before. Using the video as an introduction proved to be very effective. Not only did it give people a basic idea of what the Soul Station was about, but it also gave them the opportunity to consider what life would be like if a constant supply of spiritual nourishment was available. People were jubilant, and their excitement increased.

Dr. Bees had written a sermon with Ethan and Claire's help that he planned to give when the video ended. However, when he stood, he crumpled up his notes, threw them on the floor, and spoke from the heart.

"I can't believe I just did that. I spent all day on that. It was a darn good sermon that discussed point by point how the Soul Station was designed on biblical principles. It would have been a rather intellectually stimulating sermon, if I say so myself.

"However, when I saw your reactions to the video, the Holy Spirit told me to speak to your hearts and not your minds. There just is something supernatural about the video, which filled my soul with an overwhelming majestic peace. The more I watched it, the more I felt as if somehow God was inviting me to draw closer to Him in a deeper and more intimate way.

"For me, watching the video was a truly life-altering experience because it seemed to fill the void like nothing else could. It reminded me that just as our bodies need to rest so we can function, if we want to have the energy to do the work Christ has called us to do, we must rest. God created the Sabbath because He knew how important it was for us to take time out to rest. Some may think that the Sabbath is merely a day to go to church, but it is actually a day to rest and recharge.

"It's obvious to me that many do not understand the concept of spiritual rest. Many gather the wisdom and strength they desperately need by attending church, praying, and going to Bible study. This is good; however, upon learning about the Soul Station, I understood Jesus' command, 'Come to me, all you who labor and are heavy laden, and I will give you rest' in a new way. The Bible tells us that Jesus is always with us and will never leave us. Yet, when we grow weary from our long endless trek through the wilderness, we long for a place to go for comfort and to be refreshed. We also long for the solace of knowing that we are not alone but have a Savior who will help and guide us every step of the way.

"People often associate the idea of spiritual rest with a retreat which does give people a fresh perspective on life. The problem is that retreats happen infrequently, and the effects last only a few weeks. The fact is people need a place of ongoing spiritual rest. Throughout my years of being at this church, I can't tell you how many people long for a local retreat where they can just be still, escape from the confusion of their noisy worlds, and experience God's presence.

"Ethan and Claire, through the Holy Spirit's power, understand the deep longing people have to feel at one with God constantly and have the foresight to take a leap of faith and create the Soul Station. I admit this is a radical, new concept; but I am convinced we desperately need to build one in our community. It will offer a unique opportunity to form a closer relationship with God and help us experience spiritual rest.

"A common line I hear as a pastor is, 'I pray and pray, but God doesn't answer. Why?' Do we ever take time out to listen? Do we know how to quiet ourselves so that we can listen to the still, small voice inside of us? The fact is Jesus promises Christians that He will live inside us and if we seek first the kingdom of God and his righteousness, 'All these things will be added to you.'

"Indeed, watching the video helped me see the potential that the Soul Station will offer. I am convinced that if people took Jesus' command seriously and put Him first above all else, our lives would be much different. Jesus tells us that his disciples must be a special people who are in the world but are not of the world. Furthermore, He tells us not to look to the world for comfort but to turn to our Father who is the ultimate source of comfort. As I watched the video, I took a hard look at myself and wondered why we are so eager to ask others for help or advice instead of going to our Father for help.

"The kingdom of God resides in the hearts of all true believers. If we took Him at His Word, asked, were still, and listened, God would draw us to Him and bless us immensely. The question therefore becomes how do we turn off our incessant internal tape recorders so that we can hear the still, small voice inside of us? Experiencing God's presence is definitely the pinnacle of what it means to be human.

"Being at one with God should be as natural as it is to breathe. However, despite trying many techniques, some simply cannot experience God's presence because they cannot still their minds and tune out the external noise of the world. Some try their best, but in the end become so frustrated that they simply give up.

"As Christians, we know God calls us to separate our hearts and minds from the world. Jesus also promises us that if we trust implicitly and do as He commands, He will be our God and we will be His people. We may know this; yet, because life is so hectic and we are plagued with so many responsibilities, somehow our priorities have shifted. I understand this, but I feel perhaps God in His mercy created the Soul Station as a way to help us get our priorities straight.

"The invitation that God has extended to us is surely an incredible one. Accepting it requires us not only to abandon the ways of the world and our religious preconceptions that weigh us down, but also to fix our eyes on the kingdom of God and His righteousness above all else. Sometimes people fantasize about what it was like to be a disciple when Jesus asked them to pick up, leave everything, and follow Him wherever He leads. Dreaming about this is one thing. Now that God is inviting us to draw closer to Him, even for a short time, we need to ask ourselves two questions: Are we willing to let go of what ties us to earth and follow Him and what is holding us back?

"At times it seems as if there is a barrier between God and us. Despite our fervent attempts to penetrate the barrier of silence and to get close to God, we get nowhere and become very frustrated in the process. Although I don't have all the answers, I want to end this conference by discussing some ways the Bible tells us that we can penetrate this barrier.

"What I'm about to say will certainly offend some people, but as your pastor I feel it's time for some stark truth. From reading the

Bible, I discovered that the early Christians were a powerful people because they devoted their entire lives to doing the will of God and they depended on Him for everything. They understood that they were on earth for a distinct purpose and refused to conform to this world.

"I believe the reason we are not powerful Christians is that we live with one foot in heaven and one foot in the world. The world teaches us to be independent and to stand on our own two feet. Jesus teaches us that if we want to be His hands and feet, we must rely on Him for everything, for we cannot do anything under our own power.

"The story of Peter walking to Jesus on the water illustrates just how helpless we are under our own power. If we truly believe that we can do all things through Christ who strengthens us, we must do our best to seek God and do His will and not allow worldly distractions to sidetrack us from fulfilling our mission. Understanding this requires us to look to Him to meet our every need and desire. Compared to carrying out the will of Christ, everything else is insignificant.

"The video has helped me know that God has heard His people and that the Soul Station is a mechanism to help people cultivate a relationship with Him. I don't think it was an accident that God had us watch this video. He had us see it to show us what to do as a follow up to this extraordinarily powerful conference. In fact, I feel strongly that we could easily renovate one of our unused Sunday school rooms. The only question we must answer is if we have the drive required to follow Jesus and carry out His will."

Confident that he had delivered the most thought-provoking, powerful sermon of his lifetime, Dr. Bees sat down and smiled to himself. As the hymn "Surely the Presence of the Lord Is in This Place" played, he wondered how the people would react to the idea of opening a Soul Station. He was fully aware that his sermon had altered the dynamics of the church forever. In his opinion, whatever backlash he faced would be well worth it, for he was confident that Christ had given him and his church this opportunity. Given the week's activities and his experience at Divine Towels, Dr. Bees decided not to play it safe. Rather, he was going to trust Christ completely and not fear the consequences of his actions.

Listening to the hymn, he observed that many people seemed to be in a contemplative state. Indeed, they were captivated and profoundly moved by the majestic words they had just heard. They felt the Soul Station would satisfy their hearts and souls in a new way and allow them to and experience God's presence firsthand.

Most congregants felt this way. However, a few objected! The sermon had hit a nerve that challenged their idea of who God was and it made them squirm. Once Dr. Bees spoke about the radical concept the Soul Station as a practical application, they believed that he had gone too far and was on the brink of committing heresy!

Initially, the Soul Station seemed like a good idea, and Dr. Bees made some compelling arguments why opening it could be beneficial. From reading Mark 6:31, they understood how important it was to take a break and refuel for the next leg of the journey. The idea of opening a Soul Station as a local retreat center to help people develop a more intimate relationship with God was interesting. The problem was that they believed that the Bible is the Word of God, and that everything anyone might need comes from it.

It was admirable that Dr. Bees was trying to do his job and helping people get closer to Jesus. However, it was clear that he was going off on a tangent. As they sat listening to the song, they realized it was not so much that the concepts were wrong because, on the surface at least, some did seem to be biblically based. Still, they were traditionalists who did not see a need to try something new.

Once the song ended, Dr. Bees planned to give a quick benediction and then prepare for the board meeting. However, he sensed that not everyone accepted the concept of the Soul Station. After taking a deep breath, Dr. Bees stood up and began. "If I had any sense, I would stop right here, let the seeds settle, say a quick benediction, attend the wrap-up session of the committee for the year, and get back to the status quo. The problem is something happened, and I'm unable to continue doing the same old thing. I didn't plan for this to happen. It just did.

"Before I begin, let me say that the conference is officially over. Anyone who wants to leave is welcome to do so. I now invite anyone who wishes to speak to come to the microphone and voice his opinion. It is obvious from looking at your faces that some of you want to talk about your concerns. Rather than having a wrap-up session, because this involves everyone in the congregation, I want us to begin a conversation about where to go now. So without further ado, let the games begin!"

At this time, one of the pharies could not hold her tongue any longer. She had had enough. "Good evening, Dr. Bees," Margaret, a 75-year-old woman began. "I have always had the highest regard for you, but what you have done tonight is way, way over the top; therefore, I must object. I understand that you are trying to help people form a closer, intimate relationship with Jesus. Although this is good, the Bible is the ultimate authority and everything else is a staged gimmick. You dare to tell us to depart from following the letter of the law and adopt a new reality? Look, I understand that Jesus often scolded the Pharisees for being rigid; however, unless we hold to our traditions, we are riding down a slippery slope. I don't mean to ruin this party, but sometimes it's better to hold fast to the line."

Although people understood what she was saying, many were infuriated and felt that the pharies were being shortsighted and very legalistic. In fact, if the people felt strongly about the need to open a Soul Station, hearing the lady say this helped them see why they wanted it even more. Many knew the Word but were still spiritually starved. They saw the Soul Station as a mechanism that would allow them to break through the barrier of silence and have the personal, intimate relationship with God that they always wanted.

When the lady finished, Lisa, who was the quiet type and kept to herself, stood and spoke. "I have been a member of this church for many years and always liked coming here. However, this is without a doubt the best conference I have ever attended. It has breathed new life into my soul. I don't know about you, but to me, the entire feeling in the church has changed radically since the conference began. It's as if a surge of positive energy has enveloped us, and it's clear to me that the Holy Spirit has started a great work.

"Given what has happened here this week and the compelling sermon we just heard, I am incredulous that anyone would suggest that we return to our old ways! I believe God is giving us a tremendous opportunity to move forward and know Him more intimately.

"I don't know about you; but, personally I can't wait for the Soul Station to open because it has the potential to be a true blessing that it will transform lives in ways we cannot imagine. I realize this is all new; nothing like this has been done before. But if we truly want to have life and have it more abundantly, we must be willing to trust Jesus and follow Him wherever He leads. I believe that the kingdom of heaven is within us and that the Soul Station will help us not only get to know Jesus more intimately but also to discover a hidden world that resides within our hearts. Are we willing to listen to our hearts and take a leap of faith the way Ethan and Claire have or are we happy to trudge along in life doing the same old thing, wondering what if?"

The congregation gave a thunderous round of applause, indicating their approval.

"Lisa, I totally agree," Steve said. "The conference was amazing, especially tonight. As many of you know, I'm retired and have always been an active member of the church. I enjoy various maintenance chores around the building. However, as I listened to tonight's sermon, I felt that the Holy Spirit created something in my soul. I feel called to do whatever it takes to get the Soul Station up and running.

"I'm sure many of you are thinking, 'Doesn't he have any respect for the rules and know that anything of this magnitude needs to go before the board and be approved?' To this I ask why do we have to go through this bureaucratic process? It is obvious to me that the idea comes from the Holy Spirit. So why don't we just save ourselves a lot of time and effort, be bold and have a vote? Let's just have a show of hands.

"Why I am so insistent? Why won't I let it go through the normal process? The fact is the idea is wonderful, and I don't want to see politics get in the way, especially when people need it immediately. It is for this reason that I want to make a motion: to convert an unoccupied Sunday school room into a Soul Station." The congregation was surprised by what Steve had proposed. Yes, many of them, including Dr. Bees, were thinking it, but what Steve had done was so bold that people couldn't believe it.

"How dare you! You have no right to make such a statement!" Margaret snarled in total disgust and disbelief. "This is not even a board meeting, and you are not on the board. This violates every bylaw imaginable!"

As she stood there yelling, people looked at her, shook their heads in dismay, and wondered why she was so set in her ways. When Margaret finished ranting, Dr. Bees stood and said, "You actually make a very good point, Steve. Look, I never thought we would ever make this much progress. However, since it is obvious that the Holy Spirit is here and moving us forward at record speed, I think we should definitely consider this motion. And as for Margaret's point, I reviewed the bylaws a few weeks ago. To the best of my knowledge there's nothing in them that states the congregation isn't allowed to hold a vote on a matter, especially since it concerns the future direction on the church."

After pausing for a moment to take a sip of water, Dr. Bees began again. "So, unless someone else has anything to add for the good of the order, I move that we vote on the motion. Since we have never done this before, let's make this simple with a show of . . . ."

"Excuse me, Dr. Bees," Margaret said. "With all due respect, what you are doing is coercion. It certainly cannot and will not be done. I forbid it!"

"Look, Margaret," Dr. Bees said, "we all understand how important it is to conduct church business in an orderly way. It is obvious to me that the congregation is in favor of taking the vote and of establishing a Soul Station. I don't quite see what is unfair about holding a vote. If it doesn't pass, it doesn't pass. At least we will know where everybody stands on the issue. So, having said that, can we please just get on with it?"

"You seem to be missing the main idea, Dr. Bees," Margaret said again. "The point is that the Soul Station is totally un-biblical, and I won't be associated with it. Reading the Bible is the only comfort I need. Why experience it when you can read it?"

"Look, Margaret, it's getting late," Dr. Bees said with an annoyed tone in his voice. "People know how you feel about the matter. Please sit down and let the matter come to a vote." You may have been a founder of the church, but you do not have the right to micromanage and dictate how everything is done.

The vote began. With the exception of a few people voting in the negative, there was an overwhelming positive response. Consequently, it was time to stop deliberating about whether to do it and just roll up their sleeves and make it happen! Obviously people were tired of following the letter of the law and wanted to experience the spirit of the law.

Over the next few months, the Soul Station was built and it thrived. Through the Soul Station, the curtain separating people from God was removed. This allowed people to have a personal encounter with Jesus and learn that He is truly present in their daily lives and wants to be their constant companion and friend.

Spreading Goodwill

Life changed dramatically in Coppertown. There was a tangible transformation in attitude. Although no one could quite explain the sudden explosion of positive energy, it was obvious that the Soul Station was having a powerful effect on those who visited it. Indeed, there was not only an overwhelming peace that came over them, but people who visited the Soul Station also seemed to think differently and seemed to find extraordinary solutions to problems. Others looked at them, were amazed and wondered if they were taking some new type of medication, for there was an amazing clarity in which they thought. It would have been extraordinary enough if it had occurred in just one area of their lives; but it seemed to transform every facet of their being! What was even more amazing was that nothing bothered them and they always seemed eager to take on a new and tougher challenge.

Once everything was up and running, the Lord gave Dr. Bees a new challenge. While he was reading the Acts of the Apostles, Christ came before him and gave him a message that changed his life forever. "My son, you are to be commended greatly for trusting me and doing something quite risky in this age. Because you trusted me, I have laid my hand on you the last few months and allowed your church to flourish.

"The last few months have also been a training time for you where I have tested you to see how you would handle this task. You have acquired many skills that have prepared you well for the task I am about to ask of you. I know this will probably overwhelm you; however, I am confident that you are up to the task. You have worked tirelessly with your congregation to develop the foot-washing ministry as well as a network of support to help those in need. You have changed the image of the church from a building filled with hard wooden pews into a house where people can come and be cared for. I want you to take what you have learned and apply it on a larger level to turn this country into a faith-based nation. I want to provide people with a way out of their mental prisons, just as I freed the Israelites when they were slaves in Egypt. You can think upon this as a modern day Exodus, and I have chosen you to lead the people out of bondage.

"To start, my son, write a letter to the headquarters of all Christian churches and share your story. Explain how one day you woke up and realized that preaching compelling sermons just was not enough to help people get through the week. Tell how you met with people from your church who challenged you to shepherd their congregations in a new way as part of the evangelical conference. Tell what happened at Divine Towels and how life has changed because you trusted me and began a foot-washing ministry at your church. My Holy Spirit has illumined the darkness and has resurrected the Acts of the Apostles. If they are serious about doing this, then I want them to begin by replicating what you have done here."

Though Dr. Bees was delighted that Christ had granted him the opportunity of a lifetime and was quite anxious to do it, he also had no idea if he as a pastor of a small congregation could possibly have any influence on the direction the Church was going. While he supported the larger church by attending meetings and doing his part to support them financially, he did not like the politics of the church. On the surface, it appeared to be all about serving Christ;

however, he knew from experience that part of the Church was corrupt and revolved around money and power.

Until now, serving had been relatively easy, but now that God was demanding more, things did not seem as exciting. At this moment, a slew of questions ran through his mind. How would the letter be received and what would be the outcome? Would the headquarters of the churches be responsive and welcome this new attitude or would they dismiss the whole notion as coming from one of those pastors who was a radical fundamentalist?

If he did as Christ commanded, Dr. Bees knew that in the end things would work out even though the seas would be quite choppy. When he considered this from an intellectual standpoint, if the letter was not well received, his career and everything he had ever worked for would be over. Thus, he found himself on the fence and felt as if a battle of the wills was raging inside of him. For several days, he tried to find what he should do, but it did not help him resolve the issue. He tried praying and asking for guidance about the matter, but nothing helped.

Then one night a dream made the path clear to him. Christ appeared and said, "My son, do not worry about what people think, for truly it is inconsequential. I have a plan and you must trust me. Throughout the ages, I have asked my children to undertake bold initiatives that they thought they could never accomplish. My son, I realize what I am asking you to do is not easy. However, do not fear for you will not be doing this alone. My angels and I will guide you every step of the way."

Dr. Bees awoke and composed the letter. Normally, writing such a letter would be quite challenging. However, he knew that Christ was already with him as He promised. The words flowed as if he were conversing naturally. When he finished, he had the secretary type it and send out a massive pile of mail. Dr. Bees planned a strategy to implement his ideas on a broader level while he waited for responses to the letter.

Though the Church always had a reputation for doing the work of Christ and ministering to those in need, when the leaders of the churches received the letter, many were stunned. They received thought-provoking letters from time to time, but this one was distinctly refreshing in many ways. Instead of rehashing the problems that everyone already knew about, Dr. Bees' letter spoke to core issues, leading many to examine where they planned to lead the church in the future.

One would expect all leaders of the Church to be thrilled at the opportunity to expand their ministries and serve their congregations in a new way, but some felt Dr. Bees' ideas were extreme and wanted no part of them. And some felt it was rather presumptuous for another clergyman to call them to change their leadership style.

There were other officials, however, who were touched by the letter and were reminded of the aspirations they had upon entering the ministry when they had looked forward to inspiring people and spreading the Gospel. They also longed to be shepherds and help the church play an integral role in people's lives. However, as time went on, they had grown weary of the constant uphill battle that came with every new initiative they tried to implement. They tried to convince their people a change would be beneficial. However, after a while they decided they did not want the constant battle.

When they looked at what Dr. Bees' church was accomplishing, they were ashamed and knew they had become lax. They were eager to recapture the passion they had for the job upon entering the priesthood. Yes, they were angry at themselves for compromising their ideals; however, some felt they had been given a second chance.

When the ministers read about everything that was happening with Dr. Bees, they were excited. By virtue of their positions, they knew they could do much to resuscitate the church and give it a new image in society. Adopting such views would create quite a stir for the people under them, but it was time to stop preaching empty words and start putting the Gospel into action.

To gain a sense of where they ought to begin, many turned to the essays they had written when they applied for the positions they currently held. Given the maturity they had acquired over the years, reading the simplistic goals and dreams they had when they were young now seemed unrealistic. Yet, those aspirations were the ones that truly mattered.

Were the people who owned the store extremists who were out to destroy the clergy, or were they genuinely interested in helping to empower people? While they were not sure what to make of it, after visiting the store's Website and reading their mission statement, some officials felt that Ethan and Claire did not have a hidden agenda but truly sought to better humanity.

Before they decided to create a spiritual whirlwind, the ministers would visit the store. Though they were busy people and could have easily sent their representatives to report on what was happening, they were so inspired from reading all the literature that they were eager to take time out of their busy schedules and make an unannounced visit to the store.

Even though they had attended similar evangelical events and they thought they knew exactly what to expect upon arriving, the church leaders were fascinated. They sensed the optimism in the air and saw the way people's eyes sparkled with delight, and they knew God was there and was doing something very special.

Once the ministers visited the store and saw the transformations taking place, they were compelled more than ever to make this become a reality. As they composed the letter, they were quite excited. However, after a few minutes, an unsettling feeling began to brew inside their souls. While they wanted to send the letter to all their clergymen and hoped for a positive response, they knew from past experience that it was best not to waste the postage on the intellectually elite who were autocratic and set in their ways. Not only would such clergymen not read the letter to their parishioners, but they also would do everything they could to undermine them and cause trouble.

What had started out to be joyful was turning into a political nightmare. Their hearts were troubled, and soon they did not know quite what to do. They obviously needed serious help and knew Christ was the only one who could truly help them. "Father, you have answered our prayers and have led us to discover Divine Towels. Yes, it is an incredible ministry, and we are confident that you want us to pursue this vigorously. We understand this as a wonderful opportunity to lead the church in a new direction. Yet, we are not sure if this letter should be sent to all churches in our jurisdiction. We want this to be positive but fear it will backfire and turn into a fiasco that will jeopardize the mission of Divine Towels. Please give us the wisdom to know the most effective way to get the message out."

Opening their hearts, they were given guidance on the best way to proceed. While they did want to send the letter to all members of the clergy under them, the Lord advised them not to be afraid, and if they were to be successful, they needed to start out small. They were told to send the letter out to the parishes that had open-minded clergy who were truly committed to following the Gospel. Jesus went onto explain that once these few parishes showed prosperous results, other parishes would be quick to follow.

Once these church leaders saw how the game plan would play out, they were eager and returned to writing the letter. They explained that while this was not the official position of the church, they felt compelled as leaders to follow their hearts and invite them and their followers to take a journey of intimacy with them. This was the type of work Christ had called the church to do, and it was time the church not only preached the Gospel but also played an active role in bringing it to fruition.

PART TWO: RISING FROM THE ASHES

THE INVITATION

When people are focused on their goal, they are so consumed with what they are doing that everything else is irrelevant. While transformation is a good thing, there are people who detest seeing positive change and people triumph, especially when it affects their lifestyles and they realize they are no longer in control. It is one thing when people are enlightened, but when they refuse to tolerate the status quo and demand change, authority figures feel threatened and will go to whatever lengths necessary to regain control.

When people first received healing, the doctors in town were amazed and thrilled. Yet, as months passed and the doctors felt the economic effects from the competition, they realized they had a serious problem. Because of Divine Towels, patients were canceling their appointments and no longer needed to go to the hospital. As a result, the doctors experienced financial trouble. What had begun as a wonderful gift that was helping people soon turned into a nightmare for many in the medical community and they did not know what to do.

At first, the paradox was rather comical. The doctors, who were used to financial security, saw what it was like not to have life on their own terms. Divine Towels became a success. As the weeks became months and the trend continued, the doctors were rather angry. They did not like this new phenomenon and would not allow Divine Towels to ruin everything they had worked a lifetime to achieve. The only question was how.

The doctors tried to find a plausible solution to the problem, but they were not having much success. As time went by and the more they tried, the more problematic things became. Because Divine Towels was having such a profound negative economic impact on the entire medical community as well as drug companies, something had to be done quickly. Dr. Lows, chief of staff at Coppertown General Hospital, called an emergency staff meeting to see if together they could come up with a solution before the problem became unmanageable.

The doctors at Coppertown General were some of the most renowned in the country and were very adept at handling crises, but they had never handled anything like this before. Dr. Lows was confident, though, that as long as his team worked together and kept their common objective in mind, it would not be difficult to come up with a solution.

At eleven that morning the doctors filed into the conference room as they always did. Normally, staff meetings were routine, but because of recent events everyone was a bit tense. This was evident by all the chatter amongst the doctors before Dr. Lows called the meeting to order.

"Good morning," Dr. Lows said as he took the cap off the red marker. "You all know why I have summoned you here. So let's get right to it. How do we handle the people at Divine Towels and make them realize how much they are hurting us? I want to hear some ideas. Does anyone want to go first?"

Usually everyone was eager to voice an opinion. However, after a few moments of silence, Dr. Lows decided to take a different approach. "Look," Dr. Lows said after a deep breath, "I'm just going to level with you. It's obvious that we have never been in this situation before. I realize it's difficult to understand how this has happened and why people have fallen for all this

Jesus nonsense. I also realize how devastating this has all been for us and how unfair it seems. At one time, we were distinguished doctors who enjoyed prestige and commanded people's respect. Because of Divine Towels, people believe they no longer need us or our services. If we don't want the medical community to be destroyed, we must do something to convince people we are not a disposable commodity.

"If you think this is just about getting our patients back so we can continue living life in the way we are accustomed, you are very narrow minded! I am amused by how smart, educated people who I thought were level headed are falling for this sham. I have not visited Divine Towels, nor do I intend to. However, it is obvious the store is brainwashing people and has cult-like traits.

"It's easy to see that what I am saying is right. Just look at what is happening to the people who visit Divine Towels. Most actually believe that they are somehow 'healed' of their ailments when those frauds wash their feet. This is ludicrous! That's bad enough, but I am astounded by how this little foot washing ritual has drastically altered people's perspective on life. People whom I have known for years seem to have the vitality of a child and are dedicated to sowing seeds of truth and justice in a concrete way. They are tired of the same old stuff that never changes, are sick of being ignored, and are demanding action. It is one thing to bring problems to the public's attention by publishing articles about injustices in the local paper, but they are following up and are holding people accountable.

"These people have become very aggressive. You might think I am being ridiculous and am overreacting, but just open your eyes. We must do everything in our power to stop these radicals, or it will be too late and we will all be out of work.

"I don't profess to have all the answers. However, if we put our heads together and look at this objectively, we should be able to formulate some sort of action plan. So what do you think, doctors, shall we try it?"

The doctors were not sure what to make of this, but after a short time, they realized Dr. Lows was right. If other people could be downright assertive, so could they.

At first, the doctors thought the best way to ward off the competition and to get patients to come back was to embark on a campaign to slander and make false allegations against Ethan and Claire. The doctors realized people never appreciated those who "picked on the good guys." If people discovered what their true motive was, their plan might backfire and could possibly leave them a much bigger problem to contend with.

To prevent a backlash, the doctors decided that it was in their best interest to gain public support. Thus, they would try the diplomatic route before they resorted to other measures. Over the next two hours, they formulated an action plan. No one had all the answers, but once they began talking, one idea flowed into the next. It did not take them long to compile a list of several plausible solutions to carry out their plan.

They considered each option and consequence carefully. After more discussions, they narrowed the list down to three. They were to talk to the owners and give them a firm warning. Then they would appeal to their political allies to make washing feet a crime. Last, they would have them arrested for disrupting the peace. The doctors surmised that if they could scare the founders and make an example of them, their followers would close up shop to avoid the doctors' wrath.

The first option appeared to be the easiest, so they proceeded. They wrote the owners of Divine Towels a letter informing them that they wished to meet with them. Once the letter was written, they sent it as certified mail.

Trusting in forces that you cannot see to guide your life is not easy and is comparable to asking someone without a parachute to jump off a mountain. The question is, do you believe that invisible hands really exist, have a distinct purpose for your life, and that they will be there to act as pillows and cushion the landing before you hit the ground? It's easy to trust Jesus when you are not standing on the edge of a cliff. It's another when you are looking down and Jesus asks you to defy logic, risk it all, and put your life in His hands. Those who keep their eyes on Jesus are surprised to find that wondrous footbridges suddenly appear when they step off the cliff.

Because Ethan and Claire listened to God, Divine Towels was a thriving success. Even with all the help of students from the Foot-Washing Institute, there were always long lines of people who traveled from all over the country to visit the store.

Nancy, the mail carrier, had been delivering mail to the store since its opening and she enjoyed seeing what it had grown into. She even had Ethan wash her feet and had been healed of chronic headaches. She enjoyed delivering the mail, handing it to Jim, stopping for a quick chat, and going on her way. Today was different because she had been asked to deliver the letter from the hospital ethics board and had been given specific instructions to have Ethan and no one else sign for the letter. Nancy entered Divine Towels with the envelope and fought her way through the crowds to find Ethan. "Ethan, I'm sorry to bother you, but I have a letter for you to sign."

He signed the paper, smiled as he put the letter in his back pocket, and thanked Nancy. At closing time after everything had been cleaned up for the day, Ethan took the letter from his pocket. Seeing that it was from ethics board at Coppertown General Hospital, Ethan could not imagine why they were writing to him. Full of curiosity, Ethan ripped open the letter and began reading.

Dear Sir:

The Ethics Board at Coppertown General Hospital has been monitoring your work closely for the last few months and is aware of the numerous miracles you have performed in the community. We are admirers of your work, especially in the cancer support groups. We also consider you and your mother to be valued additions in the medical community. Over the last few months, you have developed quite a reputation throughout the town and country.

Though you may practice alternative medicine, your results are impressive and you have had such a profound impact on the lives of others. You have caused their spirits to be revitalized and have a renewed purpose in life. We are very interested in getting to know you and your mother better and learning about the extraordinary techniques you use. We would be greatly honored if you would meet with us so we can gain a better understanding of your unique gifts and exactly what you do as well as your methodology.

We understand that you and your mother are busy. Consequently, we have taken the liberty of setting some tentative dates that work for us. Please let us know which one works best for you. We look forward to hearing from you soon. Thank you for your time, and best of luck in your future endeavors.

Cordially yours,

James S. Lows, M. D.
President of the Ethics Board

P.S. If it wouldn't be too much of an inconvenience for you, we would appreciate it greatly if you would bring a few towels along to demonstrate to the board how they work.

Ethan was elated and could not believe how much God was smiling upon him and his mother. Because he had been faithful and had done what God had asked, God was blessing him even more by granting them this incredible opportunity to expand this ministry and serve a wider audience. What started out as a dream had not only turned into reality, but was on the verge of growing by leaps and bounds. Ethan was so overjoyed that he squealed with delight, and he could not wait to share this wonderful news with his mother.

Ethan walked into the back room where Claire was working on the computer and stood there smiling with the letter in his hand. "Mom," Ethan said, "you have to read this. Something extraordinarily wonderful has just happened."

"Okay, I'm always up for a good surprise. Let's see what all this excitement is about."

Claire could not believe what she was reading. It sounded like a dream come true. Claire was excited that they had been invited to this meeting and hoped that it would be a positive experience. Yet, something about the tone made her uneasy.

"This is certainly interesting, I'll give you that much," Claire said as she folded up the letter. "However, I must be honest with you. While I am excited about the possibilities of working with them, there is something disturbing about it. I can feel it. Just think about it for a minute. We have been open for nearly four months and now the ethics board at the hospital wants to meet with us. Don't you think it's a bit strange that we're being summoned to appear before this board, especially when we don't even do any business with the hospital?

"You probably think I'm overreacting, Ethan, but that's my take on the situation. Then again, I could be totally wrong. Perhaps it is legitimate and is the next logical step God is guiding us to take. I suppose it's worth going and finding out what they want. The worst-case scenario is that we get up and walk out if we don't like what they have to say. Go ahead, call them. Let's hear them with an open mind."

Initially when Ethan read the letter, he was exuberant. However, after hearing his mother's reaction and rereading the letter, he wasn't quite sure what to think. The letter appeared to be genuine, but perhaps it was a vehicle meant to lull them into a false sense of security. Had Ethan become so focused on expanding the business that he was willing to be tantalized by whatever bait came along? If this were the case, Ethan had no business being Christ's instrument.

Because Ethan was not sure how to proceed, he got down on his knees and asked for guidance. "Father, thank you for giving us this opportunity. I know that this is a gift from you, but I'm not sure what to do. Mom sees it one way, and I see it another. My intention is to serve you and do your will in all things. Please instill me with your Holy Spirit and give me clear direction on what You want us to do. I ask all these things in the name of Jesus. Amen."

Ethan sat in silence and focused on quieting his mind and opening his heart so he could receive wisdom from above. He imagined that Jesus was in the room and was enveloping his being with warm tingling light. The more aware he became, the more he tuned out the distractions around him. Soon he found himself in the middle of a Beautiful garden surrounded by exotic flowers of every color. After a few minutes, a man dressed in a white robe approached him. As they gazed in each other's eyes, somehow Ethan knew that Jesus was in front of him.

Jesus bid him to sit down. "Oh, blessed child," Jesus began as he stroked Ethan's head, "I am very proud of all you and your mother have accomplished. You have trusted and have done what I have asked. Now that I have seen that you have done well with what I have given you, others doors are about to open. You and your mother are well liked in the community and have rekindled a spark of hope that has been lost for so long, but be warned. There are forces at work that cannot stand the progress you have made, and they are planning your failure. However, my child, do not fear what lies ahead for I am with you.

"Over the years many of my people have been very faithful to me and have tried their utmost to carry out the Great Commission and empower others along the way. Many have made significant contributions and have changed lives in ways they are not even aware of. Yet, as is too often the case, there are times when my people feel that their years of hard work and dedication have all been in vain. They feel that, no matter how hard they try to do the right thing, a force is constantly trying to undermine their efforts. While it is the desire of my servants' hearts to carry out my will, after a while they become frustrated. Realizing there is nothing else they can do to win the battle, they reluctantly give up and spend the rest of their lives agonizing over their defeat.

"I have seen the great disappointments on my children's faces, have heard their cries for help, and have decided to act. For too long, the enemy has done everything possible to make life as hard as he can for my beloved people who yearn to do my will and to reward those who do the oppressing. I have decided to intervene and help my people by starting a revolution, and I need your help. Your mother and you are doing a marvelous job and have helped people to come to know me more profoundly and have gone on to do mighty works for me. Now that I see that you are faithful no matter what the circumstances may be, I have chosen you, as I have chosen others throughout the ages, to make a difference in the world.

"I could easily give you a preview of some significant events that will occur over the next few months, but it is much better if I guide you step by step. Though your mother and you are very strong, if I were to make my plans known to you, it would overwhelm you and your mother to the point where you would not be able to carry out the work I need done. However, suffice it to say, people will no longer be complacent but will feel empowered to stand up and refuse to be oppressed ever again. If you trust me, the world will never be the same again! I promise you that. Although you would love to stay here with me, it is time for you to return and get busy. Remember, I am with you always; I will never forsake you."

Ethan returned to his mother's desk and saw things with enormous clarity. He said to her, "You make a valid point. While I do want us to meet with them, it is very important that we stand our ground from the start so there is no chance that we are misunderstood. We are there to explain that we are merely the vehicles that Christ uses to heal people. If they can accept that healing is given to those who have faith, then I would like to work with them. On the other hand, if they are not receptive, then I agree we should shake the dust off our feet and move on. While I will feel sorry for them, we have far too much work to accomplish to worry about what 'the officials' think. Besides, we are not in control of any of this anyway. We are merely here to be Christ's instruments, and He is the one who will ultimately decide how He wants to use us."

Claire smiled, indicating that she agreed with this approach. She knew Ethan was perceptive, and it pleased her to see how he was able to discern what was truly happening. Once they agreed on a plan, Ethan called and made an appointment to meet with the doctors the following week. Ethan and Claire were quite excited about the meeting; they were confident that the Holy Spirit would be with them and would guide them on what to say. Consequently, they agreed not to talk or think about the meeting but rather to keep their attention on living in the present and doing the work Christ had called them to do. Many people still needed their help, and if they were to divert their attention from their mission, they would be doing a disservice to the people in the community and would be undermining the mission to which they had been called.

It would have been quite easy for Ethan and Claire to allow their excitement to go to their heads. However, they had read stories and seen others who had started out with the same noble intentions as they did. Though many of these people remained true to their calling, others enjoyed the attention and allowed it to feed their ego. Instead of remaining humble, keeping their eyes on Christ, and trusting Him to guide their every step, such people soon became highly impressed with themselves and bragged about the tremendous gift and power they had been given. Although these people may have started out with the best of intentions, they succumbed to greed and power, turning the gift Christ had given them to help people into a mockery.

Much to their dismay, Ethan and Claire had seen many friends do this sort of thing and it sickened them. They understood the severe consequences that went along with going astray and distorting a beautiful gift for their own gain. While it saddened Ethan and Claire to see this, they dared not even to venture to put a single toe on that slippery slope. For while it truly was exciting that Christ had given them this opportunity, if they wanted to remain true to the mission Christ had called them to, they had to be humble and trust Him completely. Because of their unending dedication to the accomplishment of this goal, they were to experience many glories that they would never have otherwise.

During the next week, Ethan and Claire were very involved tending to the needs of others. They hardly had time to think about their meeting at the hospital until an hour before it was t.ime to go. As they drove to the hospital, their apprehension grew. They tried the best they could to put the matter into God's hands and to trust that the Holy Spirit would guide them on what they were supposed to do and say.

Ethan and Claire entered the room where the meeting would be held, and the doctors and administrators who sat on the hospital's board greeted them quite cordially. After setting up the room and five minutes of chitchat, Dr. Lows called the meeting to order.

"Well, let's get started then. We have a lot to do and this might take a while. On behalf of the board, let me start by thanking you both for accepting our invitation. We know you are extremely busy these days, and we are very appreciative that you took time out of your schedules to come talk to us and explain what it is that you do."

"You're welcome," Claire said. "We are always willing to discuss our ideas with people like you who wish to be enlightened."

Dr. Lows continued. "I'm sure you both have been wondering why we wanted to meet you. Since we are all adults, let's get right to the point. The purpose of this meeting, as we see it, is twofold. One, we want to learn how the so-called "healings" occur, and two, we want to voice a few concerns we have. While we have much to ask you, we would like to engage in an open dialog.

"We have heard about and seen many people who claim that you have healed them from their many ailments simply by washing their feet with a towel. At first when we heard that this was happening, I must admit I dismissed it as some sort of fluke. However, when more and more of our terminally ill patients came in and we saw the results of their tests, we could not help but be amazed. Yes, maybe we could understand it if it had happened to a handful of people, but this just kept on repeating itself.

"Many in the medical community are talking about the work you are doing. We think it is quite wonderful that God has given you the power to heal others. We, who are trained in the science of medicine, are amazed by this phenomenon and would like you to demonstrate to us how you heal others. After all, we are colleagues and if one of us has found a novel way to treat people with their medical or psychiatric problems it is best for all if this knowledge is shared so more people can be helped. Wouldn't you agree?"

"Yes," Claire said with much hesitation. Although the men were making sense with what they were saying, there was something about the snide way Dr. Lows spoke that got under Claire's skin. However, in order to help the patients, she refrained.

"Good. For demonstration purposes, we have selected Sara, a patient who is paralyzed. We have treated her with the best medicine available, but unfortunately there is nothing more the medical community can do for her. Maybe you can help her."

Since doctors and administrators would be watching their every move, Ethan and Claire felt a bit uncomfortable about performing the healing. However, upon thinking about Sara was suffering, they gave in. Ethan and Claire realized that the board would carefully scrutinize their actions. They understood that they were not here to amuse the doctors, but rather to help the patients. Therefore, it really did not concern them what those who were "in charge" thought. They had a job to do, and they were not going to allow this annoying distraction to get in their way.

"Okay then," Claire said after a brief pause pretending not to be perturbed by Dr. Lows' sarcastic attitude. "Bring her in and let's get started. Will one of you be kind enough to fetch us some water?" Once Claire had gotten everything setup for the demonstration, she told Sara to please come forward.

Sara Wash was a 19-year-old girl whose aspirations to become a world-class horseback rider were shattered one day during a practice run in preparation for a national championship. Her prized horse shied away five feet from jumping over a fence, and Sara was thrown off. She suffered a spinal cord injury that left her paralyzed.

Despite intensive physical therapy and other interventions to help her regain feeling in her limbs, the prognosis was dim because the nerves had been damaged. Sara, who had been an energetic girl with much enthusiasm, spent her days in her wheelchair looking out the window for hours on end in a state of dismay. She asked herself repeatedly why this happened to her and she tried to figure out what was she going to do with the rest of her life. Her dreams had been shattered and she held out little hope for the future.

Sara had been depressed for three years, and she just did not feel like talking to anyone. No one understood her frustration and anger, and nothing that anyone could say would give her back the life she once had. Sara's mother visited and cared for her every day. However, as time passed Sara did not improve. Her mother grew weary. Sara sensed that her mother was tired and wanted to resume a normal life. Sara knew her mother loved her, but it killed her to see what her mother's life had become because her daughter was crippled and could no longer care for herself.

Sara spent much time reminiscing about the past. However, it was but a passing thought as life seemed to drag on without any relief in sight. Sara hated her disability and longed for life to return to normal, but how? Sara cried, but there was no one to hear and no solution to her problems. Doctors prescribed drugs to help her deal with the psychological turmoil. Although they had good intentions and empathized with her, they knew that until she ultimately came to terms with her lot in life that she would never have peace.

Before the accident, Sara took long walks in the woods to clear her head. Now that she was confined to a wheelchair, she found it impossible to escape. She knew the doctors were right, but she was filled with so much uncontrollable anger at God for placing her in this situation and taking her dreams, that she just did not know how to deal with it. Specifically, the three things that proved to be the most difficult were the confinement, her total dependence on others and her inability to help anyone else.

Sara was a deep thinker and had always sought to live life to its fullest, making the most out of every moment. She was curious and enjoyed watching other people. After talking to people she discovered that beneath the facade they put on, they were tired of their mundane routines and sought escape from living their lives on automatic pilot. While she empathized with them, she vowed to do everything possible to prevent herself from becoming complacent.

Sara had been through a great deal in her life and had always managed to rise above every stressful situation she encountered. Ever since the accident, everything was different. Losing her ability to walk and to function independently was something she was entirely unprepared to deal with. Sara didn't have much faith, but she found herself pleading with God for mercy and to deliver her from this horrific situation. She hated it and had no qualms telling God just how angry she was. It wasn't fair! It just wasn't fair! She had every right to be angry. There just didn't seem to be any logical explanation why this tragedy had to happen to her. She was a good person and didn't deserve this! Didn't God love her, and if He did, why was He abandoning her?

In the midst of Sara's great despair, just when it seemed that all hope was lost, the course of her life changed. One night as she was flipping through the television channels, she inadvertently stumbled upon a weekly news show which featured a segment about a miraculous store in a town that was a 15-minute drive from the hospital. According to the news report, this store was taking the region by storm. People went to this store and were healed of their ailments. These same people also underwent unusual transformations. They could not really describe what happened but felt as if their central nervous system had been shocked. Consequently, they saw life in a different way and started to act in a new way.

When she saw this segment and the amazing things people were doing, something clicked. For the first time since the accident, she felt energized and thought perhaps there was a reason to live. It was as though an earthquake had shaken her out of the depression she had been in for years. Watching the show, she realized that though her body did not function, it did not mean she was not useful. Sara had a good mind and had much to offer the world. While Sara was not sure what she was supposed to do, she wanted more than anything to go to Divine Towels and have her feet washed.

With this new mindset, Sara turned on her powered wheelchair, went into the hallway, and asked the nurse for a phone book. The nurses stood there in disbelief. It was the first time in three years that she had left her room and asked any of the nurses for anything.

"Excuse me," Sara said, "could you look up a number and dial it for me?"

"Why certainly," a nurse replied as she grabbed the phone book. "Whom do you want to call?"

"Ah, I think the name of the store is Divine Towels, but I'm not sure," Sara said with a level of uncertainty in her voice.

"Divine Towels, Divine Towels," the nurse repeated as she flipped through the pages.

That name sounded familiar to the nurse, but she just could not remember where she had heard it, and by now it was driving her crazy. Fortunately, Sara's regular nurse, Sandy, overheard this and joined the conversation.

"Sara," Sandy replied, "I was just heading to your room to talk to you about something. If you are interested in going to Divine Towels, don't bother. I got an email from Dr. Lows yesterday announcing that the people from Divine Towels will be coming here next week to demonstrate how the towels heal people. Dr. Lows is looking for volunteers and wondered if you were interested in participating."

"Yes, yes, I am interested," Sara answered without hesitation. "I don't want to live the rest of my life like this. I am willing to try everything and anything, if there is a possibility that it could improve the quality of my life or even give me my old life back. Only a fool would say no to an opportunity like this!"

Until the time Sara had seen the story on television, her day consisted of watching television, sleeping, and staring into space. However, the show acted as a stimulant. It awakened Sara from her mental coma. Now that she was alert again, Sara spent a good deal of time contemplating her life, trying to make sense of what was happening.

Sara had not had a relationship with God before and she did not know how to pray, so she pretended there was someone in the room. As Sara began to talk, the dam of emotion that had been building up inside her for years cracked. She admitted that she felt hopelessly lost, abandoned, trapped in a body with no way out, and could not stand to live like this any longer.

Sara lamented the fact that she had spent the last three years of her life sitting in her room depressed about being trapped in her body and not being able to do a thing about it. Now she realized she had to stop feeling sorry for herself and make decisions to change her life. Unless she did this, nothing in her life would get any better.

Sara knew what she needed to do but could not make it happen, despite how hard she tried. Yes, a positive attitude can help you get through anything, but the fact remained she would have to live in an institutionalized setting for the rest of her life because of her accident. She prayed and asked God to help and show her what to do, but she felt trapped. Not only did her disability affect her body, but it had imprisoned her mind as well. Initially, Sara was frustrated and couldn't understand why God was ignoring her when she needed Him most. Yet, when she stopped and remembered that she would meet with the people from Divine Towels the following week, she wondered if this would be God's way of answering her prayer. Hence, Sara was anxious for the following week to come so she could see what God had in store for her.

Finally, the day came for the people from Divine Towels to visit the hospital. Unsure of what to expect, Sara was apprehensive. However, she became calm when she entered the room and saw Claire. At that moment, Sara realized that God had allowed her to become paralyzed for several reasons. The first was so she would understand what it was like to experience loss. The second was so she would have the opportunity to meet Ethan and Claire and see life had in store for her.

Claire went to Sara and removed her shoes and socks. As soon as she touched Sara's ankle, Claire felt a strange tight sensation in her neck. It was strange but as Claire continued to loosen Sara's shoelace, the feeling not only persisted but intensified. Ordinarily,

Ethan didn't watch his mother do the healings, but as he watched he knew right away what was happening.

The two of them had performed many healings, and on rare occasions they both met people with whom they bonded. Ethan stepped in to help Claire remove Sara's socks and shoes. Ethan helped his mother and became meshed with Sara in the same manner. This was very strange, yet he sensed that this encounter was far from an accident and that Christ had brought them together for a special reason. Rather than permitting his mind to focus on all that Christ had planned for the three of them, he concentrated on the task at hand. An uncomfortable feeling came over Ethan for he sensed that an evil spirit sought to prevent the healing. Without hesitation, Ethan snapped at the spirit, rebuking it, and commanding it to return to Christ at once for destruction. At the same time, Ethan also asked Christ to send his angels to protect them from the forces which intended to do them harm.

The shoes that had been so difficult to untie suddenly fell off Sara's feet and hit the ground. While no words were exchanged, Claire knew that Ethan had prayed. Though the next hour would be difficult, she knew that Christ would be with them and wouldn't allow them to walk through the dark, lonesome valley alone.

Once the socks were off Claire washed Sara's feet, gently rubbing her skin with her thumbs. As she did this, Claire looked up into Sara's blue eyes and asked, "Do you believe?"

Sara, who was too choked up to speak, nodded yes.

Claire picked up a towel and asked to be Christ's hands and feet in whatever way He chose. When Claire placed the towel on Sara's feet and began drying them, a current of energy started to vibrate in her hands. Once Claire placed her hand on Sara's foot, all havoc broke loose. The demonic forces that had disappeared suddenly resurfaced. Instantly, there was a tug-of-war inside Sara's body to determine which force would prevail. On one hand, a current of positive energy pulsated through her body to her brain where it short-circuited the nerve centers so synapses could occur and mend them back together. On the other hand, a negative force tried to prevent this from happening.

For years, meteorologists have studied the detrimental effects of thunderstorms when warm and cold air try to occupy the same space at the same time. Yet, when these forces enter flesh, it is difficult to determine the effects on the body. This is what happened to Sara when Claire began drying Sara's feet with the towel. When the goodness of the towel collided with the poison of her illness, it was such a tremendous shock to Sara's system that it reached a point where her poor body could not handle it any longer causing her to have epileptic convulsions. The people panicked because they had no idea what was happening or what to do. Sara had never had a seizure before, and it just seemed a bit strange that drying her feet would cause such an adverse reaction.

The doctors rushed frantically to Sara's side surrounding her with pillows so she would not hurt herself. Meanwhile, as Dr. Lows paced back and forth across the room he screamed, "What have you done to her? Just look at the mess you have created. Sara thought her life was awful before, but now look at her? Not only is her body in a vegetative state but now, thanks to you and your so-called 'healing towel,' she will probably be in a coma for God knows how long. Congratulations on taking a bad situation and making it ten times worse. I knew this was a bad idea, and I should have never allowed my colleagues to talk me into this!"

After a brief pause, he frantically continued, "What am I going to tell her mother? 'Gee, Mrs. Wash, we are really sorry. However, we would like to inform you that we tried a form of prayer that was supposed to work but it didn't, and now your daughter, whom we were supposed to be taking care of, is in a coma. What's more, we don't know how long it will last or if she will ever come out of it.' Give me a break. Just do me a favor for all our sakes, get out of town and stop this healing stuff. You, like the rest of them, are nothing but frauds and this is proof of it."

While Dr. Lows and the others were carrying on, Claire calmly held the towel tightly against Sara's foot. The doctors just could not understand why Claire was doing this. Couldn't she see what her actions had done and that holding the towel on her foot wasn't helping? Pleading with Claire to stop and allow them to do their jobs proved to be of no avail, so the doctors appealed to Ethan's rational side and begged him to intercede.

It was quite understandable why the doctors reacted the way they did. After all, their necks would be on the line; if anything were to go awry, they would be responsible. In their great haste to prevent Sara from harming herself, they missed what was occurring. Just as the doctor was about to uncap the needle and inject her with a sedative, Sara's convulsions ceased, and she became calm.

Within a few minutes, Sara opened her eyes, moaned, and slowly twitched her hands and shoulders. At first, the doctors thought this was merely a muscle flinch or something. However, when the twitches persisted and were accompanied by toe and ankle movements, the doctors were simply astounded and realized that something miraculous had happened.

Sara moved her eyes and became reacquainted with her environment. She felt something had altered the core of her being, but she didn't know exactly how to describe it. It was as if she had taken the ultimate bath and had been washed afresh. She gained a new appreciation for the intricacies and complexities of life. It was as if up until this time she had been living life in a thick, dense fog and only had a limited, distorted conception of what life was about. Now that the fog had lifted, she knew God had answered her prayer and was giving her a second chance at life. She was determined to make the most of it. Not only did she see in life in a new way, but she also felt liberated from the shackles of heaviness that had oppressed her for so long.

"What just happened?" Sara asked. "For some reason I feel tingly all over as if I just had a massage." After a brief pause, she chuckled and continued. "Despite how strange this may sound, I can almost actually feel the blood circulating through my body."

The doctors mumbled among themselves and wondered what had happened and what would happen next.

"Do you feel this?" Claire asked as she gently clasped her hands.

"Oh my God, I do, I do. Praise God in heaven above," Sara exclaimed enthusiastically.

As she said this, she moved her arms slightly. Sara soon discovered that the more she praised Christ for the miracles he had done in her, the more she was able to move. The praise continued as Sara raised her arms and sang about the wonders Christ had bestowed on her. After a few minutes, Sara felt a steady, warm flow of energy stream down her spine into her legs. Sara sensed that though she had sat in her wheelchair for three years, she was able to get up and walk.

However, before she got caught up in the moment and acted rashly, Sara decided it would be a good idea to hold onto something in case she fell. "Hey, Ethan and Claire, let's get show on the road. Why don't you come over here and help me get out of the chair that I have been in for way too long."

Ethan and Claire were more than happy to oblige. Before Dr. Lows could stop them, Ethan and Claire stood on either side of Sara and grabbed her under each arm. Within a minute, Sara placed her feet firmly on the ground and stood up. Sara was overwhelmed and realized that her faith had cured her.

All this was well and good, but then the real test came. Would she be able to walk? Everyone was excited that Sara would take a leap of faith and step forward. Wanting her to be successful, they were quiet so she could concentrate on the task.

Sara felt as though Christ was asking her to walk to Him on the water. Until this time Sara had been quite optimistic and kept her focus on Christ and praising Him; however, the idea of walking was overwhelming to her. Sara had been standing fine, but suddenly she felt weak in the knees and ended up sitting back down in her wheelchair. Everyone was a bit disappointed that she had fallen but quickly reassured Sara that she had accomplished a lot and should not be disheartened.

Understandably, Sara was disappointed but realized everyone was right; Christ had healed her so much already. She attributed her inability to walk to the fact that she was expecting too much. After all, Rome wasn't built in a day. Meanwhile, Claire, who had been deeply entrenched in prayer, received a wonderful yet frightening message. Claire was aware that Sara was no doubt very tired; nonetheless, Claire felt guided by the Holy Spirit to challenge Sara's faith even further.

After a prayer for guidance, Claire faced Sara and lovingly held her hand. "Sara," Claire said as she stroked her hand, "you have shown great faith and because of it you have been rewarded. In addition to the healing you have received, Christ has blessed you with the gift of His presence. This is a special gift. All you have to do is make up your mind that you desire to make something happen, try your utmost to make it happen, and it will happen."

Throughout life, there are a few rare moments that truly affect the core of one's being so profoundly that the course of his entire life is altered. This was definitely one of these moments for Sara. Hearing Claire's words, Sara, who had been quite pleased with herself, was troubled. She had indeed put these words into practice a few minutes ago, but she had failed miserably.

Within seconds, Sara began to cry. "I heard the words that you have just spoken and I did precisely what you said; yet when I tried to walk, my foot wouldn't move. I do believe I can do whatever I set my mind to, but sometimes circumstances are beyond our control. Surely, even you must agree with that."

Sara could have rattled off numerous examples to illustrate this point, but there was no point. The room was silent in anticipation of Claire's answer. It would have been easy for Claire to disregard Sara's comment and utter some clever witticism. But doing that would be counterproductive and wouldn't solve the issue at hand. Claire knew Sara was right and had often felt the same way on several occasions herself.

"You do raise a good point and one that I have heard from many people. Just like you, I do not have all the answers. I believe God will grant any request if we meet two requirements. We seek above all else to do Christ's will and ask for things that will make the world a better place. We must be willing to live the quote 'I can do all things through Christ who strengthens me,'" Claire said, as she gently stroked Sara's head.

These simple words were very powerful and clear. Though many had heard these words before, somehow they heard them in a new light and felt they could apply these concepts to solve the problems in their lives.

When Sara examined her actions, she identified with Peter as he walked on water. She realized her knees had buckled not because she was tired, but rather because she had taken her focus off Christ. She also realized that only with Christ's help, could she, in fact, do all things. She asked Ethan and Claire to help her to her feet once more. She repeated the phrase, "I can do all things through Christ who strengthens me," and the stiffness in her legs vanished. Slowly she lifted her foot and put it forward as she held onto Ethan and Claire's hands. Once she established a rhythm, Sara weaned herself down to only holding one hand and then none at all. Sara knew in her heart that the words Claire had spoken were truly divine. Sara realized she had been given healing so she could bear witness to others and help them discover the truth.

THE STERN WARNING

Once Sara left the room and walked away as if nothing had ever been wrong, the board members gaped. Before Ethan and Claire arrived, the board had reviewed Sara's medical history extensively and had confirmed that her medical condition was indeed authentic. However, as they sat and reflected on what had happened, they were quite confounded. What they had witnessed seemed to contradict everything they had ever learned.

After several moments, they snapped back, realizing Ethan and Claire were still there. Despite what had just happened and their own beliefs, as representatives of the hospital, they were bound to continue as planned and issue the strong warning.

"Well, then," Dr. Lows said after a brief pause. "It is clear to us that the things we hear about you are true. We have all enjoyed seeing you perform these miracles and are astounded by the positive impact these healings have had on the community. While you certainly deserve to be commended, you have caused quite a problem in the medical profession."

"What do you mean?" Claire asked innocently.

"How do I put this diplomatically? The truth is, I can't, and rather than sit here and skirt the issue, let me just be frank. You are monopolizing the health care market and have put many health care providers out of work. Sick people are no longer coming to us for treatment and our waiting rooms are empty! Many doctors are letting their help go and are unable to make a living. Therefore, on behalf of the staff at Coppertown General and the medical community at large, we implore you to stop."

What Dr. Lows was suggesting seemed so far-fetched that Ethan and Claire just looked at each other and began to laugh uncontrollably. "I'm sorry to laugh," Claire said, "but you can't really expect us to take you seriously. I mean, we are only two people with a handful of helpers who are lowly instruments through which Christ chooses to work when He wills. How can established medical doctors possibly consider us competition or be threatened by us? Besides, there are millions of people who are sick and there is no way we can possibly see everyone in the vicinity of Coppertown much less the nation."

"I'm glad you find us to be so amusing. However, we are very serious about this matter, and we hope you heed our advice. We brought you here because we like you and would hate to have to take further action."

Ethan became outraged and could have easily lunged for Dr. Lows' throat. "Just a minute," Ethan said. "Before we lose our tempers, let's just take a minute and see if we can work this out. How can you threaten to take further action against us; after all, we have not even done anything wrong?"

"Didn't you ever hear of a monopoly? Don't you know that it is against the law to have a monopoly and you could get serious jail time?" the chief of staff remarked.

"Your claims are unsubstantiated," Ethan screamed out of frustration. "Fear and intimidation tactics are not going to work with me. I understand you are afraid that your prestigious careers are in jeopardy of collapsing and will go to any lengths to keep it from happening. That is all well and good. However, have some dignity and don't stoop to this level in order to save your profession. It's a pathetic argument, and frankly, it looks as if you're just grabbing at straws.

"If you had given me a chance, before jumping down my throat, I would have told you that my motivation for doing this is not money or to gain a competitive edge over you, but strictly to help other people. However, to prove to you that this is not a monopoly, I am going to turn the other cheek and offer you the opportunity of a lifetime. As I said before, so many people are suffering that my mother and I will never get the chance to meet and heal them all.

"Lately we have been inundated by the swarms of people who seek our help. We are simply overwhelmed. It is exhilarating to see God moving in wonderful ways, but it is also exhausting. Although we have others to help us and have trained them in the art of foot washing, our business is growing at such a rapid rate that we are in desperate need of some help. We have been praying, asking God to show us the way and provide us with help. In fact. . . ." At that moment, Ethan closed his eyes for a second, received a vision, and began to laugh hysterically at the irony of the situation.

"What in the world is so funny, Ethan?" Dr. Lows asked.

"Don't you see? God has quite a warped sense of humor? We both are in need and God has put us, the odd couple, together so we can help each other. You need money to support yourselves and I need help," Ethan replied enthusiastically.

"Surely, you're not suggesting. . . ." Dr. Lows said. Ethan just stood there, with a big grin on his face, his head bobbing up and down in total amusement.

After Dr. Lows mulled it over awhile, he also laughed. "You talk about ridiculous; now that is what I call absolutely insane. My God, if we did that, we would lose so much credibility and respect among our peers and patients that we could not possibly live with ourselves. It would be like abandoning our profession that has had a long history of doing good work. What's more, why should we have to give up our ways of doing business and caring for people when you were the ones who came in, uninvited mind you, and invaded our territory? You know, you could have asked. Things were so much simpler before you came along! Listen to me. Why am I even considering this? It is humiliating and demeaning.

"You have a great nerve coming here and suggesting that we abandon our cause and help you after we had the decency to invite you here. You are the rebel who has created this situation for us. Since you and your mother can't take a hint, let me be clear. We have no intention whatsoever of joining forces with you."

"Just a minute, Dr. Lows," Dr. Nassa interrupted. "Before we dismiss this as being a crazy idea, perhaps it might be in our best interest to consider Ethan's offer. After all, we got into this business because we wanted to help people. Perhaps it would be an opportunity to write a new chapter in medical history. We don't hesitate to use a new drug that researchers develop with to fight a disease, so why would we be afraid to help wash feet if it achieves the same result? If our objective is to help our patients and we can still make a living doing it, then why wouldn't we want to use any means within our power to help our patients?"

"Excuse us for a minute," Dr. Lows said with a forced smile. "Dr. Nassa," he said in a stern voice as he pinched her arm very hard, "may I please have a word with you outside now?"

Dr. Nassa caught sight of Dr. Lows' glare and stepped outside the room. "Look, Nassa, I don't know what you're trying to pull, but it needs to stop right now! Who are you to humiliate your colleagues? You are a good doctor, and I know you care about your patients. However, part of being a good doctor also means doing what is in the best interest of the medical community, even if you don't happen to agree. Look, I'm sorry I came down hard on you, but we have to stop this from happening. before things get out of control. You have a bright future here. So just go in there, be quiet, and let me finish. Trust me, I know everyone has been quite tense lately, but don't worry. Once we deal with this, life will return to normal. You'll see."

With that, Dr. Lows patted Dr. Nassa on the shoulder and the two returned to the room and took their seats. "Sorry about that," Dr. Lows said. "As I was saying, we don't want to be associated with you in any way, and Coppertown General has authorized me to give you a check to shut down your operation and take it elsewhere." Dr. Lows slid the envelope across the table.

Dr. Nassa, who was enraged at Dr. Lows' behavior before she had been called out of the room, was unable to stomach the sarcasm anymore. She could not remain quiet any longer. With no hesitation, Dr. Nassa stood and slammed the stethoscope that had been draped around her neck on the table in a fit of rage.

"I resign as of this moment! Your behavior today has reached a new all time low, and I can't stand the thought of even being associated with any one of you. What you have just done to these wonderful people makes me sick. As doctors, we should to do everything in our power to help our patients. Now that someone has come up with a way truly to help people, we want to pay them off and get them out of town? You people are sick and are nothing but hypocrites.

"When I was in college, I aspired to be a doctor and help people. But once I became a doctor, it was not the same. Office visits consist of seeing people, ordering tests, reading results, and writing prescriptions. You don't hear from patients again until they have another problem. Bedside manner is a thing of the past. Money is the driving force. The game plan is to get them in and out fast so you can get to the next person on the table. We help people, but only if they have the right insurance.

"You don't like Ethan and Claire because they are doing what you should be doing. Whether or not you want to admit it, you envy the work that is being done at Divine Towels. Rather than allowing our jealousy to turn us into vindictive people seeking revenge to prove a point, perhaps it would behoove us to re-examine the situation."

By this time, Dr. Lows and the other committee members were livid. Dr. Nassa was accurate and to the point, but where was her loyalty to the profession? Dr. Lows banged the gavel so forcefully that he broke it. With a stern bark, Dr. Lows began with clenched teeth, "Stop it! Stop it now. You will not speak like this in here. I won't permit it! Do you hear me? You are an embarrassment to me and to your colleagues."

"Dr. Lows, with all due respect," Dr. Dimmer replied, "I am interested in hearing what Dr. Nassa has to say. Like the others members of the medical community who are sitting around this table, I am well aware of our duty as members of the ethics board of this hospital. I know all about the pledge we made about standing by our position no matter how moved we might have been upon seeing these miraculous works to do otherwise. However, when you took Dr. Nassa out of the room, we realized that what Dr. Nassa did make sense. I know you're angry, but, please, let Dr. Nassa finish."

For a few minutes, there was total silence in the room. Finally, Dr. Nassa worked up enough nerve to continue. "Perhaps if we swallowed our pride and had the courage to take Ethan and Claire up on their offer, we could do wonders. Not only would we have the opportunity to fulfill our dreams and truly help our patients live more meaningful lives, but also to take the medical profession in a new direction. What do we have to lose? Look at what all the people who have had their feet washed are doing. After seeing what these people are doing, I see that it is possible to change America.

"All my life I have been waiting for an opportunity like this to come along. I believe that God has a plan for me, but until now I never knew what it was. Hearing Ethan's plea for help helped me realize this is what I am destined to do. So, if you'll have me, I'm yours." As Dr. Nassa said this, she removed her white medical coat and walked to Ethan and Claire.

Dr. Lows clapped and spoke sarcastically. "Ah, now even I must admit, Dr. Nassa, that was truly moving. You could win an Academy Award for that performance! Say, while we are at it, would anyone else like to quit the medical profession and go join the circus? How about you, Dr. Dimmer? You seemed eager to hear Dr. Nassa's speech. Well, does anyone else want to join the Jesus freaks?"

It seemed obvious to everyone that Dr. Lows had lost control. Although there were others who wanted to go up and join Dr. Nassa, Dr. Lows had created such a tense atmosphere that people were fearful. If they moved, how would Dr. Lows react? Those moments of silence seemed like an eternity.

Finally, Ethan broke the silence. "Let's get out of here and go back to the store where we can do some good. Sometimes people are filled with so much jealousy and rage that they cannot stand to face the truth. Do not be angry with them, but pray that God will have mercy on their souls and soften their hearts. Truly they should be pitied."

When Dr. Lows heard these words, he knew that Ethan had spoken the truth. Though there was something inside him that wanted to break free from what surrounded his heart and join Ethan's crusade, stubbornness and pride prevented that from happening. As Ethan and Claire walked down the hall talking with Dr. Nassa, Dr. Lows approached. Through clenched teeth he barked, "I'm warning you, if you have any sense, you would leave this alone. Take our friendly advice and get out of town, or be prepared to suffer the repercussions of your actions because you surely do not know who you are dealing with!"

Despite Dr. Lows' efforts to intimidate them, Ethan and Claire continued down the hall with Dr. Nassa. They discussed plans about the following day and her enrollment in the Foot-Washing Institute. As for Dr. Lows, he might as well have been yelling at the wind, for no one cared what he was yelling about.

It is never a good idea to enter a situation with a preconceived notion of what will happen for your plan is likely to backfire, leaving you in a state of utter confusion. Rather, it is best to experience the situation in its entirety and reserve judgment for later. Unfortunately, Dr. Lows and his cronies planned to solve this problem using bribery and intimidation tactics. When their approach did not go according to plan, they found themselves in one messy predicament and had no idea how to get out of it gracefully. Previously, money had always proved to be a feasible solution for getting rid of annoyances that never seem to go away. However, now that Ethan and Claire did not take the hint, they were desperate to find another strategy.

Dr. Lows was outraged. Because he was used to having everything on his own terms, he was quite distressed that the world he had dedicated his life to was collapsing before his eyes. Although he might have been the president of the ethics board at one of the most prestigious hospitals in the nation, he was threatened by the power that one mother and son had because they were humble instruments for Christ. They were not only on the verge of bringing his career to a standstill, but they were threatening to turn the medical profession upside down.

Dr. Lows could not even think straight. Because people were no longer going to the doctor, Dr. Lows knew he had to do something to destroy the competition or the medical profession would be out of business forever.

Just thinking about this and its implications made him cringe. Unless he dealt with this matter quickly and decisively, his job would be in jeopardy, and the hospital would hold him personally responsible for the whole disaster. To prevent this, Dr. Lows planned to hold a strategic executive meeting immediately. They would solve this problem one way or another.

As this was happening, some of the other doctors in the boardroom felt as if their stomachs had fallen out from under them. They did not know what to think or what to do. What they had witnessed in the last hour had caused them much internal turmoil and had left many to ask why they had become doctors in the first place. Yes, many went into medicine so they could help care for people. However, as they watched Ethan and Claire work and saw how Dr. Lows had taken something Beautiful and tried to put an end to it to keep the money flowing in, some realized they did not like who they had become. Maybe Dr. Nassa was right.

The miracle the doctors had witnessed reaffirmed their belief in a higher power, and they saw life in a fresh new way. While many did not understand how the towels worked, like Dr. Nassa, they were tempted to remove their stethoscopes and trade them in for a towel and a jug of water.

Dr. Lows re-entered the boardroom. His colleagues sighed heavily, for they could tell they were in for an earful. When Dr. Lows' tablet hit the table, the room became deathly silent.

Once everyone sat down and got settled, Dr. Lows felt a strange sensation and suddenly jumped out of his seat as if something had bitten him. As he looked down in his chair to see what it was, he was repulsed.

"Oh, look what we have here," he sneered while picking up the clean, white towel with his two fingertips. "Now who was the sick perverted moron who planted this in my chair? If it was a joke, I tell you the truth, it wasn't the least bit funny. While I could go on a tirade because I feel betrayed and as if it was a slap in the face, lashing out right now would be futile and unproductive. Rather, I will use my rage as a springboard to deal with the matter at hand, the towel."

As he spoke, he draped the towel across the table so everyone in the room could see it in all its splendor. "Yes, this will work better than I ever anticipated. We have to do some heavy-duty work here. Not only has our plan backfired, but somehow instead of frightening Ethan and Claire we have, I'm afraid, strengthened their reign. Can you believe Dr. Nassa turned her back on us after all we did to help her? What a traitor! You know what I always say, 'Once a doctor, always a doctor.' We doctors have to stick together because we are, after all, the trusted healing professionals."

By now, there was growing dissension in the room. Many were sickened by the tone in Dr. Lows' voice that reeked of cynicism and sarcasm. Right now many were incensed and felt as if their blood was boiling. Consequently, it took great discipline for the majority of doctors to bite their tongues and control their instincts. Despite how much some of them wanted to get up and leave, they were curious to see what Dr. Lows was planning to do.

"Now, I'm sure many of you are as bewildered as I am by all that has happened and are not sure what to do. You probably are wondering if there is merit to what they are doing. After all, ever since Ethan and Claire came into the picture, life has changed significantly. People not only are being healed of their illnesses but have adopted a new mindset to stop talking about the rhetoric and work for positive change and reform.

"While I do support many of the reforms that have been made, they have undermined the medical profession, turned it into a laughing matter, and made us look like fools. We were here first and, unlike the Indians, I'll be damned if I will let two holy rollers who have started a cult in the name of Christ wipe us off the planet as if we don't matter. As for joining them, why? It's ludicrous, insane, and mortifying! We are scientifically trained, not the touchy-feely type. Look, I'm sorry that I came down hard on them. Really I am. However, you must admit that things have gotten out of control since they came on the scene.

"We tried to reason with them, but as history has shown, there's no way to reason with rebel rousers and the swarms that follow them. Revolutionaries are good up to a point, but as we all know, if they are not watched carefully, the uprising can get out of hand and ultimately lead to transformations that can rarely be reversed. The only way to prevent this from happening and ensure that society stays in check is to destroy their power base. To do this, we must find a way to destroy the power that resides in the towels.

"I have heard the power does not come from the towels themselves, but rather from Christ who uses the towels as a device through which to heal others. I'm not a theologian by any means; however, it seems to me that if we could prevent the supply of towels from reaching them and destroy the supply they already have, our problem would be solved. All we have to do is figure out a way to do this in an inconspicuous manner, and not get caught. If we just put our heads together and work as a team, it shouldn't be hard to devise a plan. What I would like to do now is hold a brainstorming session and come up with a way to do this as a team. I'm all ears. So, who wants to go first?"

The doctors were horrified. At one time, Dr. Lows had a reputation for being a wonderful administrator who always kept the best interests of patients in mind when it came time to make sound business decisions. Now they wondered if Dr. Lows was having a psychotic breakdown. Coppertown General had always been such a reputable hospital, known for providing the best care to patients. While the doctors knew that Dr. Lows was under pressure to oust Ethan and Claire, it just seemed so out of character for someone with such great integrity to be thinking about doing something so vicious.

What would happen if the administration found out that the president of the ethics board had done something so shady? Even though the hospital's reputation would certainly be tarnished for a while, they wondered if the community would be better off if the towels were destroyed or if taking such action would make the problem worse.

The doctors sat in silence for a time and considered these things in their hearts. They didn't know what to do and felt as if they had just received a blow to their heads. Ten minutes passed and no one uttered a word. Sick of the silence, Dr. Lows grew impatient. In a rage, he stood up and yelled, "Well, don't any of you morons have any ideas on how to achieve this goal? Do you plan to just sit there like passive little weasels and watch our careers go down the drain without a fight? Why am I always the one who has to come up with a way to save the ship from sinking?"

Dr. Lows' frustration peaked, and he reached in his pocket and took out his lighter. Holding the lighter in his hand flicking it on and off, he laughed with sheer delight. He had finally figured out a way to reclaim the upper hand and he felt an exhilarating rush of power. Suddenly, he grabbed the towel on the table, set it ablaze, and said as he grimaced with delight, "Don't worry. By the time I'm finished, they will wish they never messed with us. We tried to reason with them, but they simply laughed. People think they are so clever and that God is behind their doings, but they are frauds! The quicker we prove it and set the record straight, the faster our lives will return to normal." When they saw the devious look in Dr. Lows' eyes, the doctors knew that he had formulated an action plan. Although they had no idea what he was up to, once Dr. Lows had made up his mind to do something, there was no way to appeal to his sense of reason.

The doctors had expected the meeting to be awkward and confrontational, but they never imagined that it would turn out so ugly. They knew Dr. Lows could be aggressive and downright arrogant when need be. While they understood the human element of wanting to protect one's profession that they had spent a lifetime building, there comes a time when people need to look at the larger context. As they left the boardroom, not only were they nauseated by how low Dr. Lows had stooped but they also sensed that something bad was going to happen. No matter how hard they tried to chalk his reaction up to utter frustration, they just could not forget how he played with the lighter and the sheer delight on his face as he set that towel on fire.

Understandably, the doctors felt as if their emotional batteries had been completely drained, and now their stomachs were wrenching with anguish. Life as they knew it was never going to be the same, for everything they had ever worked to achieve had suddenly collapsed before their eyes. They decided to calm their nerves at a local bar, have a few drinks, collect themselves, and try to figure out what to do next. At first, they just looked at one another and could not believe how this predicament had gotten so out of hand. Some were in such a state of bewilderment and wished they could just wake up from this horrific nightmare. Yet, facts were facts, and pretending that this was not happening would merely prolong the inevitable.

In light of all that had just transpired, the doctors could not in good conscience continue to work under the auspices of that vicious menace. Some even contemplated alerting the police as to Dr. Lows' behavior. But the hospital's management structure was hierarchical in nature and the "good old boys mentality" was at work. There was no point in reporting the incident because the higher ups would simply deny the whole thing and sweep it under the rug.

The doctors at Coppertown General had always considered each other family and stuck together no matter what. When the doctors saw him set the towel on fire and the diabolical look in his eyes, they were frightened. What would happen next? The act was so reprehensible that many were sickened and thought about resigning then and there, but if they did, what would they do?

Initially, some considered just going to work for another hospital, but the problem was more widespread and did not affect only Coppertown General. Life was going fine before Ethan and Claire came into town and disrupted everything. Because of those "divine towels" that could instantaneously cure any ailment, life was no longer the same. Understandably, the doctors were incensed and wondered who Ethan and Claire thought they were to seize their established territory, especially when they did not have any medical knowledge whatsoever. They could not understand why God had given this gift to Ethan and Claire. It just was not fair, especially since they had not done a blessed thing to earn it.

The doctors could have easily been sidetracked and harbored resentment. However, the problem remained. Their careers were in serious jeopardy, and they had to make a hard decision. Because they had no other choice, many considered doing the unthinkable - joining Dr. Nassa and others at the Foot-Washing Institute.

Familiarity is something we all enjoy to a certain extent because we know what to expect. Having this sense of security in some aspects of our lives is good, but if we become too comfortable and never venture forth, we stagnate. God, who has a distinct plan for each of His children, often puts us in situations to get our attention, hoping we will realize that something is going on and will ask for His help. It is like being locked in a jail cell for years. Suddenly someone hears your cry and comes to unlock the door. Some are so accustomed to being in the jail cell that when they are free to leave, they are afraid to go.

Many doctors had been at the Coppertown General since medical school and were frankly tired of it. They liked helping the patients, but the passion they once felt had dwindled. Many were sick of the drudgery of their routines and yearned to become part of something that actually mattered. Divine Towels was a welcome disruption of the monotony of their lives and they felt it was an answer to a prayer and were greatly relieved.

The doctors' curiosity was aroused when patients told personal stories about how they were healed. Initially, they wondered if it was some strange phenomenon; however, when patients kept relaying the same personal stories, they wanted to see what the latest craze was about for themselves.

Researching the claims turned out to be the ember that shook the doctors from their complacency. They were inspired to see that Divine Towels was not only healing people from their debilitating illnesses and was freeing them from pain but had also rekindled a flame of passion. It amazed the doctors to see the way the healings had breathed new life into people causing them to become charitable and to treat others as if they were extensions of their own family.

The stories the doctors heard were compelling and reminded them of why they had gone into the profession in the first place, to help people live healthy lives. They enjoyed helping people, but some were lured by power and prestige, which caused them to divert their attention. Because of their ambitions, some made unscrupulous deals and compromised their principles in the process. Indeed some made money; but in the end, it was not worth it. Many were filled with guilt for what they did. They were sick of engaging in questionable practices and just wanted a second chance.

The doctors thought they knew what to expect from the healing process of the Divine Towels, but witnessing Sara's healing proved to be a life-altering experience. There was something about watching Ethan and Claire wash feet that spoke to them and stilled the turmoil in their restless souls. It was the first time their stream of consciousness was silenced. They felt the Holy Spirit's presence, experienced overwhelming peace, and knew that all was well. No words were uttered; yet, it was obvious that the doctors had found a safe place where they could be accepted for who they were.

The life Ethan and Claire lived was appealing because it was genuine and reminded them of what it might be like to be a true disciple. Many were struck by the simplicity of the act and found that it soothed their souls like nothing before. While some could easily imagine themselves working alongside them, they realized that choosing this type of life would require them to make some difficult decisions. They found themselves standing on the precipice of life asking simple yet profound questions: would they be willing to forgo whatever was required to fulfill the desire of their heart or would they retreat to their safe little world where nothing was at risk? How they answered the questions would determine the rest of their lives.

After spending many heart-wrenching days agonizing with these emotions, wrestling with who they were, and pondering the type of legacy they wished to leave behind, they became exasperated and could not think clearly. In their hearts they knew what they wanted to do; yet, they were tired and did not want to be tormented any longer. Just when the doctors thought they could not stand another minute, they shut their eyes and prayed for help. Suddenly, they saw a towel in their mind's eye and realized that they were the ones who were weak and needed help. While they were not quite sure which towel they would need, they were sure that Ethan and Claire would know just what to do.

The strange part was that during this time none of the doctors who considered helping Ethan and Claire communicated with one another. Filled with anguish, they eventually called the store and asked for help.

Three of the seven doctors arrived at the store the next morning announcing that they no longer wished to be associated with the hospital. Instead they longed for a simple life of being a foot washer. Claire was pleased. Though she worried that it had all happened too quickly, nonetheless she welcomed them and was willing to work with all who sought to serve no matter where they were spiritually.

While both professions dealt with healing, the divine type that Ethan and Claire were dedicated to turned out to be much more draining and complex than they ever imagined. The physical act of washing and drying feet was only a small part of what was involved. For a healing to occur, the person doing the healing needed to believe that he was merely an instrument in which Christ's power flowed. Claire and Ethan explained that being a channel for Christ required doing things His way. The doctors' expressions showed that they grasped the gravity of what they were about to undertake.

At first glance, being Christ's instrument may not seem all that difficult. After all, it was Christ Himself who called His people to be ambassadors on the earth when He returned to heaven. Yet after watching Ethan and Claire work for a while, the doctors realized the men and women who truly brought mankind closer to their creator were humble servants who sought to do Christ's will above all else.

Ethan and Claire might have been present physically, but it was obvious that a greater force was present and was at work. In that moment they experienced true beauty and realized that if everything else were stripped from their lives, the one thing that would matter was what they did to help and care for others.

Claire was about to see another customer when the phone rang. She took the call immediately when Bill told her it was Dr. Dimmer.

"Hello," she said with much anticipation, "this is Claire speaking."

"Claire, I'm not sure if you remember me. I am Dr. Dimmer. I was in the store a few weeks ago."

Judging by the speed at which Dr. Dimmer spoke, Claire knew he needed to get something off his chest. She answered, "Yes, I remember. How can I help you?"

Feeling more comfortable, he said, "I have had some real trouble lately; my life is a mess because of you. I know I'm a hypocrite for calling the person I should hate for ruining my life. However, when I was in your store, I was reminded of what life is truly about. Life isn't about things; it's about nourishing the soul. I knew this as a child but somehow I have forgotten it. I need your help. I am sorry I left the store in a hurry. My mind was overloaded, and I just could not think.

Claire was surprised by his candor and knew God had answered her prayer. "I understand these feelings and the shame one feels about becoming shortsighted. But there's no use dwelling on the past. What is important is that we learn from our mistakes and change our lives and behavior accordingly. From what you have told me it seems obvious that you desire to serve others. I know you are afraid to take the next step. We all are. But you're not alone. Life is scary, I admit, but we do not have anything to fear. Christ is ultimately in control and will take us on the ultimate adventure if we allow Him to guide our footsteps."

Dr. Dimmer understood what Claire was saying, but he could not conceive that something so wonderful could happen to him. After all, he had helped plan their failure but still they had mercy on him. He was awed by the opportunity he had been given and felt God had brought him to this moment.

After a long pause, Dr. Dimmer said, "You have a gift with words. I must admit I am amazed by what has happened to me over the last few days. I am convinced Christ loves me and has called me to work with you in some capacity. Yet right now, my head is spinning and I can't seem to think straight. Please help me stop the tape in my head so I can think. It's driving me crazy and I can't stand it anymore!"

"I know you can't, and you don't have to. That's the Beauty of it. Come in and let me help you. You have suffered enough," Claire said with exasperation in her voice.

"I'll be right over. If I don't come now, I'll just sit here and be tormented until I do. Tell you what, if I'm not there in ten minutes, call me and harass me until I come."

In exactly ten minutes, Dr. Dimmer was at the store. As he stood in line, he felt a bit apprehensive. Despite this uneasy feeling, something pressed him forward. As he neared the front, Claire saw him out of the corner of her eye. Immediately she stopped and with a twinkle in her eye called, "Dimmer, I've been waiting for you. Now let me see those feet of yours. As you can probably see, we are swamped as always and need all the help we can get. Yet before the instrument goes to work, let's ask the Master for a tune up, shall we?"

After laughing for a minute, Dr. Dimmer followed Claire and removed his shoes and socks. She stilled herself and prayed that

Christ would touch him in whatever way he needed. As she washed his feet, she inhaled and felt a cleansing breath of air enter and fill her body. When she exhaled, all toxins were discharged and she felt that the Holy Spirit had taken over her entire being. As she dried Dr. Dimmer's feet, the energy that had enveloped her flowed into him in the form of radiant energy and heat. When this happened, he felt tingly all over and heard a voice say, "Child, come harvest for me and you shall be with me in paradise." At that moment he knew that the only things that mattered in life were the relationship he had with Christ, treating others the way he would treat Christ, and bringing people to an understanding that this was what life was truly about.

THE CONSPIRACY

Dr. Lows in his great wisdom believed he had scored a mighty victory when he kicked Ethan and Claire to the curb. Over the last few months, things had definitely gotten out of hand, especially in the medical community all because of those holy rollers who claimed to be healers. Sure, it was wonderful that people were getting better and were living productive lives, but it had come at too great a cost. Dr. Lows realized he came down very hard on Ethan and Claire, but he had to send a clear-cut message to them that continuing to disrupt society in this manner would not be tolerated.

For the next week, Dr. Lows walked around the hospital feeling confident that his stern talk had solved the problem. However, upon arriving at work the following Monday, he was summoned to an emergency meeting in the president's office. As he headed up to see Dr. Rogers, he expected Rogers to have a bottle of chilled champagne on hand as a way of saying congratulations for handling the healing matter.

"Good morning, Dr. Rogers, how are you today?" Dr. Lows asked as a way to lighten up the tenseness that seemed to be in the air.

"I'm just fine. However, I'm afraid we have a serious problem that is mainly my fault. Please come in and shut the door; we need to talk." Dr. Rogers began, "I hate to do this after you followed my orders, but I'm going to have to terminate your position at Coppertown General immediately. You were a little too aggressive when you threatened Ethan and Claire, and now the hospital is facing severe scrutiny. I'm not mad at you. Goodness knows you tried. Unfortunately, we must do some damage control because our plan has backfired. Don't worry about money. You will still receive your full salary and will be reinstated when this thing blows over. For now, I think it's in everyone's best interest for you to keep a low profile."

"What exactly happened that brought all this on?" Dr. Lows asked.

Dr. Rogers took the pile of letters out of the manila folder and threw them on the desk. "Since the day you threw Ethan and Claire out, nine out of 12 members of the ethics board resigned claiming that you were arrogant. They claimed they were intimidated at the meeting when you yelled and set the towel on fire. When I read that, I had to chuckle. I always knew you were a passionate guy but never thought you, of all people, would do something that crazy.

"Maybe you did get a little out of hand. However, rather than having empathy for you, realizing that you were fighting for them to save their jobs, they have revolted and sided with those holy rollers. Those traitors not only said they no longer wished to be associated with the hospital because you were a menace, but that they were also going to tell their patients to go to that damn store and be healed of their ailments."

Dr. Lows had no idea all this was going on. "When did this all happen? Why didn't you alert me sooner, perhaps I could have helped or at least been there to support you? After all, we are in this thing together."

"I was going to call you, but then it snowballed, and I found that I was simply overwhelmed. Somehow, everything has gotten out of control because of those radicals. They all start out the same with their ideals and then rile the crowds into believing they can change their fates by lobbying against the system. The reason we are in the situation we are in today is that people have discovered how to liberate themselves and have undertaken bold initiatives to change their situations.

"Yes, it's wonderful, but it has uncovered many deficiencies. People we always helped in times of crisis have now turned against us making us look like fools. We warned them, but they didn't take the hint. Therefore, we must take the next step and crush these people before they can do more damage. The only question we need to answer is how."

Dr. Lows was deeply immersed in thought trying to figure out a way to achieve this goal. He thought about the towel incident for several moments, and then he remembered what he had been thinking at the time. He came up with the best of all solutions and knew they could pull it off eloquently, if they could find a pro to do the job.

After a few minutes, Dr. Lows stood up and began to pace the room. "I do have an idea that might just work if we plan it properly and have it professionally done. It could be risky, but if we don't get caught and the job gets done, what do we have to lose?" Dr. Lows said with his hands on his hips.

Dr. Rogers looked at him pensively and wondered what his friend was up to. "What is it?" he asked with great intrigue.

"Let's just suppose we were to hire someone to take care of this problem for us. Don't worry about the details, I'll handle everything. We pay them cash and make sure there is not a trace of evidence left behind. There is no way anyone could link us to it. We accomplish our mission and everyone lives happily ever after. Sure people will be angry and cry, but after a while they will get over it and continue living. Yes, people will feel sorry for them and say they didn't deserve it, but they won't rebuild again. I hate to resort to violence, but some people just don't get it when you talk nice."

Dr. Rogers listened attentively, and though he was not keen on the idea of taking the law into his own hands, he realized they really had no alternative. People no longer required their services and it made him furious. The medical profession was dying and the only way to save it was to crush the competition.

Grinning, Dr. Rogers said, "Dr. Lows, I knew there was a reason I hired you. You are a genius! Boy, they certainly did pick the wrong people to mess with. They would have been fine if they had limited the healing to their own little congregation, but since they went public, they will have to pay. God, I love you, we are a great pair. Because of you we will soon thrive again."

After congratulating Dr. Lows for a few minutes, Dr. Rogers started right in again. "Now that we have a plan, the next thing we must do is decide how to carry it out. Let's see, who do we know who might be able to pull off a stunt like this? Since nothing is coming to me right now, let's consult the ultimate source of information, the Internet."

After clicking the mouse five times, they stumbled upon a newspaper article that got them thinking. Though they didn't know exactly where this would lead, they decided to go back to their alma mater, Preics University, and hang out at the local bar. If Murphy's was anything like the old days, it was still full of young, aspiring med students who went there at night unwind after becoming bleary eyed from poring over medical textbooks. It should be easy to persuade one of them to perform an historic act to help resurrect the endeared medical profession. In exchange for his cooperation, the doctors would use their influence and guarantee the medical student a job upon graduation at one of the most distinguished hospitals in the country. All they had to do now was choose a victim.

Though Dr. Rogers and Dr. Lows had never done this before, they decided to hang out a Murphy's and scope things out. Murphy's was no doubt as dingy as ever, with lousy food and loud music. Nevertheless, since they were going to spend the next several weeks there looking for the right person for the job, they figured they might as well have some fun while they were at it. There was nothing wrong with pretending they were young again and back in college: wearing blue jeans, sipping girly beer, hooking up with a few broads, playing pool, and listening to Jimmy Buffet.

For the first few nights, they felt a little awkward being back in their college bar. However, after being there for a while and offering to buy the poor med students a few rounds, they formed a bond with the guys. Before long, the doctors felt as if they were back in school, especially when they played pool and heard the guys complain about the same teachers the doctors had had. The doctors empathized and told them that if they got in a jam and needed help that they would be happy to answer a few questions.

While it may appear that the doctors were having fun and had forgotten all about carrying out their plan, everything was going as they wanted. They had studied psychology and knew it was much easier to get someone to go along with you upon developing a rapport. Hence, now that the med students looked up to them, it was time for the doctors to act. They knew that the key element was timing and selecting someone at a vulnerable moment when they weren't thinking clearly.

One night, they overheard David, a regular, talking to one of his buddies. "I am just so sick of them. I have been slaving over these courses and now I received a letter from the treasurer's office saying that I am delinquent on my tuition bill. I just got off the phone with my parents and they gave me this line, 'Well we never agreed to pay your tuition bill.' They had paid all the other years, and now that I am in my final year, they pull this! How could they do this to me after all the hard work I put in to get to this point?

What am I going to do now? How am I going to get that kind of money? I need an easy way to make a quick buck."

"I'm sorry, bud," his friend replied. "I wish I had a good idea for you, but I just don't."

Hearing David's misfortune, Dr. Lows seized the opportunity to comfort the poor boy. "Excuse me, but I couldn't help overhearing what you were talking about. David, I am truly sorry that your parents did this to you. You have every right to be angry. However, there's no use lamenting this, for it will only deter you from focusing on what you need to do next. I realize you don't know what to do, but if you're interested, I think I may be able to help you."

"Are you kidding?" David exclaimed. "I would be most appreciative of any help you could give me."

"Okay, David, you seem like a nice enough guy. I have a problem that I desperately need help with. If you help me out, I will not only pay your tuition bill but will pay you an additional $5,000."

"Sounds great," David said with a nervous laughter. "What exactly is it that I have to do? It's not anything illegal, is it?" David's friend opened his eyes wide and was eager to hear what the great doctor wanted.

Dr. Lows was about to answer right away; but David's friend was so eager to hear the details, Dr. Lows decided it was best to take a different approach. "David," Dr. Lows said as he wrapped his arm around David's shoulder, "let's go over and join Dr. Rogers, have a couple beers, and discuss this matter. Tonight is going to be a long night, so we might as well get comfortable. We have a lot to tell you."

David did not know what Dr. Lows was up to. There was just something about his tone that left David with an uneasy feeling. David should have followed his instincts and walked away. Desperately needing money, he followed Dr. Lows to the table and agreed to listen to what they had to say.

After they sat down, Dr. Lows began. "David, it would be nice if Dr. Rogers and I could pal around with you like we always do. However, we are in a difficult situation, and the longer we stall, the harder the situation gets for us. I understand your situation and will be happy to pay your tuition if you agree to help us. You might think being a doctor is all about making money, but sometimes, as you will learn, the bartering system can come in very handy. I believe it can often be better than money. People help each other with what they need and no one goes without. Isn't that the way life should be?"

David smiled as Dr. Lows took a sip of beer. "David," Dr. Rogers said in a sincere tone of voice, "as you are aware, people have always respected doctors and considered them trusted friends who help them in times of need. However, the past few months have been quite devastating for us. We feel as if the people we have always cared for and been loyal to have turned their backs on us, and frankly we are hurt. That is why, my friend, we desperately need your help."

By now, David realized he had possibly judged the doctors too fast and was quite interested to hear where Dr. Rogers was going with this. "Well, what exactly do you need help with?" David asked innocently.

"Good question," Dr. Lows added. "The truth is we know what is causing the problem. The medical community began to notice it a few months ago when patients began canceling their appointments. At first, we didn't think anything of it. However, when this continued and people didn't reschedule their appointments, we became quite concerned.

"We had our receptionists call a handful of patients to find out what was happening, and we were shocked by what we discovered. A new store called Divine Towels had opened in town, a store that claimed to heal people of any ailment, as long as they had 'faith' in God. People were anointed with the gift of healing so they could, in turn, heal others. Obviously, this was the most preposterous thing we had ever heard of, and we believed our receptionists were playing a joke on us. Yet, when they continued to tell the story and we saw the Divine Towels Website, we realized we had another form of competition to contend with.

"We were never crazy about alternative medicines, but at least they only helped people with certain types of diseases. The reason the medical community feels so enraged by what is being done at Divine Towels is that the owners have the audacity to claim they can heal any ailment. At first, we thought people were exaggerating but from all we can surmise, the claims seem to be true. We are happy that people are being healed; yet, it is hurting us deeply, especially in the wallet. It was bad enough to have high-paying patients get better because they had been healed by one of those quacky television evangelists. Yet, now that one of those quacks has opened a store in town, it is obvious that unless we take immediate action and put them in their place, we soon will be out of a job."

"I am beginning to see what you mean. However, I still don't see what any of this has to do with me. I'm not even a resident yet," David replied matter of factly.

Dr. Lows held up his hand in protest and said, "I understand what you're saying, David; however, if you will just hear me out, you will see where you fit into all of this. As I was saying, we invited these 'healers' to the hospital and tried to make them understand how they were hurting the medical profession. We explained that because of them, our waiting rooms were empty and that we could no longer make a living. We told them they had established an illegal monopoly and that we would be most appreciative if they left town. Instead of honoring our requests, not only did they refuse to take the money we offered them but had the audacity to suggest that we come work for them and help heal others.

"Dr. Rogers and I have been discussing what to do with these people who are on the verge of ruining our lives and yours, for that matter. We tried to tell them that their actions were hurting us and even begged them to stop. But they continued to do whatever they pleased and we couldn't understand why they didn't think about what impact their actions were having on us. At first, we were hurt that they did this to us; however, since they don't want to take the hint that they are not welcomed here, we have decided to say it in a way they might be able to understand better."

"What might that be?" David asked.

Dr. Lows squirmed but after looking around to make sure no one was listening, he mumbled, "Destroy it."

For a second, David looked as if he could not believe what he was hearing. He became quite uneasy once he figured out what the doctors were implying. Rather than become upset, he decided to play along and see what would happen next.

"Destroy it. Wow, that's quite a strategy! How would you do it and why are you telling me, a stranger, about this?" David asked nonchalantly.

The doctors looked at each other and began to laugh, Dr. Lows said, "Oh, come on, David, think? Why do you think we are telling you this? We need you to do this job for us. As I said in the beginning, we need each other's services. You need financial help, and we need you to put Divine Towels out of business. Seems like a perfect arrangement, if you ask me."

When David heard what the doctors were planning, he did not know how to react. Since David was studying to be a doctor, he could totally empathize with the doctors. After all, their very livelihoods as well as his own were definitely on the line, and they certainly did not want fundamentalist Christians ruining everything they had worked for. As long as Divine Towels and their counterparts were washing people's feet and healings occurred, it was obvious that there would be no way they could possibly practice medicine. Something had to be done.

David agreed with the doctors in principle; however, because he had grown up in a home where good values were taught, he found the doctors' approach quite reprehensible. What the doctors were planning to do violated everything that doctors were supposed to stand for. Yes, it was true that Divine Towels was damaging the doctors' business, but people did, after all, have a right to choose where to have their medical needs met. Just because people were no longer going to see the doctors, it didn't give the doctors the right to destroy a competitive venue.

David understood that the doctors were not used to being the underdog and would resort to any means they could to be successful again. Yet, unlike the doctors, David could not help but see the problem from a different angle. The doctors could easily destroy the store. However, once they did, would the problem be solved or would it make the problem worse? There were many times that people thought they had been victorious, but in retrospect were seen as failures; for in winning, they had not only compromised their integrity but had trampled on people's dreams in the process.

As the doctors sat laughing about what they perceived to be the perfect solution to all their problems, David found himself in quite a predicament. He was ethically opposed to helping the doctors do their dirty work, but he realized that if he wanted to do his residency and have a career at one of the most reputable hospitals in the country, it would be in his best interest to concede a point. The most despicable part was that the doctors knew David was in a bad financial situation and had chosen him specifically because he would have a hard time saying no.

David listened, but he did not know what to do or say. "What's the matter, kid? You look as if you peed your pants or something. Did we catch you off guard?" Dr. Lows asked when he saw the terror in David's eyes.

Hesitating as he took a gulp of beer, David said, "You sort of did. It's not that I am unwilling to help you; I'm just surprised. I am sorry the store has brought the medical profession to a screeching halt, but I wonder if this is the best way to eliminate the problem or if it will make the problem worse."

"Oh, and how do you think it would exacerbate the problem if we destroy the source of the problem? Yes, we know the people who were 'healed' claim it is Christ who heals through the person, but it's all just a trick the owners told people. If we destroy the towels and the store, we eliminate the root of the problem. It's as simple as that. I'm curious, oh wise one, if we achieve this, how could our plan possibly backfire?"

"Have you ever stopped to consider what would happen if people somehow found out that it was you who did this? What makes you so sure it is the towels that are making people well and not Christ's power especially if there are people in other places who are washing feet and healing people as well? If people continue healing others after you destroy the store, then what? Where will you draw the line or will you destroy every place where people are healing others? If this is the case, then all will be afraid of provoking the infamous doctors."

Though David did raise several good points, the doctors did not have any good answers. They became defensive. The more they listened to what David had to say, the more they realized their plan was weak and needed serious help. "Stop it, just stop it! We are the ones running the show, not you! Besides, who asked for your opinion anyway?" Dr. Lows clamored, as he was about to strike David for being so disrespectful.

David shouted back. "First you ask for my opinion, and then when I give it to you, you go psycho on me. No wonder people don't like you." David paused, took a sip of beer, and continued. "However, that's irrelevant. All you really care about is if I will help you destroy the store so you can continue living life in the manner you are accustomed to. Am I right?"

When David said this, Dr. Lows said, "You may be a little antagonistic, but you certainly do catch on quickly. So now that we have gone through the niceties, will you help relieve our suffering?"

The moment of truth arrived. The doctors' hearts pounded, as they awaited David's decision. Would David help them or would he report them to the authorities?

David knew how eager they were for him to answer. However, since David had an advantage over them, he decided to make them squirm a little. "I feel as if I'm sitting on a fulcrum and am not sure which way I'm leaning. On one hand, I want to be a doctor so I can help people, yet I also feel an obligation to help my colleagues. For when one of us suffers, we all suffer. If I do what you're asking, please understand I am not doing it to save you, but rather so I could save the medical community and take it in a new direction.

"On the other hand, destroying what another person has built is not only a crime but is unethical as well. I never heard of Divine Towels before now; however, from what I surmise you want to destroy them because you can't deal with not being in control. You both want to help people get better but rather than trying to work together as a team, you decide Divine Towels is insignificant and not worth bothering with. This is not only narrow-minded, but arrogant as well."

By now, David could tell that he was getting on the doctors' nerves. He should stop or he would be sorry. "Having weighed both options, I have decided, against my better judgment, to help you. You probably don't care why, but I'm going to tell you anyway. I don't particularly want to do this; however, I am in a difficult situation. I must remember that sometimes the end justifies the means."

Although the doctors wished David was more enthusiastic about helping them, at least he was willing to do the job. Once David agreed to do the deed, Dr. Lows pressed on. He tossed an envelope across the table and said, "Now, I imagine you have never done this type of work before; however, never fear because we have you covered. We have done some research on the most effective flammables and remote control devices experts have used when they have carried out this kind of thing. If you can bake a cake, you can do this. Follow these guidelines, use your head, and everything will be fine."

After taking a sip of beer, Dr. Rogers continued, "As long as you do the job in the next week and the store is destroyed, we don't really care what method you use. To show you we are men of our word, here is a wad of cash that will cover half of the balance you owe the school. I want you to deposit the money in your account tomorrow. You will then write a check to the school and tell them that you will pay the rest within two weeks. As long as the school sees that you will pay what you owe them, you will remain in school. Once you do the job and we see for ourselves that the store has indeed been destroyed, I will give you the remaining cash. Nothing complicated about it, just a straightforward business transaction. Any questions?"

Dr. Rogers handed David the money and smiled. Though he knew he ought to have been happy, he looked at the cash. He was deeply troubled and wondered if he had the nerve to go through with this. David knew this was a bad idea from the get-go, but he was in a no-win situation.

David decided it was best to end the meeting on a positive note. "Thank you. You won't be sorry you picked me. I won't disappoint you." David yawned and looked at his watch and continued, "Gee whiz, it's 1:30. I best get home. I have a long day tomorrow and need to hit the sack. I will read the information and call you if I have any questions. If you don't hear from me, it means that I am set. I will call you once I have completed the job, and we can arrange a time to settle up. Again, it is nice doing business with you." Having said this, David shook the doctors' hands and departed.

It had been a busy week for Ethan and Claire, just as it had been for ages. They were overjoyed that Christ answered their prayer and allowed them to devote their lives to helping those in need and changing lives. Nevertheless, their schedules were quite grueling. A typical day now consisted of working in the store during the day, teaching others to wash feet, and doing countless speaking engagements at night to heal those who were ill.

Claire and Ethan were tired; everything was taking its toll on them. The thought of going home, getting under the covers, and going to sleep for the night was especially enticing since it was a cold, misty night. By 8:30 that night, both Ethan and Claire were snug in their freshly laundered beds and were ready for a deep, sound sleep.

On nights when Ethan was so tired that he could not even see straight, it was customary for him to take the phone off the hook. However, on that particular night he was just too overtired to care. It was a good thing that the phone had remained on the hook, for at two that morning, the phone rang.

"Hello, I hate to bother you at this hour, Ethan, but this is Captain Haines."

Ethan, who had been in a deep sleep when he answered the phone, quickly snapped out of it. "Hi," Ethan said, "has something happened?"

After a brief pause, Captain Haines began. "I hate to be the one to have to break this to you, but 20 minutes ago we got a 911 call from someone who told us that your store was on fire. Although it is too soon to determine the cause of the fire, if I had to venture a guess, my hunch would be that it was arson. Since this is a 3-alarmer, we doubt that anything worthwhile can be salvaged. Nonetheless, you should come down here anyway."

At that time, Ethan's heart sank; for in that moment everything in his entire world that he had ever worked for came crashing down. Ethan knew there were people in the community who felt threatened by what he was doing and could not stand to see this progress being made. However, he never imagined that they would go to such drastic measures to plan his destruction; then again, look at what they did to Christ.

Ethan, who had always been very perceptive, came to an awesome discovery in that instant. He realized that from the time he surrendered everything to Christ and asked to be His hands and feet on the earth, Christ had bestowed the ultimate gift on him and his mother. Ethan realized that from that moment the life he and his mother had led paralleled the life of Christ.

Ethan was paralyzed with fear for he knew the story of Christ and wondered what would happen next. Despite his fear, he recollected Christ's words that everything was in His hands and not to fear because He was in control. Even though Ethan had great confidence in Christ and trusted him totally, he panicked. Ethan paused and tried to regain his composure. Ethan began, "Yes, of course, I'll be right down. By any chance, did you call my mother?"

"No. But, if you want me to, I will," Captain Haines said.

"Ah, I don't know what to say or what to do. I am just in shock. On second thought, could you take me to the scene? I'm too upset to drive."

Ethan managed to remain calm until they arrived at the scene. When he saw the flames envelop the store along with the sea of television reporters who were waiting to interview him, reality struck and Ethan lost his composure. He felt as if his life was over and he no longer had a reason to be alive. "Oh God, what am I going to do now? Why did this happen just when things were heading in the right direction? How am I ever going to break this to my beloved mother? For a long time we dreamed of opening this store and have invested all of our savings to make this a reality. We did it not for selfish gain, but rather so we could help and empower others, the way Christ did when He was on earth. And look at where it has gotten us. Nothing but a pile of smoldering ash. Why would anyone want to do this to us?" Ethan screamed in anguish.

Captain Haines wished he could do something to comfort his friend, but there was nothing to say. It was sickening that everything had been destroyed. Captain Haines was determined to bring justice to those responsible. Haines was definitely enraged, but right now he needed to help Ethan get through this ordeal.

As Haines embraced Ethan, he said, "Life is not fair. However, I believe that occasionally God prunes even His most prized trees, so they can blossom even more. Think about this. Since this store has opened, great changes have come about in this and surrounding communities. Congregations have grown, and people have been empowered to do great works for Christ. I know you don't understand why this tragedy has occurred. However, trust me, I know God did this for a reason and will work a miracle in some way from these ashes. I know you don't believe me, but just look at what God did after Jesus died. He raised Him from the dead after three days and saved the world from eternal damnation."

THE PHOENIX

When Ethan and Claire woke up the next morning and smelled the residual smoke on themselves, they remembered that their dream had gone up in smoldering ash. They were frustrated and angry for they believed their whole reason for living was gone. For the first few hours, Ethan and Claire cried uncontrollably and could not get themselves back together. They just could not understand why God, who had blessed them with this incredible gift, had allowed this to happen, especially when they had done their utmost to carry out His will.

In an effort to understand this and receive much needed solace, they thought about what people did to Jesus because they felt threatened. They saw amazing parallels between Jesus' life and their own. Suddenly, they saw what God was doing and had to laugh at God's sense of humor. Despite what people did to prevent the higher good from being done, God refused to allow man to write the end of the story. They surmised that God had allowed Divine Towels to burn down so a greater wonder could happen. Ethan and Claire had no idea what God was going to do, but they felt that God was about to do something miraculous.

While they knew God would work things out, they wondered who would be capable of committing such a heinous act. After thinking about it for a while, it was obvious to them that the doctors had committed this desperate act because they did not know how else to handle the situation. They knew Dr. Lows was enraged, but they never imagined he would take such drastic measures. In retrospect, if they had seen that he was obsessed, they would have taken his threats more seriously.

Ethan and Claire could not prove who was behind this act; nonetheless, they were determined not to allow the doctors to prevail. As they cried, they asked the Lord what was the best way to defeat their unseen, cowardly enemy. They were eager to rebuild and to get back to healing and empowering others again. Yet, they realized that until they addressed the underlying issue, there was no point in trying to rebuild. If they rebuilt the store, which would not be a problem, what would prevent Dr. Lows or his other counterparts from doing this again? Even if he and his conspirators were caught, it was just a matter of time before someone would try something similar.

At this time, Ethan and Claire began to see the war on terror in a new way. They understood that the war on terror should not merely be aimed at external forces that sought to disrupt the norm of society. Rather, the true war on terror needed to be against the unseen forces that sought to oppress the human spirit. Coming to this realization gave them insight as to what was going on and how to handle the situation. It was obvious that the doctors had burned down the heart of the healing ministry as an intimidation technique hoping that Ethan, Claire, and their team would cease healing out of fear of the repercussions that might befall them next. Hence, if they truly wanted to lead the war on terror in a new way, they had to lead by example and not allow fear to paralyze them. They had to trust Christ and reopen their store as quickly as possible.

The prospect of reopening the store and preparing others to fight relentlessly against the unseen forces that sought to oppress the human spirit was exciting. They understood how it was for the forces of good to prevail and to be victorious. This was all well and good strategically speaking. However, in thinking about this, many questions came to mind. How would they implement the vision and get people to see themselves as soldiers fighting an all-out war against evil. They knew what to do but needed help figuring out how to carry it out.

At seven that evening, the team met at Claire's house. They were delighted to be together again and eager to hear what was going on. After a brief chitchat, Ethan got everyone's attention. "Good evening, everyone. I wasn't planning to make a speech, but here I am. Yesterday was quite devastating for us all. We were all making such good progress, and I don't know about you but somehow my mother and I felt as if, for a few weeks, we had reenacted the Acts of the Apostles.

"No matter how much good we all do, there is a force that hates our work and will do anything to deter us from our mission. Look at what has happened to our store," Ethan said as he broke into tears. "I'm sorry. I thought I could get through this on my own, but I can't. Mom, please take over for a few minutes."

Claire hated seeing her son cry and almost told the team members to come back another time so she could comfort her son. However, Claire realized that if they really were a team and a community, as they claimed, then the team had to get through this together. In an effort to keep the momentum going, Claire took a deep breath and continued.

"Ethan's right. We cannot allow the demented people who burned down the store prevent us from pressing forward! It was a horrific act, and the people who did this will be brought to justice when God deems it fit. I'm sorry Ethan and I did not call you right away. However, we needed time to think about what we should do next. We believe that the doctors burned down the store because we were a threat to them and assumed it would be the easiest way to make their problem go away. If we had sense, we would take the hint, count our losses, and not put up a fuss. The problem is that Ethan and I know Christ has chosen all of us to fulfill a special mission for Him: to open people's eyes and let them know that through Christ's power they can change the world. Thus, we will not allow anything to deter us from accomplishing our mission!

"When we opened the store, it was a given that some people would loathe us and do everything in their power to plan our failure. Now that it has happened, I know we are making progress. Not only do I want us to come back twice as hard but to launch an all-out, aggressive war on the forces that seek to oppress the human spirit. If we intend to move forward, we must use nonviolent techniques to kill the forces of tyranny that oppress the human spirit. Unlike other wars, this one can be won only by pursuing justice and seeking the highest good in every situation.

"This will not be easy, but I believe all we have to do is put a different emphasis on what we are already doing. Now that you have an idea of what we have in mind, we want to get your input on it as well as any ideas you may have on how we can put our plans into action."

For several moments, everyone sat in silence and thought about what Claire had just said. At this time, the Holy Spirit came upon Kathy, and she began to speak. "Bring it on, I say! I agree with everything you have just said. If Christ is on our side and we do as He commands, He has promised that He will be with us. He will protect us. I know this seems strange to say, given that the store was set ablaze. I do not know why this happened, but I am sure we will find out. I believe the best way to deal with this situation is to take it head on. From how I see it, this is our hour to lead and show the world that, through Christ, we can take this horrific situation and make good come of it.

"Absolutely, we must reopen the store. It will be difficult, and no doubt people will be angered by our resolve. However, this is nothing new. We have charted unfamiliar territory before. If we are united in our efforts and rely on Christ for guidance, we will succeed. The doctors might have burned down the store, but this has strengthened my commitment to do the work of Christ. From the moment I first entered this store, I knew I was born to be here and serve the Master. Through Christ, we are changing the world, and there is no way I am going to allow our work to be destroyed. It really doesn't matter what obstacles are put in our path. The question is not if we should rebuild, but when.

"I believe the most effective way to spread our message is to hold a press conference. I see it as the ideal venue to announce our plans. Declare an all-out, get-in-your-face war against the forces that want to harm the human spirit. Invite all those who want to see good triumph to join our movement. Since no one is expecting Divine Towels to rise from the ashes, it is the perfect way to rally our troops and put the enemy on notice that anymore outbursts will not be tolerated!"

Kathy finished and everyone was moved. She had spoken what they all had been feeling. Kathy's words not only reassured them but gave them the energy to move forward.

"Thank you, Kathy," Ethan said after a moment of silence. "You are absolutely right. We can do all things through Christ who strengthens us. Yes, let them bring it on and wear themselves out. It will certainly take more than this to break us down. We have done a lot through Christ, and the devil has no power over us. If Christ is on our side, nothing can harm us.

"Let's get busy. We have a lot of work to do, but if we plan this methodically, we can have the store up and running in no time. By the time we make our statement and explain what we are planning, I'm sure people will be happy to lend a hand. However, before we get started, let's get a couple of those enormous dumpsters and a bulldozer for the debris. Until this is done, we can't begin rebuilding."

During the several months that Divine Towels had operated, people who had received healing often reacted the same way. Most people not only gave generous donations to the store but also had often left their business cards. Initially, Jim tacked the cards to a corkboard, but soon it was full. Because he saw much value in this information, Jim created a database and stored it on his laptop so he could retrieve it wherever he went in case anyone ever needed help. Little did Jim ever expect to have to use it on such an eerie occasion.

"Jim," Bill said, "I think I remember a man a while back who owned a demolition company. Perhaps we could call him and see if he will help us."

Within seconds, Jim had retrieved Mr. Sloan's information. "Good thinking. I'll get right on it. What's next, Ethan?"

"Well, to tell you the truth, Bill," Ethan said, "we haven't fully thought it out. However, I still think the original blueprint Jim did works well. We should rebuild the store the same way, unless you all can think of any structural alterations that would help us."

The group nodded signaling that they concurred.

"Good," Ethan continued, "Jim, I still have the receipts of everything we bought. Will you take tomorrow and reorder the materials we used the first time as well as anything else we might need? I estimate it will take a week to clear everything out and then let's get started right away. Let's also update our website and let our accountability board know what we are doing. Perhaps they can recruit some of our volunteers to come help us. I know I am rambling and know this is a team effort, but like Kathy, I felt compelled to say this."

At that moment, the group became silent and smiled at one another. Although no words were exchanged, it was clear that this tragedy had deepened their resolve to continue their mission. Now that the plans were in place, it was time to launch an all-out attack against the enemy. The funny part was that they suddenly realized it had only been two days since the fire had happened. Just as Jesus died and rose on the third day, their assignment to rebuild Divine Towels and expand the ministry would also begin on the third day.

Once the team devised the plan, they met for an additional two hours and sprang into action! Jim and Bill spent the time sending out the press release to the local media, announcing that they would hold a meeting the following morning to discuss their setback as well as to unveil their plans for the future.

Meanwhile, the other team members gathered around the table and wrote a well-crafted speech that Kathy would deliver at eleven the following morning. The goal of the speech was simple: to tell the world about the wondrous, future plans God had for Divine Towels and to recruit people to help bring them to fruition in whatever way they could. While the goal was simple, because the Lord sprang this entire thing on them at the last minute, they felt somewhat overwhelmed by the whole thing and were not quite sure how to begin. In the end, with the Holy Spirit's help, they wrote a speech that clearly articulated their vision and put everyone on notice that Divine Towels was more than a store. Indeed, it was a force to be reckoned with! The team then realized that it had been only two days and that their assignment to rebuild Divine Towels would begin on the third day, just as Jesus rose on the third day.

When people saw the front page of the paper and read about that Divine Towels had been set ablaze, the air in Coppertown changed considerably. There was no getting around the fact that Divine Towels had transformed the attitude of the town as nothing had before. Yes, attending church gave people's souls a much-needed weekly boost. However, the Holy Spirit was at work at Divine Towels and surely invigorating and empowering them to feel they could do all things under Christ's power.

Learning about the tragic story behind the fire, people were incensed and eager to seek revenge. Deeply disturbed, those who had received healing at Divine Towels were resolute to see the phoenix rise from the ashes and triumph over the darkness once and for all. The only question was how. There was an outpouring of support. Many called, wrote letters of condolences, and offered to do whatever they could to help. The Divine Towels staff appreciated the help and planned to use all the resources at their disposal, but it was not until the Holy Spirit directed them could they determine what type of help would be needed.

"Good morning," Kathy began. "Thank you all for coming out on such short notice. As you all can imagine, the last two days have been very devastating for everyone. We are sick and tired of the fact that whenever something good happens someone always has to come along and botch it up! There was absolutely no excuse, no reason why something like this had to happen. Ethan and Claire are good people. They did not deserve this; none of us did. This is not just another local fire you read about in the paper where you feel bad for the owner one day, bake him a cake, and then go on living. No, this tragedy has not only affected this community, but people all over this nation who have been touched and healed. We are outraged and feel violated! Therefore, we do not intend to be passive and let the dust settle as it may on this one. Rather, we will deal with this matter lawfully, vigilantly, and decisively, according to a well-developed plan.

"Ethan and Claire planted a good seed by opening Divine Towels. However, what good would all of their work be if we allow the seeds to go unfertilized? If this happens, all the work they have done would be for nothing. The Lord would never forgive any of us. The power of God is at work.

"If those responsible intended to burn Divine Towels down hoping all associated with the store would become so frightened that they would cease, their goal has not been achieved. I can ensure everyone that those who have been healed and have committed their lives to empowering have not been deterred. In fact, this tragedy has strengthened our resolve, and now we plan to take our ministry to a new level. My friends, the time has come for us to become Christian warriors and do our ultimate duty. Wage war against the unseen forces that seek to hinder the human spirit once and for all.

"We not only plan to hunt down the arsonist responsible for this and rebuild a bigger and better Divine Towels in Coppertown but also to build a chain of Divine Towels in every major city throughout the United States. The fact is the Holy Spirit has transformed the lives of many who have had their feet washed at Divine Towels.

"People have come from far away to be healed. We can and will rebuild Divine Towels; however, if we want people throughout the nation to experience the Holy Spirit's power like those in Coppertown, we must build Divine Towels in cities throughout the country! Then all people can benefit from this miraculous store. We know this announcement will surely enrage those who oppose what we are doing. However, we say bring it on because good will prevail! Through Christ, the work of Divine Towels has become a beacon of hope in the world, and there is no way a fire is going to stop us from doing the work Christ has commissioned us to do. It really does not matter what obstacles they put in our path. Let them bring it on. Eventually, they will tire of failing, and we will reclaim the world for Christ.

"Divine Towels has taught us the lesson that with Christ we can accomplish whatever task comes our way. It has been said that one person cannot change the world; however, I beg to differ. Just look at the miraculous works Christ has performed through humble, willing instruments like Ethan and Claire who have surrendered their lives unconditionally and agreed to do whatever Christ asked. The fire has strengthened our resolve and made us see that we have only begun to wage war against tyranny. Much hard work lies ahead. We will be challenged in many ways. But with Christ's help not only will we do it, but we will win!"

Once Kathy finished, there was silence. The journalists covering this story were astounded. They knew that tragic events often brought people together and compelled them to undertake bold and courageous action, but it had been such a long time since they had seen such a united, organized movement, that they were simply overwhelmed. The doctors, who thought they were victorious when they set the store on fire, now had a raging revolution on their hands. The worst part was that they had played their last card and never anticipated that the tide of public opinion would turn against them.

About the Author

Jason McGlynn has lived in the Atlantic City area and has worked for the FAA as a Technical Publications Editor for ten years. He attended Saint Joseph's University in Philadelphia where he earned a B.S. degree in food marketing and a MBA in management information systems.

While Jason is quite successful, his life got off to a rocky start. When Jason was born in the coal fields of West Virginia, the doctors diagnosed Jason with Cerebral Palsy and told his mother to forget about him because he would be profoundly retarded and would be a vegetable. From that moment on, his struggles began, but he was determined not to allow them to stop him from living a full and productive life.

Living with Cerebral Palsy is hard enough, but it's even harder when you don't have an earthly support system behind you. With the exception of his dear mother, he always felt like a leper.

When people look at the many adversities Jason has overcome in life, they are often amazed. Often people will ask him how he managed to do it and why he has such a positive outlook on life. Jason attributes his success to the three things in his life:

1. His God, who is not only at his side every step of the way, but who also gives him the determination and will needed to face whatever obstacle comes his way. The Bible verse, "I can do all things through Christ who strengthens me," has always sustained him and given him the strength to do whatever he needs to do.

2. His mother, who is his best friend and role model. She has been there for him in every way imaginable. Not only has she dedicated her life to ensuring that he has had every opportunity possible, but she has also inspired him to write Divine Towels.

3. His writing, which is Jason's greatest passion. Jason definitely does have Cerebral Palsy and a speech impediment to go with it. However, when Jason becomes quiet and asks the Holy Spirit to fill his heart, his speech is no longer an issue. For the Holy Spirit blesses him with an incredible gift and tells Jason word for word what to write. The words the Holy Spirit gives him to write are

definitely inspired and are intended for a troubled world that desperately needs to hear them.

Jason can be reached by email at divinetowel1@yahoo.com